Freedom of Expression of Judges

This book addresses the impact of developments surrounding the freedom of expression of judges by building on the experience of judges themselves, legal practitioners and academics across Europe. Like everybody, judges enjoy freedom of expression. However, historically, there have been starker limitations to the free speech of judges compared to ordinary citizens, the rationale being to safeguard judicial independence, impartiality and public trust in the judiciary. Where exactly the boundary lies is a highly complex question. The recent developments in Europe have rekindled the dilemma of guaranteeing freedom of expression to judges. The rule of law crisis has led many judges to speak out against the attacks of autocratic governments targeting judges and courts. The rapid expansion of the digital world has opened up new channels of communication, and the growing role of courts in society has expanded the reach of courts to practically any social issue, even the most polarised. This work critically analyses the recent jurisprudence of the Court of Justice of the EU and the European Court of Human Rights, its reception at the national level and the contribution of national judiciaries to the discussion pervading the European judicial space. It seeks to raise awareness that judicial speech is a multifaceted phenomenon shaped by complex legal and social considerations worth further exploration. The book will be of interest to academics, researchers, and policy-makers working in the areas of Human Rights Law, Constitutional Law and Politics, and Comparative Law.

Federica Casarosa, Research Affiliate at Sant'Anna School of Advanced Studies, Pisa, and part-time Professor at the European University Institute, Florence.

Mohor Fajdiga, Teaching Assistant and PhD candidate at the Faculty of Law, University of Ljubljana.

Madalina Moraru, Associate Professor of EU Law, Department of Political Science, University of Bologna, and part-time Associate Professor at the European University Institute, Florence.

Freedom of Expression of Judges

European and National Perspectives

Edited by Federica Casarosa, Mohor Fajdiga and Madalina Moraru

Routledge
Taylor & Francis Group
LONDON AND NEW YORK

First published 2025
by Routledge
4 Park Square, Milton Park, Abingdon, Oxon OX14 4RN

and by Routledge
605 Third Avenue, New York, NY 10158

Routledge is an imprint of the Taylor & Francis Group, an informa business

British Library Cataloguing-in-Publication Data
A catalogue record for this book is available from the British Library

Library of Congress Cataloging-in-Publication Data
Names: Casarosa, Federica, 1978- editor. | Fajdiga, Mohor, editor. | Moraru, Madalina, editor.
Title: Freedom of expression of judges: European and national perspectives/edited by Federica Casarosa, Mohor Fajdiga, and Madalina Moraru.
Description: Abingdon, Oxon [UK]; New York, NY: Routledge, 2025. | Includes bibliographical references and index.
Identifiers: LCCN 2024036925 (print) | LCCN 2024036926 (ebook) | ISBN 9781032736167 (hardback) | ISBN 9781032747613 (paperback) | ISBN 9781003470779 (ebook)
Subjects: LCSH: Judicial power–European Union countries. | Freedom of expression–European Union countries. | Freedom of speech–European Union countries. | Judges–European Union countries. | Justice, Administration of–European Union countries.
Classification: LCC KJE3655 .F74 2025 (print) | LCC KJE3655 (ebook) | DDC 347.4/012–dc23/eng/20240813
LC record available at https://lccn.loc.gov/2024036925
LC ebook record available at https://lccn.loc.gov/2024036926

ISBN: 978-1-032-73616-7 (hbk)
ISBN: 978-1-032-74761-3 (pbk)
ISBN: 978-1-003-47077-9 (ebk)

DOI: 10.4324/9781003470779

Typeset in Galliard
by Deanta Global Publishing Services, Chennai, India

Ad Alba, meravigliosa e coraggiosa
Federica Casarosa

Ženi Ani ter hčerkama Zarji in Pavlini, ki v moj sivi vsakdan prinašata barve življenja
Mohor Fajdiga

Pentru Andreas, lumina vieții mele, care îmi aduce inspirație în fiecare zi

Madalina Moraru

Contents

Contributors

Raluca Bercea
West University of Timisoara

Federica Casarosa
Sant'Anna School of Advanced Studies and European University Institute

Sietske Dijkstra
Court House of Groningen

Mohor Fajdiga
University of Ljubljana

Pierpaolo Gori
Italian Court of Cassation

Jarosław Gwizdak
Institute for Law and Society Warsaw and SWPS University of Social Sciences and Humanities

Gábor Halmai
European University Institute

Ágnes Kovács
Eötvös Loránd University

Madalina Moraru
University of Bologna and European University Institute

Oreste Pollicino
Bocconi University

Boštjan Zalar
Administrative Court of the Republic of Slovenia

Part 1

Judicial free speech standards emerging from the European courts jurisprudence and other horizontal issues

1 Should judicial voices be heard? Judicial interactions between national and European courts reframing freedom of expression as a tool to protect the European rule of law

Federica Casarosa, Mohor Fajdiga, and Madalina Moraru

Introduction: navigating judicial free speech in an evolving legal landscape

Like all individuals, judges also enjoy freedom of expression, belief, association, and assembly.[1] However, even in legal systems governed by the rule of law, there have traditionally been stricter limitations on these fundamental rights for judges than ordinary citizens. This has been done to safeguard important competing interests such as judicial independence, impartiality, and public trust in the judiciary. Determining the exact boundary between these two competing values is a complex question, with the answer in each case depending on a multitude of factors and specific circumstances. The recent rule of law developments in Europe and worldwide have reignited the dilemma of guaranteeing these fundamental rights to judges. The rule of law crisis has prompted many judges to voice their concerns and protest against the attacks of autocratic governments targeting judges and courts. The rapid expansion of the digital world has created new avenues of communication, which has led to the decline of traditional media. Social networks have emerged as the new digital marketplace of ideas, with all their vices and virtues. The growing role of courts in society, particularly the judicialisation of politics, has expanded the range of topics brought before the courts and increased the instances where courts deal with much more contentious disputes than ever before.[2]

1 Bangalore Principles of Judicial Conduct, UN Judicial Group on Strengthening Judicial Integrity, November 2002, para. 4.6.

2 Ran Hirschl, 'The Judicialization of Politics' in Robert Goodin (ed), *The Oxford Handbook of Political Science* (Oxford University Press 2011); David Kosař, Jiři Baroš, and Pavel Dufek, 'The Twin Challenges to Separation of Powers in Central Europe: Technocratic Governance and Populism' (2019) 3 European Constitutional Law Review 427; C Neal Tate and Torbjorn Vallinder (eds), 'The Global Expansion of Judicial Power' (NYU Press, 1997); Kim Lane Schep-

DOI: 10.4324/9781003470779-2

These developments challenge the conventional understanding of the judiciary's role and conduct, both on and off the bench. Simultaneously, they have triggered an unprecedented wave of cases concerning the freedom of expression of judges before European and national courts, which has resulted in important jurisprudential developments. For instance, the European Court of Human Rights (ECtHR) has refined the nature of the judicial function. Judges are now regarded as a special category of civil servants whose loyalty lies not with their superiors or the state but with the rule of law.[3] Furthermore, the Court has recognised the crucial role of judicial expression in safeguarding judicial independence and the rule of law by confirming that:

> [T]he general right to freedom of expression of judges to address matters concerning the functioning of the justice system may be transformed into a corresponding duty to speak out in defence of the rule of law and judicial independence when those fundamental values come under threat.[4]

The Court of Justice of the European Union (CJEU) has also been very active in addressing the new threats to the independence of judicial power. Notably, it has prohibited any interference with the right of judges to request the interpretation of EU law from the CJEU under the Article 267 TFEU procedure, even when this would place national courts in conflict with judgments of their national constitutional courts.[5] Strictly speaking, the right to refer preliminary questions to the CJEU is not covered by freedom of expression, but it can be used – and indeed was used – many times as a tool for conveying judicial protest against harmful reforms and pressures, undermining judicial independence.[6]

---

pele, 'Democracy by Judiciary. Or, Why Courts Can Be More Democratic than Parliaments' (2005) 25 Rethinking the Rule of Law after Communism 44.

3 *Bilgen v Turkey* App No. 1571/07 (ECHR, 9 March 2021), para 79; *Grzęda v Poland* App No. 43572/18 (ECHR (GC), 15 March 2022), para 264. See also David Kosař and Katarína Šipulová, 'The Strasbourg Court Meets Abusive Constitutionalism: *Baka v. Hungary* and the Rule of Law' (2018) 10 Hague Journal on the Rule of Law 83.

4 *Żurek v Poland* App No. 39650/18 (ECHR, 16 June 2022), para 222. See also *Baka v Hungary* App No. 20261/12 (ECHR (GC), 23 June 2016), para 168. The Venice Commission considers that a democratic crisis or a breakdown of the constitutional system is an important element of a particular case and essential in determining the scope of the fundamental rights and freedoms of judges (Venice Commission Report no. 806/2015, CDL-AD(2015)018) 23 June 2015, <https://www.venice.coe.int/webforms/documents/default.aspx?pdffile=CDL-AD(2015)018-e>, accessed 29 April 2024.

5 See Joined cases C-558/18 and C-563/18, *Miasto Łowicz* (CJEU, 26 March 2020); Case C-564/19, *IS* (CJEU, 23 November 2021); Joined cases C-357/19, C-379/19, C-547/19, C-811/19 and C-840/19, *Euro Box Promotion and Others* (CJEU, 21 December 2021).

6 See the contribution of Raluca Bercea in this volume. Cf. *Kayasu v Turkey* App No. 64119/00 and 76292/01 (ECHR, 13 November 2008), where the Court found a violation of the prosecutor's freedom of expression for bringing criminal charges against individuals who had attempted to carry out a *coup d'état* in 1980.

Moreover, various soft law instruments are currently sprouting at the national and supranational levels. Some, for example, Opinion 25 of the Consultative Council of European Judges from December 2022, cover the topic of judicial speech in general, whereas others concentrate on narrower issues such as the use of social media by judges.[7]

However rich and insightful, the literature on the freedom of expression of judges has not exhaustively analysed the challenges and trends in the exercise of freedom of expression of judges following the rule of law crisis and the digital shift in judicial communication.[8] For instance, the literature on freedom of expression is either geographically limited (focusing on one country or only on common law countries)[9] or substantively limited (e.g. addressing freedom of expression among other facets of the rule of law or the digital reform, or only focusing on the EU level, without adding a comparative legal analysis perspective).[10] In addition, with a few notable exceptions, much of

7 See UNODOC, 'Non-binding Guidelines on the Use of Social Media by Judges', <https://www.unodc.org/res/ji/import/international_standards/social_media_guidelines/social_media_guidelines_final.pdf>, accessed 29 April 2024; CEELI Institute, 'Practical Guidelines on Use of Social Media by Judges: Central and Eastern European Context', November 2019 <https://ceeliinstitute.org/wp-content/uploads/2022/01/CEELI_SoMe_Guidelines_ENG_Upd2021.pdf>, accessed 29 April 2024.

8 Jannika Jahn, 'Social Media Communication by Judges: Assessing Guidelines and New Challenges for Free Speech and Judicial Duties in the Light of the Convention', in María Elósegui, Alina Miron and Iulia Motoc (eds), *The Rule of Law in Europe: Recent Challenges and Judicial Responses* (Springer 2021) 137.

9 Common law jurisdictions have devoted much more attention to the phenomenon of judicial speech than civil law jurisdictions. Some contributions from common law countries include: Hoong Phun Lee (ed), *Judiciaries in Comparative Perspective* (Cambridge University Press 2011), which gives an account of the freedom of expression of judges in six common law countries: Australia, Canada, New Zealand, South Africa, United Kingdom, and United States; Shimon Shetreet and Sophie Turenne, *Judges on Trial: The Independence and Accountability of the English Judiciary* (2nd edn, Cambridge University Press 2013); A. Wayne MacKay, 'Judicial Free Speech and Accountability: Should Judges Be Seen but Not Heard?', 3 National J. of Constitutional Law (1993) 159; Robert H. Alsdorf, 'The Sound of Silence: Thoughts of a Sitting Judge on the Problem of Free Speech and the Judiciary in a Democracy' (2002) 30 Hastings Constitutional Law Quarterly 197; Stephen J. Jr Fortunato, 'On a Judge's Duty to Speak Extrajudicially: Rethinking the Strategy of Silence (1998) 12 Georgetown Journal of Legal Ethics 679; Nancy Gertner, 'To Speak or Not to Speak: Musings on Judicial Silence' (2004) 32 Hofstra Law Review 1147; Rónán Kennedy, 'Extra-Judicial Comment By Judges' (2007) 5 Judicial Studies Institute Journal 199; Brian MacKenzie, 'Extrajudicial Speech: Judicial Ethics in the New Media Age' (2012) 2 Reynolds Courts & Media Law Journal 185; Lynne H Rambo, 'When Should the First Amendment Protect Judges from Their Unethical Speech' (2018) 79 Ohio State Law Journal 279.

10 Sietske Dijkstra, 'The Freedom of the Judge to Express His Personal Opinions and Convictions under the ECHR', 13 Utrecht Law Review (2017) 1; Kosař and Šipulová (n 3) 83; Anja Seibert-Fohr, 'Judges' Freedom of Expression and Their Independence: An Ambivalent Relationship' in María Elósegui, Alina Miron and Iulia Motoc (eds), *The Rule of Law in Europe: Recent Challenges and Judicial Responses* (Springer 2021).

the literature lacks systematic analysis of recent jurisprudence, particularly that related to the rule of law crisis and digital revolution.[11]

Furthermore, despite this increase in case law concerning the freedom of expression of judges, the European courts still have to cover many scenarios. Legal standards are currently under accelerated development. Numerous cases pending before the ECtHR[12] show that the topic is far from settled. There seems to be no consensus on the precise margins and limitations of the freedom of expression of judges in Europe,[13] let alone worldwide. The scope, content, and justiciability of the freedom of expression as recognised by the CJEU and ECtHR is still subject to both scholarly divergence and States' contestation. States enjoy a certain margin of appreciation, which has certainly been narrowed down by recent European developments, but the differences from country to country remain significant.

Given a relatively weak academic interest in the topic before the outbreak of the rule of law crisis, there is currently a significant gap in the scholarly literature comparatively assessing the limit of the freedom of expression of judges in Europe. This edited volume does not entirely fill the extensive gap and settle this hot issue. It is only the first step in a challenging quest to shed more light on this fascinating topic. Its strength is that it is not a purely academic contribution to the debate. The edited volume includes three chapters written by sitting judges and one from a former judge, which means that the book is itself a manifestation of the phenomenon under scrutiny – the freedom of expression of judges. Moreover, the edited volume draws from two projects: "Trust, Independence, Impartiality and Accountability of Judges and Arbitrators

11 Other contributions in this field include: Sietske Dijkstra, *Walking the Tightrope: The Judge and His Freedom to Express His Personal Opinions and Convictions* (Eleven International Publishing 2023); Neha Jain, 'Separate Judicial Speech' (2020) 61 Virginia Journal of International Law 1; Mohor Fajdiga and Saša Zagorc, 'Freedom or Feardom of Expression of Judges? Exploring the "Chilling Effect" on Judicial Speech' (2023) 19 European Constitutional Law Review 249; Joan Solanes Mullor, 'Spain, Judicial Independence, and Judges' Freedom of Expression: Missing an Opportunity to Leverage the European Constitutional Shift?' (2023) 19 European Constitutional Law Review 271; Mohor Fajdiga, 'Freedom of Expression of Judges on Social Media: A Case Note on the Order Ds-Ss 1/2021 of the Disciplinary Court of the Judicial Council of the Republic of Slovenia' (2023) LXXXIII Ljubljana Law Review (Zbornik znanstvenih razprav) 221.

12 *Chaves Fernandes Figueiredo v Switzerland* App No. 55603/18 (ECHR, communicated 28 August 2019); *Bakradze v Georgia* App No. 20592/21 (ECHR, communicated 6 October 2021); *Wróbel v Poland* App No. 6904/22 (ECHR, communicated 31 March 2022); *Gąciarek v Poland* App No. 27444/22 (ECHR, communicated 10 June 2022); *Morawiec v Poland* App No. 46238/20 (ECHR, communicated 4 July 2022); *Ferek v Poland* App No. 22591/22 (ECHR, communicated 7 November 2022); *Coadă v Romania* App No. 616/20 (ECHR, communicated on 5 April 2023); *Chinita Rodrigues v Portugal* App No. 17655/19 (ECHR, communicated 29 August 2023).

13 Venice Commission (n 4); Seibert-Fohr (n 10). For a very recent example, see *Danileţ v Romania* App No. 16915/21 (ECHR, 20 February 2024), in which the distribution of votes of ECtHR justices reveals the different perceptions on the topic within the Court itself.

Safeguarding the Rule of Law under the EU Charter" (TRIIAL)[14] and "Trust, Independence, Impartiality and Accountability of Legal Professionals under the EU Charter – Part 2" (TRIIAL 2).[15] It elaborates on the findings emerging from the set of 15 cross-border training events where more than 350 legal practitioners discussed the pressing issues of European judiciaries, among which freedom of expression of judges stood out as the most frequent topic.[16]

The edited volume features two parts and an epilogue. The first part looks at the most recent standards on freedom of expression of judges (and prosecutors) that rely on varied interlinked legal sources, ranging from national constitutions to the European Convention on Human Rights and EU law, as interpreted by relevant jurisprudence. The second part offers perspectives from four different countries: Italy, one of the founding members of the European Union and a consolidated democracy with its own specific challenges in the justice sector; and, on the other hand, Hungary, Poland, and Romania, where the rule of law crisis has struck the hardest. These chapters go beyond the mere descriptive analysis of the situation on the ground in these judiciaries and examine how these judiciaries were successful in grasping the developments on the European stage. Instead, they work as in-depth case studies, providing new perspectives on certain yet unexplored aspects of wider European relevance. The epilogue provides the personal experience of a European judge, reflecting on the new factual and legal circumstances that have evolved in Europe, which considerably affect the standards of the rule of law. According to the judge, the adoption of a meritocracy-based structure of the judiciary will serve as a means to protect the rule of law.

This introductory chapter begins by providing an overview of the topic, tracing the evolution of societal understanding regarding the freedom of expression of judges (and prosecutors).[17] Second, it briefly outlines the devel-

14 TRIIAL project is a DG Justice-supported project (G.A. No. 853832). See more at: https://cjc.eui.eu/projects/triial/.

15 TRIIAL 2 project is a DG Justice-supported project (project no. 101089737). See more at: https://cjc.eui.eu/projects/triial-2/.

16 Six workshops were dedicated to the topic of freedom of expression of judges within the framework of the TRIIAL project (n 14) and two under the TRIIAL 2 project (n 15).

17 The ECtHR seems to treat cases concerning the freedom of expression of prosecutors along the same lines as those concerning judges (see the chapter by Sietske Dijkstra in this volume). However, this might be a consequence of the fact that most cases come from jurisdictions, in which the status of public prosecutors is comparable to the status of judges. Relying on *Eminağaoğlu v Turkey* App No. 76521/12 (ECHR, 9 March 2021), para 125 and *argumentum a contrario*, one could argue that the ECtHR could treat prosecutors differently in cases when the status of judges and prosecutors under national law differs. However, there are other persuasive arguments for treating judges' and prosecutors' expressions alike: some prosecutors' tasks are very similar to those of judges (plea bargaining, proposal of sanctions, decision-making on the dismissal of criminal complaints, ordering of (secret) investigative measures), they must enjoy a certain level of independence (autonomy) and public trust and must conduct their tasks professionally and without discrimination.

opments that request a reconsideration of the traditional approach to the freedom of expression of judges. The chapter then delves into the latest phase of this evolution, which is unfolding before our very eyes. It highlights unresolved questions that have become increasingly pertinent amidst the backdrop of the rule of law crisis and the rise of social media. The chapter analyses the recent jurisprudence of the European courts, examining their impact on the jurisprudence of national courts. Without envisaging to provide clear-cut answers, the analysis shows the current standards applied to the fundamental right to free speech and procedural guarantees and avenues for its protection. The chapter concludes with a succinct statement of the book's objectives.

The evolution of judicial freedom of expression in Europe: from speaking exclusively through judgments to explicit recognition of freedom of expression

At first glance, for most of the 20th century in continental Europe, it seems that the prevailing understanding was that once appointed to a judicial office, judges gave up their freedom of expression.[18] In the democratic West, this was predominantly due to high standards of what was deemed decent and appropriate for judges. In the Communist East, judges, who were downgraded to some kind of servile bureaucrats, relied on restraint and discretion mainly as a shield against the omnipresent control of the state.[19] The fall of the Berlin Wall and the wind of change it brought started a process where judicial independence was put at the forefront of debates on the judiciary.[20]

In the early 2000s, Bangalore principles explicitly recognised that judges enjoy freedom of expression.[21] However, their role in the democratic society directly influences the forms and manners through which such a right can be exercised. As courts have to be regarded as appropriate fora for dispute resolution, judicial free speech has to be limited to safeguard the independence, impartiality, and authority of the judiciary.[22] This is why the ECtHR

18 Christine Matray, 'En marge du film "Ni juge ni soumise": quelques rappels sur la liberté d'expression des magistrats' (2019) <https://www.justice-en-ligne.be/En-marge-du-film-Ni-juge-ni>, accessed 29 April 2024. Cf. Federica Casarosa in this volume, where it is explained that in modern Italy, judges and prosecutors have always had an important voice in society.

19 Aleš Galič, 'The Aversion to Judicial Discretion in Civil Procedure in Post-Communist Countries: Can the Influence of EU Law Change it?' in Michal Bobek (ed), *Central European Judges Under the European Influence: The Transformative Power of the EU Revisited* (Hart Publishing, 2015).

20 Kosař, Baroš, and Dufek (n 2); Michal Bobek, 'The Fortress of Judicial Independence and the Mental Transitions of the Central European Judiciaries' (2008) 14 European Public Law 99; Nuno Garoupa and Tom Ginsburg, 'Guarding the Guardians: Judicial Councils and Judicial Independence', 57 *AJIL* (2009) 103.

21 Bangalore Principles (n 1), para 4.6.

22 See, for instance, the decision of the Italian Constitutional Court n. 100, 8 June 1981. In the words of the ECtHR, '[judges] should show restraint in exercising their freedom of expres-

and national courts[23] require judges to exercise their freedom of expression with moderation and restraint. They should, in principle, avoid communication through the media even in response to provocation.[24] Moreover, they should not address specific issues, such as, most obviously, the content of the proceedings that the judge is currently deciding, but also sensitive cases where the judge may express opinions that may not be interpreted as personal but rather as presenting the views of the judicial institution. These conflicting values must be protected not only with specific reference to the concrete exercise of judicial functions but also as a deontological rule to be observed in all behaviours in order to avoid independence and impartiality in the performance of the assigned task being justifiably doubted by the citizens.

Despite these important limitations on judicial freedom of expression, courts call for caution whenever this right is at stake. Since *Wille v Liechtenstein* in 1999, any limitation to the freedom of expression of judges calls for close scrutiny[25] and should be justified based on the existence of an equally important legitimate interest.

Rule of law crisis and digital world: a push towards a new understanding of freedom of expression of judges?

Freedom of expression of judges has acquired a new layer of complexity, particularly in light of its role in confronting threats to the rule of law, emanating not only from the (authoritarian) governments but also from within the third branch (the judiciary). In the last decade, several Member States have witnessed an unprecedented decline in the rule of law, one of the Article 2 TEU values upon which the European Union is founded. Polish and Hungarian judicial "reforms" have led to a structural breakdown, eroding the independence and impartiality of their judiciaries.[26] While some Member States currently

sion in all cases where the authority and impartiality of the judiciary are likely to be called in question' (e.g. *Wille v Liechtenstein*, App No. 28396/95 (ECHR, 28 October 1999), para 64; *Baka* (n 4), para 164; *Kövesi v Romania* App No. 3594/19 (ECHR, 5 May 2020), para 201; *Morice v France* App No. 29369/12 (ECHR (GC) 23 April 2015), para 129).

23 As it emerges from the results of the TRIIAL project, national judiciaries addressed this balancing exercise, elaborating on the standards that emerge from the European Court of Human Rights. See Madalina Moraru, Mohor Fajdiga, and Federica Casarosa (eds), *TRIIAL National Reports: Belgium, Hungary, Italy, Poland, Portugal, Romania, Slovenia, Spain, The Netherlands* (2006) Working Paper, EUI RSC, 2022/52, Centre for Judicial Cooperation <https://cadmus.eui.eu/handle/1814/74814>, accessed 29 April 2024.

24 *Di Giovanni v Italy* App No. 51160/06, (ECHR, 9 July 2013), para 80; *Kudeshkina v Russia* App No. 29492/05 (ECHR, 26 February 2009), para 93.

25 *Wille v Liechtenstein*, App No. 28396/95 (ECHR, 28 October 1999), para 64. See also *Baka*, supra n. 4, para 165.

26 Case C-791/19, *Commission v Poland (Régime disciplinaire des juges)* (CJEU, 15 July 2021), para. 64.

maintain a semblance of stability, the resilience of their institutions against present and future assaults on judicial independence is increasingly in doubt.[27]

Traditionally, legal professionals, especially judges and prosecutors, have adhered to a code of silence to uphold the impartiality and the credibility of their institutions. The duty of restraint has been regarded as a prerequisite for public confidence, necessary for the successful fulfilment of the role of the judiciary in a democratic society. However, nowadays legal professionals more often than ever find themselves in a difficult position: they have a (moral) duty to speak out against assaults on the rule of law, yet fulfilment of such a duty could expose them to disciplinary and other types of sanctions.[28]

Could the current challenges to independent judicial systems be regarded as a call for a re-examination of the duty of discretion and perhaps for adjustments to the existing norm, especially as the perception that legal professionals should show restraint could be abused as an excuse for disciplining the independent-minded?[29] What are the risks of leaving more freedom (of expression) to legal professionals[30] and what are the advantages of exploring new means to defend this fundamental right?[31] What role do the European courts play in shaping the European standards of freedom of expression of judges, and how do judicial interaction techniques contribute to safeguarding the rule of law? How has the rule of law crisis influenced developments regarding freedom of expression in supranational and national courts?

This edited volume raises these questions while examining the recent jurisprudence from the European courts and assessing its influence on national courts' decisions. However, the scope of this book extends beyond a mere legal analysis of judicial speech standards. It addresses various socio-legal issues, with special attention to the contextual nuances of speech, the "chilling effect", and the strategic use of judicial free speech. These aspects are crucial

27 For Romania, see: ECJ, Joined Cases C-83/19, C-127/19, C-195/19, C-291/19, C-355/19, and C-397/19, Asociația 'Forumul Judecătorilor din România'; *Euro Box Promotion and Others* (n 5); Case C-430/21, *RS* (CJEU, 22 February 2022); Case C-817/21, *Inspecția Judiciară* (CJEU, 11 May 2023). On the rule of law issues in Belgium, Hungary, Italy, Poland, Portugal, Romania, Slovenia, Spain, and the Netherlands, see *TRIIAL National Reports* (n 23).

28 Joined Cases C-83/19, C-127/19, C-195/19, C-291/19, C-355/19, and C-397/19, *Asociația 'Forumul Judecătorilor din România'* (CJEU, 18 May 2021) (indirect criminal sanctions); *Miasto Łowicz* (n 5); *IS* (n 5) (disciplinary proceedings); *Kövesi* (n 22) and *Baka* (n 4) (premature termination of mandate); *Żurek* (n 4) (audit of judge's financial declaration, inspection of his work, and premature termination of mandate as a member of the National Council of the Judiciary (NCJ) and its spokesperson); *Miroslava Todorova v Bulgaria* App No. 40072/13 (ECHR, 19 October 2021) (disciplinary sanctions and administrative controls of judicial work).

29 See the chapter by Gábor Halmai and Ágnes Kovács in this volume.

30 See the chapter by Jaroslaw Gwizdak in this volume.

31 See the chapter by Pierpaolo Gori and Oreste Pollicino in this volume.

for comprehensively understanding the complex phenomenon of judicial free speech in the era of digital innovation and the rule of law crisis.

Refinement of the existing case law or next major step in the evolution of freedom of expression of judges?

The rule of law crisis in several EU Member States has forced European and national courts to refine their case law. The Court of Justice of the European Union has rediscovered the fundamental importance of the rule of law as an EU value and judicial independence as one of its central elements. From the seminal *ASJP* judgment delivered in February 2018,[32] the Court has carefully construed the narrative around the rule of law and judicial independence as cornerstones of the organisation of the judiciary, guarantees for the operation of the preliminary ruling mechanism, and consequently for the functioning of the European Union as a community based on law. The ECtHR has also underlined the importance of these values. The rule of law challenges have become the key topic of the Court in the last few years.[33] For example, in *Astraðsson v Iceland* and its progeny,[34] the Court subjected national judicial selection procedures to its scrutiny. In *Bilgen v Turkey* and *Grzęda v Poland*,[35] it has refined the status of judges, who are now considered loyal to the rule of law and not their superiors or the holders of state power.

This entrenchment of the rule of law and judicial independence as fundamentals of modern democratic states has had a tremendous impact on the judicial free speech standards. As explained by Dijkstra regarding the ECtHR, it seems there is very little room for limitations of the freedom of expression of judges (and prosecutors) when they speak in defence of the rule of law and judicial independence.[36] Starting from *Baka v Hungary*, the Court has consistently adopted a very judge-friendly approach. It has been willing to treat official speech, even stemming from a legal duty to give an opinion on judicial reforms, as an exercise of the right to freedom of expression.[37] It has shifted the burden of proof regarding the causal link between public expression and

32 Case C-64/16, *Associação Sindical dos Juízes Portugueses* (CJEU (GC), 27 February 2018).

33 Robert Spano, 'The Rule of Law as the Lodestar of the European Convention on Human Rights: The Strasbourg Court and the Independence of the Judiciary' (2021) 27 European Law Journal 211.

34 *Guðmundur Andri Ástráðsson v Iceland* App No. 26374/18 (ECHR (GC), 1 December 2020); *Xero Flor w POLSCE sp. zo.o. v Poland* App No. 4907/18 (ECHR, 7 May 2021), *Reczkowicz v Poland* App no 43447/19 (ECHR, 22 July 2021), *Dolińska-Ficek and Ozimek v Poland* App No. 49868/19 and 57511/19 (ECHR, 8 November 2021); *Advance Pharma sp. zo.o v Poland* App No. 1469/20 (ECHR, 3 February 2023); *Besnik Cani v Albania* App No. 37474/20 (ECHR, 4 October 2022).

35 *Bilgen v Turkey* (n 3); *Grzęda v Poland* (n 3)

36 See the chapter by Sietske Dijkstra in this volume.

37 On the impact of *Baka v Hungary* at the national level, see the chapter by Gábor Halmai and Ágnes Kovács in this volume.

the sanction suffered by a judge from the applicant to the state. It has found that governmental measures served no legitimate aim (e.g. *Kövesi*, *Baka*), a finding the Court makes extremely rarely, and even relied on Article 18 of the Convention to conclude that the state abused the limitation clause for furthering an illegitimate aim (*Miroslava Todorova*).[38] Moreover, in cases where judges raise their voices to defend the rule of law, only a narrow margin of appreciation is afforded to the national authorities (*Baka*, *Kövesi*, *Żurek*, etc.). In *Żurek v Poland*, the Court even ruled that judges have a duty to speak out when the rule of law is at stake. As shown by Dijkstra, such a duty is most probably a moral one. Nevertheless, it is a strong sign of support for judges in backsliding states to know that their freedom of expression will be safeguarded in Strasbourg.

Like the ECtHR, the CJEU has been an important ally of national judges in hardship.[39] It has taken a strict stance on the right of national judges to refer preliminary questions,[40] namely that

> [I]t is an inherent guarantee of the independence of national judges that they will not be subject to disciplinary proceedings or sanctions because they have exercised the option to apply to the Court under Article 267 TFEU.[41]
>
> Also thatthe mere prospect of being the subject of disciplinary proceedings as a result of making such a request (or deciding to maintain that request after it was made) is likely to undermine the effective exercise by the national judges concerned of the discretion and the functions of national courts in the framework of Article 267 TFEU.[42]

As also affirmed by AG Bobek, such a right should not be interpreted as absolute.[43] Nevertheless, in the context of a rule of law crisis, national judges are able to seek support from the Court of Justice by smartly channelling their opposition to harmful reforms or other phenomena detrimental to judicial independence through preliminary questions under Article 267 TFEU.[44] This is a much wiser approach compared to open public criticism of the government

38 *Miroslava Todorova v Bulgaria* (n 28).

39 Case C-564/19, *IS*, Opinion of Advocate General Pikamäe, 15 April 2021, para 1, where AG notes that in some cases, preliminary questions 'are appeals for assistance from national judges concerned by or even subject to disciplinary proceedings'.

40 Ibid., paras 44 and 48.

41 *Euro Box Promotion and others* (n 5), para 227. See also Judgment of 26 March 2020, *Miasto Łowicz* (n 5), para 59.

42 *Miasto Łowicz* (n 5), para 57.

43 See Opinion of AG Bobek in *Euro Box Promotion and others* (n 5), paras 238–245; Case C-379/19, *DNA-Serviciul Teritorial Oradea*, Opinion of AG Bobek, paras 93–95.

44 Of course, judges must make sure that the preliminary question they are raising is relevant for determination of the concrete case. If they fail to do so, the Court finds that the question is

since judges express themselves solely through legal mechanisms, whose legitimacy is beyond doubt.[45] Judges can rely on Article 6 ECHR to defend their right to refer preliminary questions since, at least in some cases, unduly reasoned rejection of a party's request for a preliminary ruling violates the right to a fair trial.[46] Arguably, another avenue worth exploring is to claim that the interference with the judge's right to refer a preliminary ruling violates the right to information, as one of the aspects of Article 10 ECHR.[47] Freedom of expression is defined very broadly by the ECtHR and covers "formal" speech[48] and arguably even instances when a judge (or a prosecutor) expresses his or her opinion through a legal act.[49]

For now, the Court of Justice has not yet directly addressed the issue of freedom of expression of judges, a right guaranteed under Article 11 of the EU Charter of Fundamental Rights (the Charter). The reason is that the competence to regulate judicial conduct remains within the purview of the Member States, a stance reiterated by the CJEU on numerous occasions. Consequently, Member States are generally not implementing EU law as required by Article 51(1) of the Charter when acting within the field of judicial organisation, and thus the Charter does not apply.[50] However, Article 19(1)(2) of the Treaty on the EU (TEU) mandates Member States to ensure effective judicial protection in the fields covered by EU law. The Court of Justice has interpreted this provision to require Member States to exercise their competencies in the field of justice in such a way that the independence of the judiciary is guaranteed.[51]

---

inadmissible. This happened in Miasto Łowicz (n 5). For more detail on this aspect, see the chapter by Raluca Bercea in this volume.

45 Boštjan Zalar, 'Strategic (mis)use of a judge's freedom of expression and its impact on the quality of the judiciary', presentation, given at TRIIAL cross-border workshop 'Freedom of Expression of Legal Professionals: Facing the Rule of Law Challenges in Europe, 21–22 October 2021'. See also the chapter by Boštjan Zalar in this volume, which builds on the above presentation.

46 *Dhahbi v Italy* App No. 17120/09 (ECHR, 8 April 2014); *Schipani and others v Italy* App No. 38369/09 (ECHR, 21 October 2015); *Baltic Master Ltd v Lithuania* App No. 55092/16 (ECHR, 16 April 2019); *Sanofi Pasteur v France* App No. 25137/16 (ECHR, 13 February 2020); *Somorjal v Hungary* App No. 60934/13 (ECHR, 28 August 2018); *Harisch v Germany* App 50053/16 (ECHR, 11 April 2019).

47 See the chapter by Raluca Bercea in this volume.

48 Ibid.

49 *Kayasu v Turkey* (n 6). See also *Chinita Rodrigues v Portugal* (n 12). However, in such cases, invoking Article 10 ECHR could turn out to be far-fetched and unconvincing, as there nevertheless seems to be a stark difference between speech originating in a professional legal duty, as in *Baka v Hungary*, and expression of opinion in a legal act, as in the case of referrals under Article 267.

50 For the same reasons, the material scope of the recently adopted Directive (EU) 2019/1937 of the European Parliament and of the Council of 23 October 2019 on the protection of persons who report breaches of Union law (the Whistleblower Directive) does not cover the judiciary. However, Member States are explicitly allowed to extend the scope of application to other fields under Article 2(2) of the Whistleblower Directive.

51 *Associação Sindical dos Juízes Portugueses* (n 32).

This provision has served as a linchpin for numerous preliminary ruling procedures and some infringement actions against states exhibiting democratic backsliding. In these cases, the Court of Justice has extensively scrutinised domestic accountability mechanisms and developed strong guarantees of judicial independence.[52] Hence, the Court has bolstered the procedural standards that apply when judges face disciplinary or similar charges for exercising their freedom of expression. Moreover, given the intrinsic link between freedom of expression and judicial independence, judges may invoke Article 19 TEU to defend their freedom of expression whenever they assert that their independence has been compromised.[53,54]

The refinement of the case law we have witnessed in the last 15 years has made an invaluable contribution to slowing the backsliding of the rule of law. However, its impact outside the context of the rule of law crisis remains uncertain. Nevertheless, the developments undoubtedly bear a tremendous prospect for further bolstering the standards of freedom of expression even outside that context.

In addition to the rule of law crisis, other phenomena challenge the prevailing understanding of where the limits of judicial free speech lie. The first one is the role and authority of the judiciary in modern society. According to the ECtHR, it should not be understood in the sense that judicial actors should not be criticised. The Court understands this limitation clause essentially as a synonym for public trust in the judiciary, meaning that the courts are recognised by the public as appropriate fora for the resolution of disputes. Constructive criticism is not harmful but beneficial to the authority of the judiciary,[55] even when it comes from the mouth of a fellow judge. The social legitimacy of the judiciary is crucial for the everyday functioning of the judiciary as well as for the resilience of the third branch against a "hostile takeover" by the government since courts and formal institutions cannot resist authoritarian attacks without public support.[56] If people felt that it was not only

52 For an overview of the case law concerning the rule of law, see: Laurent Pech and Dimitry Kochenov, 'Respect for the Rule of Law in the Case Law of the European Court of Justice A Casebook Overview of Key Judgments since the Portuguese Judges Case' SIEPS 2021:3 <https://www.sieps.se/en/publications/2021/respect-for-the-rule-of-law-in-the-case-law-of-the-european-court-of-justice/>, accessed 29 April 2024.

53 Laurent Pech, Alberto Alemanno, Vlad Perju, Joelle Grogan, 'The Good Lobby Profs statement in Support of Romanian Judges' <http://www.forumuljudecatorilor.ro/index.php/archives/4409>. The authors argue that the disciplinary proceedings against judges who criticised judicial reforms in Romania in a closed Facebook group are contrary to Article 19(1)(2) TEU.

54 See Mohor Fajdiga, 'Thematic booklet: Freedom of Expression and Association of Judges', TRIIAL 2 Project, 10–11, on file with the author.

55 *Morice v France* (n 22), paras 129, 167, 170.

56 Tom Ginsburg, Aziz Z Huq, and Mila Versteeg, 'The Coming Demise of Liberal Constitutionalism?' (2018) 85 The University of Chicago Law Review 239, p. 258; Andrew Arato: Populism and the Courts, VerfBlog, 2017/4/25, <https://verfassungsblog.de/populism

some court but their court that was under pressure, we would not have such large-scale meddling with the judiciary by political actors.[57] The question is what makes people feel that these are *their* courts and what kind of negative statements towards the judiciary may weaken their trust.

If the authority of the judiciary is, in fact, the level of public trust in judges, this should mean that the higher trust one has in judges (and prosecutors) as individual components of the judiciary, the more eagerly they will support the freedom of expression of judges. If we trust judges judging, why should we not trust them when they are using their free speech? There is some logic behind this rationale. However, judges have not been trained for public communication of their opinions outside the courtroom. Training is crucial in this respect, as was recently recognised by the CCJE in its Opinion No. 25 on the freedom of expression of judges.

This is even truer now than it was 15 years ago. With the advent of social media, the means of communication, the tone of expressing one's opinion, as well as the reach and availability of channels for public communication, have changed dramatically. What does this mean for judicial free speech?[58] It is hard to draw general conclusions, but these developments seem to push the boundaries of what is deemed appropriate communication for judges. Some general principles, such as discretion and restraint, the requirement to avoid communication through the media, even when provoked or the prohibition to comment on the case the judge is handling, have not been seriously questioned yet but could come under stress in the coming years.[59] Such general prohibitions are hardly consistent with the logic of human rights, which is allergic to sweeping rules that take little account of the different circumstances in which such rules are applied.[60] During one of the TRIIAL project workshops, a judge contemplated whether it would be better to inform the media about inadequacies in the judiciary, especially after exhausting other internal remedies. At the end of the day, this might help bring positive change to the functioning of the judiciary, which is a topic of great public concern. Besides, judges know the judicial system best and fully understand its functioning in practice, which is often different than on paper.[61] Their opinion could, hence,

-and-the-courts>, accessed 29 April 2024; David Kosař, 'Freedom of Speech and Permissible Degree of Criticism of Judges' (LL.M. thesis, Central European University 2007), p. 7; Bojan Bugarič, 'Can Law Protect Democracy? Legal institutions as Speed Bumps', (2019) 11 Hague Journal on the Rule of Law 450.

57 'Understanding Social Legitimacy of the Judicial Power – Tomasz Koncewicz, TRIIAL Transnational Training, Accountability and Freedom of Expression of Magistrates and Attorneys in Europe', EUI, 16–17 June 2021. <https://www.youtube.com/watch?v=1Vu-0lLImZk>, accessed 18 January 2023.

58 See the chapter by Gori and Pollicino in this volume.

59 See the chapter by Dijkstra in this volume.

60 In the United States, such rules are regularly found to be overbroad and thus unconstitutional.

61 David Kosař, 'The Heterogeneous Systems of Accountability of Magistrates in Europe', presentation at TRIIAL Transnational workshop 'Accountability and Freedom of Expression of

turn out to be priceless for strengthening our judiciaries or defending them against outside (or inside) pressures. Moreover, it seems that excessive restrictions on the freedom of expression of judges, in effect, conceal from the public upright, independent, and professional judges, and thus, the judiciary as a whole loses its reputation, which is not built on the "immaculateness" of the institution, but on the excellence of the individuals who make it up. If we want judges to be truly public intellectuals who contribute to debates in the public interest, we must also encourage them to responsibly[62] use social networks. However, judges should be mindful of the dangers social media communication entails. Former judge and court president Jaroslaw Gwizdak offers an insightful account of some judges in Poland's often unbarred use of social media and the consequences this entails for the public image of the judiciary.[63]

However, our moderate scepticism towards the general rules outlined above should not be understood as a call for their abandonment at the normative level. They should be taken into account when balancing the competing interests, but alongside other factors, which could sway the decision in the other direction. If these rules are used too rigidly, they can become tools for disciplining independent-minded judges who feel obliged to speak out in the face of affronts to the rule of law. When these judges are systematically penalised, a powerful chilling effect on the freedom of expression of other judges and the judiciary as a whole is created.[64] If such an atmosphere is established and maintained, the judiciary becomes an easy target for (aspiring) autocrats. This is one of the reasons why the concept of the chilling effect is so important. However, for the chilling effect to pervade the legal system and silence judges, directly sanctioning judges might not be required. The mere existence of legislation or initiation of accountability proceedings, even if, in the end, no sanction is imposed, can lead to a similar result. As governments are increasingly relying on private actors or measures that escape the purview of courts, it is important that the ECtHR adequately addresses such measures and adopts a more sensitive approach to the chilling effect stemming from

Magistrates and Attorneys in Europe' 17–18 June 2021 <https://www.youtube.com/watch?v=1V0g0xrzE3E>, accessed 29 April 2024. See also: Jerg Gutmann and Stefan Voigt, 'Judicial Independence in the EU: a Puzzle', European Journal of Law and Economics, 49(1), 83–100.

62 For personal experience on the use of social media and first-hand practical guidelines from a senior judge from the Netherlands and former president of the European Network of the Councils for the Judiciary, see Kees Sterk, 'To Post or Not to Post: Personal Experience with the Use of Social Media', TRIIAL 2 cross-border workshop 'Freedom of Expression and Association of Judges, 13–14 March 2024', <https://www.youtube.com/results?search_query=kees+sterk> accessed 29 April 2024.

63 See also the presentation of Judith Gleeson, a senior judge from the United Kingdom, at one of the TRIIAL 2 workshops, who calls social media "the wild west" – https://www.youtube.com/watch?v=zlKVc3wxzwA.

64 For a comprehensive account on the use of the chilling effect argument by the ECtHR in cases concerning freedom of expression of judges, see Fajdiga and Zagorc (n 11).

such measures to ensure meaningful protection of freedom of expression (of judges) in the future.[65] Due to its elusive nature, some doubt the true impact of the chilling effect. Even though the chilling effect is a complex behavioural phenomenon, it is very real. We have experienced it ourselves during the TRIIAL and TRIIAL 2 projects through discussions with legal practitioners. Hungarian judges, for example, seemed very hesitant in expressing their views. Their Polish colleagues were far more vocal, which could be a surprise given that authoritarian governments penalised judges who dared to speak out in both countries. The difference testifies that there are many different factors contributing to the overall chilling effect on judicial speech in a given society, *inter alia*, the normative framework, the self-perception of judges, legal culture embedded in a particular socio-historical setting, the strength of judicial associations, and the (perceived) support of civil society and European actors. Halmai and Kovács offer a comprehensive case study of Hungary to identify these socio-legal factors and how they impact judges' freedom of expression in a given society.[66] These factors, even if rarely directly relevant for the legal analysis of the phenomenon under scrutiny, carry important weight. A judge who wishes to express his or her opinion must often think beyond the legal and ethical boundaries. He or she must think strategically and come to a conclusion on whether and, if so, how and through what channel to express the opinion.[67]

Conclusion

To effectively contribute to the protection of human rights and the rule of law through this unconventional means of judicial conduct, judges need to be aware of the risks and benefits and understand the complexities of the demanding exercise of their freedom of expression: either when they themselves express an opinion, or when they are called to evaluate an opinion expressed by their colleague(s). This book can equip them to make more informed decisions about this fundamental right. It also offers a valuable perspective for other stakeholders: members of self-government bodies of the judiciary, legislators, policymakers, and academics. In an increasingly challenging legal and political landscape, the judicial voice could prove to be a priceless contribution to democratic societies and, sometimes (unfortunately), even a required stronghold for the institutions of the rule of law.

65 See the chapter by Fajdiga in this volume.
66 See the chapter by Gábor Halmai and Ágnes Kovács in this volume.
67 See the chapter by Boštjan Zalar in this volume.

2 The freedom of expression of judges in Europe: an analysis of the case law under Article 10 of the European Convention of Human Rights

The rule of law in the leading role

Sietske Dijkstra

Introduction

The judge is the holder of a state office in the rule of law. At the same time, he or she is an individual with opinions and convictions. The judge's speech is both a highly complex and a highly topical subject. The expression of opinions by judges meets specific limits, which follow from the fact that judges' opinions may negatively represent the judicial office. These limits are not easy to identify. Within a rule of law society, there are different competing interests, for instance, the protection of the adjudicatory process or the separation of powers, that may be affected when judges express their opinions. There are therefore often defensible arguments for both speaking and being silent. It is this very dichotomy between expressing oneself and restraint that is at the heart of the debate about the judge's speech. The positions in this debate range from the idea that a judge should not make public statements that go beyond a "thank-you to a boy scout who has helped him across the street"[1] to the idea that a judge's voice should be as loud as that of a tabloid reporter's.[2] In recent years, the debate has been complicated further by the impact of rule-of-law backsliding developments in some Central and Eastern European (CEE) countries. These developments have not only acted as an incentive for judges to express their opinions but also form the backdrop of new views on the expression of opinions by judges.

This chapter will examine the limits of the freedom of judges to express their opinions, both in and outside the exercise of their judicial duties, in various ways and about various topics. More specifically, it will analyse the case law of the European Court of Human Rights (the Court) on this subject under

1 M. D. Schoepf, 'Removing the Judicial Gag Rule: A Proposal for Changing Judicial Speech Regulations to Encourage Public Discussion of Active Cases' (2008) 93 Minnesota Law Review 341, 369.

2 J. Ziegel, 'Judicial free speech and judicial accountability: striking the right balance' (1996) 45 UNB Law Journal, 175, 177, quoting Bernard Levin.

DOI: 10.4324/9781003470779-3

Article 10 of the European Convention on Human Rights (ECHR), which protects freedom of expression.[3] Over the years, the Court has produced a varied body of case law based on applications filed by judges and public prosecutors about restrictions on their speech.[4] Due to space limitations, the chapter will not analyse judges' speech from the angle of Article 6 ECHR, that is, from the perspective of parties in proceedings that claim that the judge has expressed opinions and, as a consequence, has jeopardised his or her independence or impartiality.

In the next section, the chapter discusses two aspects of the applicability of Article 10 ECHR. First, it examines the specific broad interpretation of this right in the Court's case law regarding the judge's speech. It concerns a principal issue about the scope of the protection of Article 10 ECHR that has surfaced in recent case law. Second, the chapter discusses the causal relationship between the opinion expressed and the restrictive measure that is complained of. This is a difficult element in the case law which has evolved considerably in the last number of years. The following section discusses the three conditions of Article 10(2) ECHR that need to be met for restrictions of freedom of expression to be justified. The main focus here will be on the condition that an interference is necessary in a democratic society since the Court's considerations in this context generally provide the most information about the limits of the freedom of expression of judges. The chapter looks in more detail at a number of important factors that play a role in this so-called necessity test. Especially the duties and responsibilities of the judicial office, the contents of the opinion and its public debate contribution are factors that receive attention.

3 See about the case law on this subject under both Article 6 and 10 ECHR up to January 2023: S. Dijkstra, *Walking the Tightrope: The Freedom of the Judge to Express His Personal Opinions and Convictions* (Eleven 2023). See for more general information about Article 10 ECHR among others: Council of Europe, *Guide on Article 10 of the European Court of Human Rights; Freedom of Expression* <www.echr.coe.int/documents/guide_art_10_eng.pdf>, accessed 28 March 2024; J. Gerards, *General Principles of the European Convention on Human Rights* (Cambridge University Press 2019); P. van Dijk and others, *Theory and Practice of the European Convention on Human Rights* (Intersentia 2018); D. J. Harris and others, *Harris, O'Boyle and Warbrick: Law of the European Convention on Human Rights* (Oxford University Press 2018).

4 Although the Court has recognised the characteristic position of the public prosecutor, it has generally dealt with these cases along the same lines as the cases of judges, for instance, *Kövesi v Romania* App No. 3594/19 (ECHR, 5 May 2020), [201]. *Goryaynova v Turkey* App No. 41752/09 (ECHR, 8 October 2020), [56], warrants the conclusion that a differentiation between judges and public prosecutors may be relevant when the national legal system does not regard the prosecution authorities as part of the judiciary. See under Article 6 ECHR: *Eminağaoğlu v Turkey* App No. 76521/12 (ECHR, 9 March 2021), [36].

Article 10(1) ECHR

When assessing a case from the point of view of Article 10 ECHR, the first question is whether Article 10 ECHR is applicable. This section discusses two points: the specific broad interpretation of this right in the Court's case law and the requirement that there must be a causal relationship between the opinion expressed and the restrictive measure complained of.

The scope of Article 10(1) ECHR

In general, the Court has given Article 10 ECHR a wide scope. Freedom of expression covers numerous types of expressions, including those of an artistic[5] and commercial[6] character, and it is standard case law that Article 10 ECHR is applicable to information and ideas that are favourably received or inoffensive as well as to those that offend, shock, and disturb.[7] In the case law regarding the judge's speech, the Court has interpreted Article 10 ECHR broadly in another, highly specific way.

This specific interpretation concerns the origin of the judge's statements. Most cases are about judges who express an opinion in a private capacity, that is, as persons who do not act in any official capacity. Examples of such activities are handing out political pamphlets in the streets,[8] watching a PKK-related television channel,[9] sharing an article on the judiciary on Facebook,[10] or writing and publishing a personal letter on the internet.[11] The case law also includes cases about judges who express an opinion during the performance of their judicial duties. An example is the case of *Pitkevich v Russia*,[12] which concerns a judge who was dismissed for, among other things, having entered into prayer during court sessions and for promising parties to the proceedings a favourable outcome of their cases if they joined the church she was a member of, all of which had negative consequences in the form of recusals and delays. However different the contexts of these cases, all are about the expression by judges of a personal viewpoint, one that originates in his or her private convictions.

The case of *Baka v Hungary*[13] has introduced a new approach. In this case, the Court seems to have abandoned the idea that an opinion needs to

5 *Müller and others v Switzerland* App No. 10737/84 (ECHR, 24 May 1988); *Ulusoy and others v Turkey* App No. 34797/03 (ECHR, 3 May 2007). See also extensively about the scope of Article 10 ECHR, Harris and others (n 3) 593–609.

6 *Markt intern Verlag GmbH and Klaus Beermann v Germany* App No. 10572/83 (ECHR, 20 November 1989).

7 *Handyside v the United Kingdom* App No. 5493/72 (ECHR, 7 December 1976).

8 *E. v Switzerland* App No. 10279/83 (EComHR, 7 May 1984).

9 *Albayrak v Turkey* App No. 38406 (ECHR, 31 January 2008).

10 *Kozan v Turkey* 16695/19 (ECHR, 1 March 2022).

11 *Panioglu v Romania* App No. 33794/14 (ECHR, 8 December 2020).

12 *Pitkevich v Russia* App No. 47936/99 (ECHR, 8 February 2001).

13 *Baka v Hungary* App No. 20261/12 (ECHR, 23 June 2016).

originate in the individual's convictions. This is also seen in the cases *Kövesi v Romania*[14] (2020) and *Brisc v Romania*[15] (2018). Baka and Kövesi were magistrates in high legal offices: Baka was President of the Supreme Court and of the National Judicial Council, and Kövesi, a public prosecutor, was the head of the National Anticorruption Directorate. Both were confronted with legislative reforms that impacted their professional fields. One of Baka's legal duties as President of the National Judicial Council was to comment on draft legislation that affected the judiciary.[16] Baka had made critical statements about the comprehensive constitutional and legislative proposals initiated by the coalition of Fidesz and the Christian Democratic People's Party in 2010/2011, referring to the proposals as, among other things, unconstitutional.[17] The Court considered these statements as the fulfilment of an official duty: "it was not only his right but also his duty as President of the National Council of Justice to express his opinion".[18] Kövesi had publicly criticised the political choice to decriminalise corruption offences and the revision of laws that could affect the independence of the judiciary. As in the case of *Baka v Hungary*, the Court considered the expression of these views as part of the duties of the magistrate's office.[19] In both cases, the Court applied Article 10 ECHR, although in the Baka case the judgment was not unanimous.[20] This broad interpretation of Article 10 ECHR is also visible in the case of *Brisc v Romania*, which concerns a public prosecutor with the task of providing information to the press on criminal investigations, who was accused of having disclosed confidential information.

In these three cases, the Court applied Article 10 ECHR to the expression of views that is rooted in the judge's official tasks. This is different from the other cases, where, even though an opinion may be expressed *during* the exercise of official duties, as in *Pitkevich v Russia*,[21] its source is always the judge's own convictions. The difference becomes especially tangible when it is considered that the officeholder may personally disagree with the statements he makes on behalf of the office. The approach in these cases therefore testifies to a principal broadening of the scope of Article 10 ECHR.

This interpretation of Article 10 ECHR draws attention to Article 34 ECHR. Article 34 ECHR reserves the right to submit an application to the Court for persons, non-governmental organisations, and groups of individuals. Applications that are not aimed at the protection of the rights of individuals,

14 *Kövesi* (n 4).

15 *Brisc v Romania* App No. 26238/10 (ECHR, 11 December 2018). See later also (partly) for this approach *Żurek v Poland*, 39650/18 (ECHR 16 June 2022).

16 *Baka* (n 13) [44], [168].

17 Ibid., [16], [21].

18 Ibid., [168].

19 *Kövesi* (n 4), [205].

20 *Baka* (n 13) (Judge Wojtyczek).

21 *Pitkevich* (n 12).

but that serve the interests of state(-related) authorities, are excluded.[22] The sharp distinction the Court made in the case of *Demirbaş and others v Turkey*[23] is illustrative. In this case, a mayor and members of a municipal council complained that Article 10 ECHR was violated because the Minister had disbanded the municipal council and dismissed the mayor after they had decided to offer municipal services in the Kurdish language. The application was inadmissible because its aim was to protect the interests of the council, a part of the state, instead of safeguarding the individual rights of the mayor and council members.

In the cases concerning the judge's speech, this distinction is not visible. It can be said, however, that if a judge makes statements that do not originate from his own convictions, but in the exercise of an official duty, it is not the individual but in effect the judicial office that is complaining and issuing an application. A restriction of that speech is a curtailment of the office's exercise of its powers, not the limitation of the exercise of an individual's right. This observation about Article 34 ECHR finds support in the dissenting opinions in several of the Court's cases.[24] The essence of the dissent is that the exercise of an official duty cannot be equated with the exercise of personal freedom by the individual who holds the office. It is difficult to ignore this criticism. Freedom of expression is undeniably a construct that exists to protect individuals, especially against state power; it is not meant to protect state offices against other state offices, however important their function may be.

The causality question of Article 10(1) ECHR

The application of Article 10 ECHR also requires a causal relationship between the expression of an opinion and a negative action by the authorities: the public authorities must somehow have restricted the expression of the opinion to the public debate.[25] Sometimes the Court makes an explicit decision on this issue, especially when the existence of the causal relationship is in dispute. This

22 The ECtHR does not see it as its role 'to examine disputes between institutions or over internal politics': *Assanidze v Georgia* App No. 71503/01 (ECHR, 8 April 2004), [149]; *María Carmen Forcadell I Luis and others v Spain* App No. 75147/17 (ECHR, 7 May 2019), [17].

23 *Demirbaş and others v Turkey* App No. 1093/08 ECHR (9 November 2010).

24 Baka (n 13) (Judge Wojtyczek); Żurek (n 15) (Judge Wojtyczek); Brisc (n 15) (Judge Kūris and Yudkivska).

25 See, for instance, *M.D. and others v Spain* App No. 36584/17 (ECHR, 28 June 2022): the authorities initiated disciplinary proceedings but did not impose any sanctions because signing a political manifesto was regarded as a legitimate exercise of the judges' freedom of expression. Cf. *mutatis mutandis Ayuso Torres v Spain* App No. 74729/17 (ECHR, 8 November 2022) where the Court found Article 10 applicable even though the disciplinary motion was found to be time-barred and no concrete sanction was imposed. Nevertheless, the Court found that the declaration of the disciplinary body that the expression at hand went beyond the limits of freedom of expression created a chilling effect on the applicant's future exercise of his freedom of expression.

sometimes requires a detailed examination on the part of the Court that goes beyond the facts as they are presented by the parties.[26]

Part of the causality question is an examination of whether the measure is essentially related to the judge's professional ability to properly exercise his or her function. When this is so, the complaint is not covered by Article 10 ECHR. This is seen, for instance, in the case of ***Harabin v Slovakia*** from 2004.[27] Judge Harabin was confronted with a proposal by the Minister of Justice to revoke his appointment as President of the Supreme Court. Harabin claimed that this was a punishment for his views concerning the position of the judiciary. The ECtHR disagreed:

> … the Court considers that the disputed measure is essentially related to the applicant's ability properly to exercise the post of President of the Supreme Court, that is to the appraisal of his professional qualifications and personal qualities in the context of his activities and attitudes relating to State administration of the Supreme Court.[28]

The application of this criterion is difficult. In the case of ***Simić v Bosnia and Herzegovina***,[29] the complaint fell outside the scope of Article 10 ECHR although the expression of opinions by a judge features prominently in the case. The case concerns the dismissal of a judge of the Constitutional Court who had previously been the vice-president of a political party. His independence from the political sphere was questioned after a letter of the judge to the president of the political party in question was published in a newspaper. In addition, the judge had expressed serious allegations in the press about corruption in the Constitutional Court, without providing any evidence. The case shows similarities with the case *Erotocritou v Cyprus*,[30] which concerns far-reaching unproven accusations of bribery by a magistrate in a press conference directed at an attorney general. This case, however, did fall within the ambit of Article 10 ECHR. The reasons for the difference in approach are difficult to identify.

In other cases, the causality question does not concern the judge's professional abilities, but the relationship between the opinion and a subsequent event with a negative impact on the judge's freedom of expression. In the

26 For instance, *Baka* (n 13); *Kövesi* (n 4); *Miroslava Todorova v Bulgaria* App No. 40072/13 (ECHR, 19 October 2021).

27 *Harabin v Slovakia* App No. 62584/00 (ECHR, 29 June 2004).

28 See a later case initiated by *Harabin* App No. 58688/11 (ECHR, 20 November 2012), [151], for a similar consideration. See *Tuleya v Poland* 21181/19 and 51751/20 (ECHR, 6 July 2023), [516], for a more accessible formulation: measures that are mainly related to the applicant's capacity to perform his or her duties.

29 *Simić v Bosnia Herzegovina* App No. 75255/10 (ECHR, 8 December 2016).

30 *Erotocritou v Cyprus* App No. 15783/16 (ECHR, 25 May 2021).

case *Baka v Hungary*[31] the question was whether there was a relation between Baka's criticism and a subsequent reorganisation of the judicial system that prematurely ended his mandate as President of the Supreme Court and of the National Judicial Council. The Court's Grand Chamber reconstructed the events leading up to the legislation and saw in the "sequence of events in their entirety", supported by documents, "prima facie evidence" of the existence of a causal relationship. In view of this evidence, it was up to the national authorities to convince the Court of the incorrectness of this assumption. They did not succeed in doing so. Article 10 ECHR was therefore applicable. In the post-*Baka v Hungary* case law, this shift of burden of proof has been repeated several times.[32] The *ratio* behind this is not unlike in cases concerning other Articles of the Convention,[33] that the authorities are likely to have exclusive access to the information that is necessary to corroborate the applicant's position.[34]

The three conditions of Article 10(2) ECHR

When it has been determined that the measure of the public authorities interferes with Article 10 ECHR, it must be examined whether the three conditions of the second paragraph of Article 10 ECHR are met: the measure must be prescribed by law, serve a legitimate aim, and be necessary in a democratic society.

A violation of the condition of lawfulness is rare. The term "law" refers to a broad spectrum of regulation, provided that it meets certain quality standards, more concretely that it is accessible to the person concerned and that the consequences of a transgression are sufficiently foreseeable for him or her.[35] In *Tuleya v Poland*,[36] the case concerning one of the most well-known representatives of judicial opposition in Poland, the underlying moral of these criteria comes through clearly: there must be proper safeguards against arbitrariness and abuse of power by the authorities. Tuleya had been confronted, among other things, with disciplinary proceedings and with a decision to lift his immunity and suspend his judicial duties. The preliminary inquiries were terminated without informing Tuleya, which was considered by the Court as

31 *Baka* (n 13).

32 *Kövesi* (n 4), [188]–[189]; *Miroslava Todorova* (n 26),[163]; *Żurek* (n 15), [121]–[122]; *Tuleya* (n 28), [518].

33 For instance, *Saveriadus v Turkey* App No. 16160/90 (ECHR 22 September 2009), [18] (Article 1 ECHR Protocol No. 1); *Ibrahimov and Mammadov v Azerbaijan and others* App No. 63571/16 (ECHR 13 February 2020), [93] (Article 3 ECHR).

34 *Ukraine v Russia, re Crimea* App No. 20958/14 and 38334/18 (ECHR, 16 December 2020), [255]–[256].

35 See, for instance, Tuleya (n 28), [431]. See also about this condition, for instance, Harris and others (n 3) 629–631. See also M. Fajdiga's chapter in this volume.

36 *Tuleya* (n 28).

a neglect of minimum procedural safeguards and as a form of pressure on the judge.[37] The decision to lift immunity and suspend judicial duties had been made by a disciplinary chamber that could not be considered a tribunal established by law in the sense of Article 6 ECHR.[38] As a result, the interferences did not meet the first condition of Article 10(2) ECHR.

The requirement that the interference serves a legitimate aim does not often lead to a violation of Article 10 ECHR either: Article 10(2) ECHR includes a considerable list of aims, including the protection of the authority and impartiality of the judiciary.[39] The cases *Baka v Hungary*, *Kövesi v Romania*, and *Tuleya v Poland* show the relevance of this criterion.[40] These cases concern magistrates who have used their speech to take a stance against bills or legislation that could negatively affect judicial independence or the rule of law and were confronted with a severe reaction by the authorities. The Court concluded that the authorities had acted with the purpose of ending the criticism. By definition, this is not a legitimate aim. In *Tuleya v Poland*, the Court formulated this sharply, referring to the authorities as operating with the purpose of intimidating and silencing the judges.[41]

It is standard case law that the third condition of Article 10(2) ECHR, "necessary in a democratic society", requires that there must be a fair balance between the fundamental right of the judge to freedom of expression and the legitimate interest of the state to ensure that the civil service furthers the purposes enumerated in Article 10(2) ECHR.[42] The Court considers the national authorities in principle in a better position than itself to make this assessment. For this reason, they are allowed a margin of appreciation for their own appraisal.[43] In this part of the case law, traditionally, a "certain" margin of appreciation has been applied, which was considered justified by the judge's civil servant status.[44] In *Baka v Hungary*, a "narrow" margin of appreciation was introduced, resulting in stricter scrutiny by the Court.[45] This line has been followed in some later cases: the common denominator seems to be that they concern statements from judges made in defence of judicial independence and

37 Ibid. [534]–[535].

38 Ibid. [538]–[541].

39 See, for instance, *Harris and others* (n 3) 631–660, about the aims and, in particular, about the maintaining of the authority and impartiality of the judiciary, 653.

40 *Baka* (n 13), *Kövesi* (n 4), *Tuleya* (n 28).

41 *Tuleya* (n 28), [544]. See also *Żurek* (n 15), [277] where these words are used in the context of the necessity test.

42 See, for instance, *Baka* (n 13), [162], and the classic case *Wille v Liechtenstein* App No. 28396/95 (ECHR, 28 October 1999), [62].

43 See extensive discussions on the margin of appreciation and the variations in the width of the margin in Gerards, Chapter 7 (n 3).

44 *Pitkevich* (n 12); *Albayrak* (n 9), [42].

45 *Baka* (n 13), [171].

the rule of law, that are not damaging to the judiciary or other judges, and that are made from a "professional perspective".[46]

The necessity test: balancing the facts

In most cases, the requirement that the interference is necessary in a democratic society forms the core of the test under Article 10(2) ECHR. This condition requires that the interests that argue in favour of the exercise of freedom of expression are weighed against the interests that argue against it, including those that are protected by other Convention rights, such as the right to a fair trial and the right to protection of private life (Article 6 ECHR and Article 8 ECHR).[47] Below, a number of the most important factors that play a role in this weighing exercise are discussed: the duties and responsibilities of the office, the opinion's contents, its public debate contribution and its negative consequences, the negative consequences of the interference, and the fairness in the proceedings at the national level. Especially the first three of these factors come forward as factors that warrant examination.

The duties and responsibilities of the office

The duties and responsibilities of the judicial office may be an important factor when assessing the necessity of a measure. An example is found in *E. v Switzerland*,[48] a case from 1984 about a criminal court judge who had publicly demanded that a group of arrested demonstrators be granted amnesty. The competent national authority reprimanded him because it was not to be excluded that the judge might one day be called upon to decide the cases of the demonstrators. This did not produce a violation of Article 10 ECHR. The relevance of the duties and responsibilities of the office as a factor has grown in recent case law. In the cases *Baka v Hungary*[49] and *Kövesi v Romania*[50] the Court identified, as part of the judicial office, a duty to defend the rule of law and judicial independence by making public statements. Baka had a legal duty to make such statements as President of the Supreme Court and Head of the National Judicial Council;[51] for Kövesi, this duty was considered inherent in the functions of the office of head of the national anti-corruption unit.[52] The expression of their criticism was therefore seen as "part of the job". In later case law, this duty was also recognised as part of the tasks of a chairman of a

46 Ibid.; *Żurek* (n 15), [223]–[224].
47 See, for instance, *Brisc* (n 15); *Panioglu* (n 11).
48 *E.* (n 8).
49 *Baka* (n 13).
50 *Kövesi* (n 4).
51 *Baka* (n 13), [168].
52 *Kövesi* (n 4), [205].

national union of judges[53] or spokesperson of a judicial council or other representative body of the judiciary.[54] In the case *Żurek v Poland*, the Court spoke about a duty for *all* judges:

> Furthermore, the general right to freedom of expression of judges to address matters concerning the functioning of the justice system may be transformed into a corresponding duty to speak out in defence of the rule of law and judicial independence when those fundamental values come under threat.[55]

This approach of the judge fits with a broader development in the case law in which the Court emphasises the independence of the judge towards the other actors of the State. In the case law under Article 6 ECHR, for instance, the judge has been qualified as belonging to a specific category of civil servants.[56] Their relationship with the State as an employer has been described as "a special bond of trust and loyalty". Initially this categorisation meant that the civil servant received no protection under Article 6 ECHR.[57] In its case law under Article 6 ECHR from 2021, the Court has explicitly repositioned the judge in his relationship with the State in the sense that the Court still refers to a special bond between the judge and the State, but not between the judge and the State as an employer, but between the judge and the rule of law.[58] The focus of the judge's loyalty is therefore not his employer, but the rule of law.

When the Court referred to a duty to speak out in defence of the rule of law, it carefully chose its words. There are good reasons for that. On the one hand, it can be said that the judge, when acting in an official capacity, may be expected to defend the rule of law: the judiciary is an important part of the rule of law, and the judge may be expected to defend the system he is part of. This duty is carried out through the reasons in the judge's verdicts, the application of human rights treaties, or, for judges in a special representative office, the fulfilment of specific communicative tasks, as was the case for Baka and Kövesi. It is, however, difficult to assume a duty beyond the judge's professional domain, in the judge's private life. Although it is beyond doubt

53 *Miroslava Todorova* (n 26), [174]; *Eminağaoğlu* (n 4), [134]; *Sarisu Peshlivan v Turkey* App No. 63029/19 (ECHR, 6 June 2023), [41].

54 *Żurek* (n 15).

55 Ibid. [221]–{222]. See also *Tuleya* (n 28), [538].

56 *Pitkevich* (n 12). See for the police and the armed forces Pe*llegrin v France* App No. 28541/95 (ECHR, 8 December 1999), [66], and for *diplomats Karapetyan and others v Armenia* App No. 59001/08 (ECHR, 17 November 2016), [50].

57 Pitkevich (n 12). *Vilho Eskelinen and others v Finland* App No. 63235/00 (ECHR, 19 April 2007) have introduced a more generous approach to civil servants' rights.

58 *Eminağaoğlu* (n 4), [72]–[80]; *Bilgen v Turkey* App No. 1571/07 (ECHR, 9 March 2021), [65]–[68]; *Grzęda v Poland* App No. 43572/18 (ECHR, 15 March 2020), [264].

that professional ethical requirements may enter the private sphere,[59] a duty to actively use speech in a specific way is difficult to reconcile with the freedom of expression of judges,[60] since that freedom implies the choice not to express an opinion and to express a different opinion.[61] In addition, Article 10(2) ECHR makes specific requirements on restrictions of freedom of expression, among other things, that they are proportionate to a legitimate aim, something which can only be determined on the basis of a fact-specific balancing exercise.

A related question is whether speaking out is such a superior an action compared to other courses of action that it can be elevated to a duty. There are always competing interests in a rule of law society that need to be safeguarded. Silence may, for instance, find strong justification in the protection of the adjudicatory process. Opposing viewpoints – speaking out or remaining silent – may well be based on arguments that are defensible in a rule of law society. An illustrative example is the successful challenge by the Dutch public prosecutor's office of the chairwoman of the Dutch foundation Judges for Judges, an organisation that defends the interests of judges worldwide. In her capacity as chairwoman, the judge had expressed herself in a highly critical way about the democratic backsliding developments in Poland. At the same time, she was handling Polish extradition cases. In the view of the Court, this judge had a duty to defend the rule of law in her position as chairwoman. However, the Dutch court that decided the challenge found a violation of Article 6(1) ECHR: the judge's statements in the media were so absolute that she had damaged her impartiality.[62]

An escape from these objections against a duty to speak out would be to view this duty beyond the official domain not as a professional duty, but as a personal moral duty: a duty that originates from the judge's own conscience and free will instead of from the (judicial) office.[63] The judge may act upon this duty within the limitations that follow from the judicial office. This duty is strictly personal and cannot be imposed on others. This approach can be

59 In the Article 8 ECHR case *Özpinar v Turkey* App No. 20999/04 (ECHR, 19 October 2010), [71], the Court explains that professional ethical demands may restrict the judge's private life.

60 *Żurek* (n 15) (Judge Wojtyczek).

61 See the recognition by the Court of such a negative right in *K. v Austria* App No. 16002/90 (EComHR, 13 October 1992) [45]; *Strohal v Austria* App No. 20871/92 (EComHR, 7 April 1994). Reluctance, however, in, for instance, *Gillberg v Sweden* App No. 41723/06 (ECHR 13 April 2012), [85]. See also *Baka* (n 13) (Judge Wojtyczek): 'The notion of freedom of expression enshrined in Article 10 of the Convention presupposes free choice as to whether to speak and what to say'.

62 Courthouse of Amsterdam, 31 March 2021 (ECLI:NL:RBAMS:2021:1576).

63 The Court's reasoning seems to leave little room for this nuance: official speech is in principle treated in the same way as private speech, implying that professional duties are private duties. In the case *López Lone and others v Honduras* of 5 October 2015, the Inter American Court of Human Rights approached a duty for judges to defend democracy by the use of their speech also as a civic duty. This approach meets with the same objections as described here.

recognised in the Commentary on the United Nations Bangalore Principles of Judicial Conduct where it is said that a judge, as a human being with a conscience, morals, feelings, and values, may experience a moral duty to speak out, which can be the basis of the expression of an opinion within the boundaries of judicial impartiality and integrity.[64]

The contents of the opinion

An obvious factor in the necessity test is the meaning of the opinion. To establish that meaning, the choice of words and style of the opinion need examination. It is the overall content of the text that is decisive, not the meaning of the separate elements.[65] The difference between statements of facts and value judgments is an important element in this respect. It is standard case law that the existence of facts can and sometimes needs to be demonstrated, whereas this cannot be said of value judgments.[66] The requirement to prove the truth of a value judgment is by its nature an impossible one. Nevertheless, the proportionality of an interference may depend on whether there is a sufficient factual basis for a value judgment; otherwise, it may be seen as excessive. Opinions motivated by personal grievances, personal antagonism, or the expectation of personal advantage do not justify much protection.[67] How subjective this interpretation may be is apparent in the case *Kudeshkina v Russia*.[68] The majority of the Chamber concluded that the judge's remarks about the lack of independence of the Moscow courts were fierce but, ultimately, had to be regarded as a fair comment on a matter of public importance. Dissenters Kolver and Steiner were of the complete opposite opinion: they viewed the remarks as part of the "settling of a personal score".[69]

The expression of opinions about the judge's own pending cases meets the Court's standard case law: judges are required to exercise "maximum discretion" with regard to the cases with which they deal.[70] A similar consideration appears in cases concerning the use by judges of the press:

64 Commentary on the Bangalore Principles of Judicial Conduct 97 [140]. <www.unodc.org/documents/nigeria/publications/Otherpublications/Commentry_on_the_Bangalore_principles_of_Judicial_Conduct.pdf>, accessed 28 March 2024.

65 See, for instance, *Panioglu* (n 11), [116]–[117]; *Perna v Italy* App No. 48898/99 (ECHR, 6 May 2003), [47].

66 See, for instance, *Morice v France* App No. 29369/10 (ECHR, 23 April 2015), [126].

67 *Kudeshkina v Russia* App No. 29492/05 (ECHR, 26 February 2009), [95]; *Lishnyak v Russia* App No. 9964/06 (ECHR, 17 September 2019), [53], a case about the letters of a (former) judge who accuse other judges of a lack of integrity.

68 *Kudeshkina* (n 67).

69 Ibid. [95] and Ibid. (Judge Kolver and Steiner).

70 See, for instance, *Baka* (n 13), [164]; *Eminağaoğlu* (n 4), [136]. The criterion originates in the case law under Article 6(1) ECHR: see, for instance, *Buscemi v Italy* App No. 29569/95 (ECHR, 16 September 2019).

> The judicial authorities are required to exercise maximum discretion and that discretion should dissuade them from making use of the press, even when provoked. It is the higher demands of justice and the elevated nature of judicial office which impose that duty …[71]

In *Manole v Moldovia*,[72] the Court also pointed to the judge's duty of confidentiality when speaking with the press on his or her own pending cases. The case concerns a judge who had informed a journalist of the reasons for her dissenting opinion before the verdict was made public.

There is considerable tension between the broad and strict "maximum-discretion" principles and the system of Article 10 ECHR. They are hard to reconcile with the (fact-specific) requirements of Article 10(2) ECHR. It cannot be said either that the strictness is justified by Article 6 ECHR, as appears from the case *Chim and Przywieczerski v Poland*.[73] When pressed by a journalist in an interview, the judge in question made remarks about the high-profile criminal case he was handling at that time: from his statements, it became clear that the judge was a champion of zero tolerance policy towards crime, but the statements were too general to jeopardise the judge's impartiality.[74] The "maximum-discretion" principles seem to be based on the debatable assumption that in such contexts, the judge's speech by definition has undesirable consequences. It is, however, not inconceivable that an explanation by the judge on a pending case would promote public confidence in the judiciary.[75] In comparison, the Bangalore Principles of Judicial Conduct[76] and the Model Code of Judicial Conduct from the American Bar Association (ABA)[77] take a more relaxed approach towards speech on pending cases. They prescribe that a judge shall not make comments that might reasonably be expected to affect

71 See, for instance, *Kayasu v Turkey* App Nos. 64119/00 and 76292/01 (ECHR, 13 November 2008), [100]; *Di Giovanni v Italy* App No. 51160/06 (ECHR, 9 July 2013), [80]; *Marcolino de Jesus v Portugal* App No. 2388/15 (ECHR, 1 June 2021), [60]; *Manole v Moldovia* App No. 26360/19 (ECHR, 18 July 2023), [65]–[66].

72 *Manole* (n 71), [66]. The Court found a violation of Article 10 ECHR because at the national level the case had not been decided in accordance with the Court's case law and because the disciplinary dismissal of the judge could not be considered necessary in a democratic society.

73 *Chim and Przywieczerski v Poland* App Nos. 36661/07 and 38433/07 (ECHR, 12 April 2018).

74 Ibid. [165].

75 Lack of freedom to react to criticism may also evoke judges to initiate libel or defamation cases against their critics, a practice that may meet with ethical objections. An example is *Tavares de Almeida Fernandes and Almeida Fernandes v Portugal* App No. 31566/13 (ECHR, 17 January 2017).

76 <unodc.org/pdf/crime/corruption/judicial_group/Bangalore_principles.pdf>, accessed 28 March 2024.

77 The *ABA Model Code of Judicial Conduct*, 2020 edition (ABA Book Publishing 2020), Canon 2.10(A).

the outcome of impending or pending cases or impair the manifest fairness in the process.[78]

Speech on the judge's potential future or impending cases may be precarious as well, as appears from the case *E. v Switzerland*,[79] about the criminal court judge who risked his impartiality by publicly demanding the amnesty of certain detainees. The case *Eminağaoğlu v Turkey*[80] shows that, in the end, here, too, the limits of speech are the product of a weighing exercise. The case concerns the criticism of a public prosecutor of the Court of Cassation on an ongoing criminal investigation, with which he had no involvement (yet). The Court on the one hand attached importance to the fact that the criticism was aimed at the preventive measures and not at the criminal case as such and that it concerned a matter of public interest, factors that argue in favour of the exercise of freedom of expression. The Court, however, also considered that there could be room for restrictions because the criticism could also be regarded as aimed at the way the judicial authorities were handling the situation. The assessment was complicated by the fact that the magistrate was also the chair of a judges' association, implying that there was also a certain duty to speak out. The conclusion that Article 10 ECHR was violated in this case is predominantly motivated by the lack of procedural protection at the national level, as a consequence of which the exact weight of the other circumstances remains unclear.[81]

The contribution of the opinion to the public debate

In many cases, the judge's opinions concern the judiciary and related issues. The Court in principle regards such opinions as a contribution to a public debate, and it is standard case law that a public debate allows for few restrictions.[82] In *Żurek v Poland*, this was further underlined by the Court's choice to afford extra protection to statements in defence of judicial independence and the rule of law made by judges in special representative positions.[83] The Court does examine whether the link with the public debate justifies the strong protection. When, for instance, opinions disparage a certain group of people, especially vulnerable groups, they are not afforded.[84] Opinions also meet the special limits of a debate about the judiciary. The case *Prager and Oberschlick v Austria*[85] has set the standard: it may be necessary to protect public confidence in the judiciary against gravely damaging attacks that are

78 The Bangalore Principles of Judicial Conduct (n 64), application 2.4.
79 *E.* (n 8).
80 *Eminağaoğlu* (n 4).
81 Ibid. [138]–[140].
82 See, for instance, *Morice* (n 66), [125].
83 *Żurek* (n 15), [222].
84 For instance, *Zhablyanov v Bulgaria* App No. 36658/18 (ECHR, 27 June 2023), [112].
85 *Prager and Oberschlick* App No. 15974/90 (ECHR, 16 April 1995).

essentially unfounded.[86] This consideration is based on the view that judges who are criticised are "subject to a duty of discretion that precludes them from replying".[87] These words do not seem to leave any room for judges to react. As with the "maximum-discretion" principles discussed above, the strictness seems to be based on the assumption that the judge's speech always has negative consequences. Here, too, the ABA Model Code is illustrative of a different approach: on the condition that the judge does not affect the outcome or impair the fairness of a proceeding, he may respond directly or through a third party to allegations in the media or elsewhere concerning his conduct.[88]

In the case of *Tavares de Almeida Fernandes and Almeida Fernandes v Portugal*,[89] the Court has nuanced its strictness somewhat. In this case, the criticism was aimed at the President of the Supreme Court. This judge is seen as having more room to defend himself in public because he fulfils tasks that are not part of adjudication, as a result of which there is also more space to criticise the judge. The room for the judge to express himself and the room for critics to vent criticism are communicating vessels. Relevant here is that the criticism was not aimed at the performance of the judge in any adjudicatory tasks, but purely concerned his career and personality.[90] In such a situation there is less risk that the adjudicatory process is damaged by an exchange of opinions between the press and the judge.

It is also standard case law that, apart from the Prager situation, the limits of acceptable criticism from judges or other critiques may be wider with regard to judges who act in an official capacity than with regard to ordinary citizens.[91] This is especially so when the criticised judge holds a visible function, as in the case *Panioglu v Romania*,[92] where the subject of the judge's suggestive letter on the internet was the President of the Court of Cassation.[93] There are, however, also cases from which it appears that judges should show restraint when they express criticism about their fellow civil servants, in particular about other judges.[94] These two seemingly contradictory approaches coexist in the Court's case law regarding the judge's speech and it is not completely clear how they relate to each other.

86 Ibid. [34]. See also, for instance, *Harris and others* (n 3), 653–657, about criticism aimed at judges.

87 *Prager and Oberschlick* (n 85), [34].

88 ABA Model Code (n 77) Canon 2.10(E).

89 T*avares de Almeida and Almeida Fernandes* (n 75).

90 Ibid. [93].

91 See, for instance, *Guz v Poland* App No. 965/12 (ECHR, 15 October 2020), [89]. See also, for instance, Harris and others (n 3), 670–674, about the bounds of acceptable criticism of specific groups.

92 *Panioglu* (n 11), [113].

93 However, because of, among other things, the modest sanction, there was no violation of Article 10 ECHR.

94 *Sarisu* (n 53), [36]. See also *Eminağaoğlu* (n 4), [136] referring to *Di Giovanni* (n 71) and *Simić* (n 29).

The negative consequences of the opinion

The negative consequences of an opinion are an element that weighs against the exercise of freedom of expression. These may take the form of damage to the judge's impartiality,[95] the authority of the judiciary,[96] or the reputation of other judges.[97] When statements impact an ongoing case, there may be a conflict between Article 6 ECHR and Article 10 ECHR, for instance, when the information disclosed could affect the secrecy of criminal investigations.[98] A balancing between these rights is then required, the outcome of which should not, according to the Court, in principle vary according to whether the complaint is lodged under Article 6 or under Article 10 ECHR.[99] The same applies to conflicts between Article 8 and Article 10 ECHR, which may occur when opinions affect the interests of others, for instance, because they have a negative effect on a person's reputation.[100]

The effect of an opinion may also depend on the audience it is directed to. In *Guz v Poland*, the judge's opinions were expressed in an "intra-judicial" context: the judge had vented criticism during the internal stage of a promotion procedure, so the opinions were known to only a few people.[101] The negative effects of the opinions were therefore regarded as limited.[102]

The negative consequences of the interference

The nature and severity of the interference play an important role in the balancing act as well. The judge may suffer the loss of a career because of a disciplinary dismissal,[103] have lessened career prospects because an offence is recorded in a personal file[104] or suffer financial consequences.[105] The national authorities are expected to examine whether appropriate sanctions are available that are less intrusive.[106] The broader effect of the interference, also described as the "chilling effect", may weigh heavily against an interference.[107] This effect refers

95 *E.* (n 8); *Pitkevich* (12).
96 *Kudeshkina* (n 67); *Goryaynova* (n 4).
97 *Di Giovanni* (n 71); *Panioglu* (n 11).
98 For instance, *Brisc* (n 15).
99 For instance, *Bédat v Switzerland* App No. 56925/08 (ECHR, 29 March 2016) [52]–[53].
100 For instance, *Panioglu* (n 11); ECtHR Guide on Article 10 ECHR (n 3) 17–18.
101 *Guz* (n 91), [90].
102 For an audience consisting of only judges: *Peruzzi v Italy* App No. 39294/09 (ECHR, 30 June 2015).
103 For instance, *Kayasu* (n 71), [105]–[106]; *Kövesi* (n 4), [209]; *Goryaynova* (n 4), [64]; *Manole* (n 71), [69].
104 For instance, *Panioglu* (n 11), [120].
105 For instance, *Lishnyak* (n 67), [58].
106 For instance, *Goryaynova* (n 4), [65].
107 See for an extensive analysis of the chilling effect in this segment of the Court's case law: M. Fajdiga & S. Zagorc, 'Freedom or Feardom of Expression of Judges? Exploring the "Chilling Effect" on Judicial Speech', *European Constitutional Law Review* 19: 249–270, 2023.

to the discouraging consequences an interference may have on the further exercise of freedom of expression by the judge in question, by other judges, or the rest of society. In *Żurek v Poland*[108] and *Tuleya v Poland*,[109] for instance, the Court saw the intimidating actions by the national authorities as a source of a "chilling effect" on the ongoing public debate about the judiciary and legislation in Poland.[110] In the case of *Kayasu v Turkey*, the Court explained why this factor is so important: society as a whole suffers, since the chill negatively affects public confidence in the ability of judicial officials to do what is necessary to maintain the rule of law.[111]

The procedure at the national level

A lack of fairness in the proceedings at the national level may strongly argue in favour of a violation of Article 10 ECHR. Sometimes there is no opportunity at all to fight the interference.[112] The premature termination of Baka's mandate, for instance, was the result of legislation at the constitutional level, which was not open to judicial review. Sometimes there is a possibility to fight the measure, but the national procedure is defective or turns out to be defective in the specific case. In the case *Kudeshkina v Russia*,[113] for instance, the judge's opinions included allegations of pressure put on her by the president of the same court that later reviewed the judge's disciplinary dismissal.[114] In some cases, the national courts have not assessed the case in a "Convention-compliant manner",[115] that is, in accordance with the framework the Court has developed in its case law.[116] In those cases, the national courts may have failed to properly examine whether the measure is necessary in a democratic society because they did not make a proper analysis of the key elements of the case, such as the nature and veracity of the opinions, the motives for expressing them, or the alleged damage caused by them.[117]

The complexity of the balancing exercise

Determining the point of fair balance between the competing interests in the necessity test may be a complex exercise. Many facts need to be taken into

108 *Żurek* (n 15).
109 *Tuleya* (n 28).
110 See also *Juszczyszyn v Poland* App No. 35599/20 (ECHR, 6 October 2022) [337].
111 *Kayasu* (n 71), [106].
112 For instance, *Baka* (n 13), [121], [174].
113 *Kudeshkina* (n 67).
114 Ibid. [97].
115 This terminology: *Gudmundur Andri Ástráđson v Iceland* App No. 26374/18 (ECHR, 1 December 2020), [278].
116 For instance, *Eminağaoğlu* (n 4), [151]; *Miroslava Todorova* (n 26), [178].
117 *Goryaynova* (n 4), [65].

consideration, and the analysis above shows that the Court's principles that guide the weighing process are not always easily reconcilable with each other. A further complexity is present in the fact that the weighing scales are emphatically placed within the national context. This is not only visible in cases that play against the background of recent democratic backsliding developments, but also in the role specific historic events may play,[118] such as the communist past of a member state.[119] In this overall assessment, the public debate about the judiciary is a factor that often sets the direction towards freedom. The cases concerning judges who speak out in support of the rule of law or judicial independence seem to form a category of their own. The Court has approached their speech as the fulfilment of a duty, which makes it difficult to conceive that the outcome of the balancing exercise would be anything other than space for the exercise of freedom of expression. After all, when acting on a duty, there is no choice but to speak.[120] In cases where the public debate about the judiciary and the defence of the rule of law is less prominent, the restrictions that follow from, especially, the protection of the adjudicatory process are felt stronger.

Conclusion

The Court's case law regarding the judge's freedom of expression has grown in momentum after the landmark case of *Baka v Hungary*[121] from 2016. Since then, the Court has handled more cases on this subject than in the entire period up to that case. The framework of Article 10 ECHR that the Court has developed in these cases is complex. Many factors play a role in the assessment of a case, often making the outcome difficult to predict, and some of the Court's considerations and guiding principles are not easy to reconcile with each other. The predicament of judges who have been caught up in the democratic backsliding events in the CEE countries has left a clear mark on the case law since 2016, adding to the already existing complexity of the framework. In cases set in a context where the rule of law is under threat, the Court has developed an approach that is highly protective of speech that defends the rule of law. In some cases, the protection of Article 10 ECHR extends itself to official statements made by judges as part of their judicial duties,[122] something that is difficult to unite with the Court's case law under Article 34 ECHR. With this, the distinction between the individual and the state as a victim of a

118 For instance, *Vogt v Germany* App No. 17851/91 (ECHR, 26 September 1995); *Panioglu* (n 11).

119 See, for instance, *Rekvényi v Hungary* App No. 25390/94 (ECHR, 20 May 1999) for police officers and *Panioglu* (n 11) for judges.

120 See also *Brisc* (n 15) (Judge Kūris and Yudkivska) about the character of a duty of a state official.

121 *Baka* (n 13).

122 Ibid., *Kövesi* (n 4), *Brisc* (n 15).

violation of Article 10 ECHR has faded.[123] The judge's speech has also benefited from the introduction in these cases of a shift of the burden of proof in the assessment of whether Article 10 ECHR is applicable to the case.[124] This construction relieves judges to a high degree from the burden of proving their claim that the national authorities have restricted their freedom of expression. The Court has also made several choices in the context of the necessity test that strengthen the freedom of judges to speak out in support of the rule of law. A narrow margin of appreciation has been introduced,[125] allowing the Court to look more critically at the case, and additional protection is afforded to statements made by judges in representative functions, such as chairman of a national union of judges or spokesperson of a judicial council.[126] Finally, the Court has referred to a duty of judges to speak out in support of the rule of law.[127] This is a very clear sign of support for both the judge and the rule of law, since the presence of a duty provides a strong justification for the judge's speech. The nuances, variations, and fragmentation of the Court's case law notwithstanding, it therefore emerges from the analysis that the rule of law is nowadays leading the way in the Court's case law on the freedom of expression of judges.

123 *Grzęda* (n 58) (Judge Woytyczek).
124 See notes 31 and 32.
125 See notes 45 and 46.
126 See notes 53 and 54.
127 See note 55.

3 Chilling effect or no chilling effect

To be or not to be for freedom of expression of judges before the European Court of Human Rights

Mohor Fajdiga

Introduction

The rule of law crisis has revealed that courts and other independent institutions are less resilient than previously thought.[1] It has also given us some shining examples of uprightness and professional courage. Judges Baka, Tuleya, Żurek, and others fearlessly spoke up to defend the rule of law. Many risked their careers to preserve judicial independence. However, these models of judicial virtue represent only a minuscule part of the judicial corps. Why did the large majority remain silent? The reasons are manifold. One of them is certainly the chilling effect: the effect of (potential) sanctions for expressing one's opinion, creating fear, which dissuades people from speaking about a certain topic at all or compels them to use milder, more indirect or subtle ways of communicating their views.

The European academic community has hardly paid any attention to this behavioural phenomenon,[2] despite its prominent role in the jurisprudence of the European Court of Human Rights (the Court). The Court often relies on the chilling effect in two stages of the review: when deciding whether the measure interferes with one of the rights guaranteed under the European Convention for the Protection of Human Rights and Fundamental Freedoms (the Convention), and when ruling on the proportionality of the interference.[3]

1 Tom Ginsburg, Aziz Z Huq, and Mila Versteeg, 'The Coming Demise of Liberal Constitutionalism?' (2018) 85 The University of Chicago Law Review 239, p. 258.

2 Rónán Ó Fathaigh, 'Article 10 and the Chilling Effect: A Critical Examination of How the European Court of Human Rights Seeks to Protect Freedom of Expression from the Chilling Effect' (doctoral dissertation, Ghent University 2019); Judith Townend, 'Freedom of Expression and the Chilling Effect', in Howard Tumber, Silvio Waisbord (eds), *The Routledge Companion to Media and Human Rights* (Routledge 2017); Laurent Pech, 'The Concept of the Chilling Effect: Its Untapped Potential to Better Protect Democracy, the Rule of Law, and Fundamental Rights in the EU' (2021) Open Society Foundations <https://www.opensocietyfoundations.org/publications/the-concept-of-chilling-effect>, accessed 24 February 2024; Mohor Fajdiga and Saša Zagorc, 'Freedom or Feardom of Expression of Judges? Exploring the "Chilling Effect" on Judicial Speech' (2023) 19 European Constitutional Law Review 249.

3 Fathaigh (n 2), 355.

DOI: 10.4324/9781003470779-4

In both stages, the chilling effect emerges as an important element in favour of increased human rights protection. In cases with a clear interference with a certain Convention right, it is hard to determine and evaluate the impact of the chilling effect on the balancing exercise, since the chilling effect features only as one of the many elements the Court considers. The paramount role of this socio-legal concept comes much more clearly through in cases where the interference itself is disputable. These are instances where no tangible sanction is imposed or when the measure is so mild that it hardly affects the legal position of the applicant. In such cases, the concept of chilling effect works as a gatekeeper of Convention protection. In other words, the Court has employed the chilling effect argument to bring the case under its purview when it is deemed that the applicant had suffered no meaningful harm.[4] Deterrence of future exercise of Convention rights served as a trigger for the application of Convention guarantees when the measure hardly affected the applicant's position. However, in other similar cases, the Court ruled that no chilling effect occurred or simply omitted any reference to this argument. This resulted in inadmissibility decisions or findings of no interference with rights guaranteed by the Convention. The Convention protection in such cases thus largely hinges upon the appearance or absence of the chilling effect argument in the reasoning of the Court. When the Court invokes the chilling effect, it finds an interference with the freedom of expression and the Convention guarantees kick in; when it rules the measure had no chilling effect, the safeguards of the Convention do not apply. This applies equally to cases concerning freedom of expression of judges. In cases where the applicant has suffered no evident harm, the protection of judges, guaranteed under Article 10 of the Convention, therefore seems to stand or fall on the notion of chilling effect.

However, the chilling effect is a behavioural phenomenon. The Court lacks sufficient expertise to properly assess its impact on future expression and hence struggles to grasp this socio-legal concept. Admittedly, this is a daunting task: since not every measure that social scientists have found to affect future expression can be relevant in court, the Court must find ways to distinguish between measures that create a legally relevant chilling effect and those that do not. On the one hand, an over-generous consideration of chilling effect could flood the Court with applications that would otherwise be inadmissible. A strict approach, on the other hand, could result in turning the Court into a toothless tiger, especially since the era of crude interferences with freedom of expression seems to be over. Instead, we are increasingly witnessing indirect, subtle, refined measures and other actions designed to fly below the radar of

4 The Court assesses such cases using the victim status requirement from Article 34 of the Convention, the no significant disadvantage rule from Article 35 (3) (b) of the Convention, and/or the question of existence of interference with the applicable article of the Convention.

courts.[5] If the Court fails to address them, there might not be much left of a meaningful protection of freedom of expression in Strasbourg. How the Court draws this dividing line is therefore an issue crucially important for freedom of expression in such cases. It is the question of "to be or not to be" for freedom of expression of judges.

Even in a narrow area of case law covering only freedom of expression of judges, the Court has not yet designed a convincing approach for distinguishing cases that merit the application of the chilling effect argument from those that do not. In *Wille v Liechtenstein*, for example, the Court found that a declaration by the Prince of Liechtenstein – the authority competent for reappointing the applicant judge – that he would not reappoint Judge Wille, constituted an interference with (and a violation of) freedom of expression, even though it clearly had no immediate impact on the applicant's position. It was a mere declaration from a private letter with no legal effect. The Court nevertheless found that such a threat created the chilling effect, affecting the applicant's future expression.[6] On the other hand, in *M. D. and Others v Spain*, the Court found that no chilling effect arose, even though the police had unlawfully created a secret file containing personal data and images of judges, which was later leaked to the media, resulting in a disciplinary procedure against judges who signed a manifesto in support of the right to secession of the Catalan people.[7] These two cases illustrate the difficulties in finding a convincing approach for determining the existence of the chilling effect. There are arguments for and against finding a legally relevant chilling effect in both cases presented. It arguably even seems that the Catalan judges suffered more in reaction to their exercise of freedom of expression than their colleague from Liechtenstein. The Court could therefore arguably come to the reverse conclusion that the chilling effect occurred in *M. D. and Others* and that there was no chilling effect in *Wille*.

To determine how the Court performs this daunting task, this chapter provides a doctrinal analysis of the Court's jurisprudence. It covers cases focusing on the existence of interference, victim status, or no significant disadvantage rule, where the chilling effect argument features in the reasoning of the Court. Relying on the rich jurisprudence of the Strasbourg court and the chilling effect theory, the chapter fleshes out and critically analyses the circumstances relevant for the Court when determining the existence of the chilling effect. To pinpoint the circumstances that the Court deems important when drawing

5 Tim Wu, 'Is the First Amendment Obsolete?' (2018) 117 Michigan Law Review 547; Zeynep Tufekci, *Twitter and Tear Gas: The Power and Fragility of Networked Protest* (Yale University Press 2017); Rebecca Tushnet, 'First Amendment Today: Not Obsolete, But …' (2019) 19; Barrie Sander, 'Democratic Disruption in the Age of Social Media: Between Marketized and Structural Conceptions of Human Rights Law' (2021) 32 European Journal of International Law 159.

6 *Wille v Liechtenstein*, App No. 28396/95 (ECHR, 28 October 1999).

7 *M.D. and Others v Spain*, App No. 36584/17 (ECHR, 28 June 2022), para 90.

the line between negligible and non-negligible chilling effect on freedom of expression of judges, the chapter draws from the case law on various articles of the Convention and concerning applicants of different professions such as journalists, teachers, judges, other civil servants, and even ordinary citizens. It shows that the admissibility requirements and their underlying rationales currently seem to have clipped the wings of chilling effect – an argument with great potential to increase the level of protection of human rights. The analysis also shows that the jurisprudence is consistent only within narrowly construed strands of case law, whereas glaring inconsistencies exist in the jurisprudence overall. The chapter argues that this is a consequence of the fact that the legal landscape in which the chilling effect operates largely determines the outcome of its evaluation, which is done by judges who are legal professionals lacking the required expertise to evaluate the actual occurrence and strength of this behavioural phenomenon.

The nature of the chilling effect and the inevitable difficulties for courts

The chilling effect – fear created by regulation or concrete measures, which forces the individual to accommodate his or her future behaviour to avoid negative repercussions[8] – is a behavioural phenomenon that is extremely hard to measure and assess.[9] Some argue that the judicial use of the chilling effect is purely speculative,[10] as judges are not experts in behavioural psychology, mass communication, or any other social science offering expertise in this field. These areas of science indicate that many different factors affect our future behaviour. Moreover, the findings of social scientists who specialise in self-censorship or related concepts[11] often diverge. Some research suggests

8 For a freedom of expression-specific definition of the chilling effect, see: Council of Ministers of the Council of Europe, Recommendation CM/Rec(2016)4 on the protection of journalism and safety of journalists and other media actors, 13 April 2016, https://search.coe.int/cm/Pages/result_details.aspx?ObjectId=09000016806415d9#_ftn1, accessed 24 February 2024, p. 23, para 33.

9 Townend (n 2), 73.

10 Leslie Kendrick, 'Speech, Intent, and the Chilling Effect' (2013) 54 William & Mary Law Review 1633, argues that the doctrine of chilling effect rests "*on nothing more than unpersuasive empirical guesswork*". In referring to the US Supreme Court's famous case of New York Times Co. v Sullivan, Schauer claims that the court's judgment "*was based on what was at best armchair economics and at worst casual speculation* ..." (Frederick Schauer, The Dilemma of Ignorance: PGA Tour, INC. v Casey Martin' (2001) The Supreme Court Review 267, p. 286). Suneal Bedi, 'The Myth of the Chilling Effect' (2021) 35 Harvard Journal of Law & Technology 268.

11 The chilling effect is a legal term. Other social sciences have established their own concepts, which are related and often overlap with the notion of the chilling effect, for example: self-censorship (Daniel Bar-Tal, 'Self-Censorship as a Socio-Political-Psychological Phenomenon: Conception and Research' (2017) 38 Political Psychology 37; Kurt Neuwirth, Edward Frederick, and Charles Mayo, 'The Spiral of Silence and Fear of Isolation' (2007) 57 Journal of

that people are very impressionable and inclined to adapt their behaviour to social norms and expectations,[12] whereas other studies raise serious doubts as to whether the fear of sanction actually has such an impact on behaviour as traditionally assumed.[13] Recently, the traditional liberal premise that people's decision-making process is rational has come under severe pressure.[14] Whether judges recognise it or not, they face an extremely demanding task: they have to assess the existence and strength of a behavioural phenomenon without having any training in this respect.

Nevertheless, it would be wrong to assume that judges determine the actual existence and strength of chilling effect. As legal professionals, they apply the legal notion of chilling effect in view of circumstances of each individual case. The nature of their assessment is legal. Various social sanctions, such as public ridicule, a cool reception, intolerance of error, ostracism, disparagement, and disrespect[15] are certainly capable of affecting our future behaviour. Practically any legislation, even if not implemented in a concrete case, is liable to raise some chilling effect if understood in the social sense.[16] However, this does not mean that the courts must recognise such chilling effect as legally relevant. Otherwise, they could strike an improper balance between the competing interests. Judges therefore must come up with an approach to distinguish

---

Communication 450), conformity (Vernon L. Allen, 'Situational Factors in Conformity' in Leonard Berkowitz (ed), *Advances in Experimental Social Psychology* (Academic Press 1965)); self-restraint and self-control (Emily Chamlee-Wright, 'Self-Censorship and Associational Life in the Liberal Academy' (2019) 56 Society 538; John Horton, 'Self-Censorship' (2011) 17 Res Publica 91); obedience (Stanley Milgram, 'Behavioural Study of Obedience' (1963) 67 The Journal of Abnormal and Social Psychology 371); social influence, group pressure, social control, groupthink (Irving L. Janis, *Groupthink: Psychological Studies of Policy Decisions and Fiascoes* (2nd edition, Wadsworth Publishing 1982)); communication apprehension (James C. McCroskey, 'The Communication Apprehension Perspective' in J.A. Daly and James C McC.roskey (eds), *Avoiding Communication: Shyness, Reticence, and Communication* (SAGE Publications 1984)); avoidance (Andrew F. Hayes, 'Exploring the Forms of Self-Censorship: On the Spiral of Silence and the Use of Opinion Expression Avoidance Strategies' (2007) 57 Journal of Communication 785); fear of social isolation as one of the central elements of the theory of the spiral of silence (Elisabeth Noelle-Neumann, 'The Spiral of Silence: A Theory of Public Opinion' (1974) 24 Journal of Communication 43).

12 See, for example, Solomon E. Asch, 'Studies of Independence and Conformity: I. A Minority of One against a Unanimous Majority' (1956) 70 Psychological Monographs: General and Applied 1.

13 Jonathon W. Penney, 'Understanding Chilling Effects' 2022 Minnesota Law Review 1451, pp. 1470–1472.

14 Ibid., p. 1470.

15 Christopher J Ryan, 'A Qualitative Approach to Spiral of Silence Research: Self-Censorship Narratives Regarding Environmental and Social Conflict' (Antioch University of New England 2011) <https://aura.antioch.edu/etds/801>, p. 186, referring to Elisabeth Noelle-Neumann, *The Spiral of Silence: Public Opinion – Our Social Skin* (University of Chicago Press 1993).

16 Frederick Schauer, 'Fear, Risk and the First Amendment: Unraveling the Chilling Effect' (1978) 1978 58 Boston University Law Review 685, pp. 700–701.

between legally relevant and legally irrelevant chilling effect. How the Court has performed this daunting task will be the focus of the following parts of this chapter.

The analysis of the Court's case law

The Court's jurisprudence concerning the concept of chilling effect is far from settled. Legal scholars have already noticed the discrepancies in the Court's case law.[17] In some cases, the Court simply does not rely on the chilling effect, even though the same argument made a resounding appearance in another arguably very similar case. Despite such inconsistencies, from the first cases in the 1980s, the Strasbourg Court has developed rich jurisprudence, which has great potential to ascertain the circumstances relevant for drawing the line between legally relevant and legally irrelevant chilling effect.

The analysis of the Court's case law, conducted for the purposes of this chapter, does not focus merely on judges' and prosecutors' freedom of expression. It has a much broader scope covering other professions such as lawyers, journalists, teachers, academics, other civil servants, and even random applicants. It relies on the premise that the circumstances the Court uses to distinguish between legally relevant and irrelevant chilling effect should be analogous in cases concerning the rights of judges as well as other applicants. In other words, considerations that determine the Court's approach to cases in which the chilling effect plays a role in establishing the standing of the applicants should be similar irrespective of the applicant's profession and the Convention right in question. In addition to Article 10, it also examines complaints concerning other Convention rights, even though the chilling effect is mostly invoked in cases concerning freedom of expression.[18] The analysis omits cases that have little to no potential of being relevant for the question of freedom of expression of judges.[19]

The HUDOC database was used to select the relevant case law by conducting three separate inquiries. The selection included judgments of chambers or the grand chamber as well as admissibility decisions. First, an alternative combination of keywords "no significant disadvantage", "victim status", "actio popularis", "manifestly ill-founded", and "interference" (regarding Articles 8, 9, 10, and 11 of the Convention) was combined with the text search "chilling effect" OR[20] "effet dissuasif". The first inquiry yielded 289 results, amounting

17 Ó Fathaigh (n 2), pp. 48–49; Fajdiga and Zagorc (n 2), p. 268.

18 Ó Fathaigh (n 2), p. 352.

19 Cases concerning government surveillance (for example, *Big Brother Watch v The United Kingdom* App Nos. 58170/13, 62322/14, 24960/15 (ECHR, 13 September 2018)) or the protection of journalistic sources (for example, *Sanoma Uitgevers B.V. v the Netherlands* (GC) App No. 38224/03 (ECHR, 14 September 2010)).

20 Boolean operator OR was used to encompass cases in English and those available only in French.

to 179 individual decisions.[21] Second, the inquiry aimed to identify cases in which the Court explicitly denied the existence of chilling effect. It relied on the text search function using the phrase "no chilling effect" OR "any chilling effect" OR "4751/07", the latter being the application number of the oldest relevant case in which the Court found that the measure entailed no chilling effect.[22] The second inquiry yielded 57 results, amounting to 43 cases, 29 of which were new compared to the first inquiry. Third, an additional inquiry, which turned out to be necessary during the analysis of the case law, again combined the text search "chilling effect" OR "effet dissuasive" with an alternative combination of keyword searches, which included "prescribed by law" requirement of Articles 8, 9, 10, and 11 of the Convention. The third inquiry found 194 results, amounting to 113 individual cases, and added another 46 new cases to the sample. The end cut-off date was set at 26 August 2023. The dataset thus included the relevant case law stretching over more than four decades.[23] All three inquiries yielded a total of 254 decisions. Cases were classified into three categories based on the chilling potential of the source of chilling effect: national legislation with the lowest chilling potential, individualised threats and legal accountability procedures with no sanctions with the highest chilling potential.[24]

Chilling effect stemming from national legislation

Legal scholars from the United States have traditionally underlined the importance of chilling effect stemming from the legislation. The debate in the United States often revolves around the legislative enactment itself, and not necessarily around the concrete application of the law at hand.[25] The US Supreme Court regularly strikes down laws that are overbroad, for example. Conversely, the Court finds a violation of the Convention on account of chilling effect created by the legislation only in exceptional cases. The Strasbourg Court is

21 When decisions were issued in a single case by more Convention bodies (chamber, grand chamber, and the commission), each decision counted as one unit.

22 In *Pedersen and Baadsgaard v. Denmark* (GC) App No. 49017/99 (ECHR 17 December 2004), para 93, the Court found that the sanctions imposed on journalists for a defamatory TV programme were not excessive or of such a kind as to have a chilling effect. The case is not relevant for my analysis since the chilling effect argument was used in the context of the proportionality test and not regarding the existence of interference or victim status. For a critical account on the use of the chilling effect in this case, see Ó Fathaigh (n 2), pp. 48–49.

23 The first case, included in the dataset – *X v the Federal Republic of Germany* App No. 9704/82 (EComHR, 16 December 1982) – is at the same time the first case in which one of the Convention bodies explicitly relies on the notion of the chilling effect.

24 The premise of different chilling potential relies on findings from Jonathon W Penney, 'Internet Surveillance, Regulation, and Chilling Effects Online: A Comparative Case Study' (2017) 6 Internet Policy Review.

25 See, for example, Schauer (n 16); Kendrick (n 10); Brandice Canes-Wrone and Michael Dorf, 'Measuring the Chilling Effect' 2015 New York University Law Review 1095.

not a constitutional court and does not perform constitutional review of the impugned legislation.[26] It is interested in concrete prejudice to the applicant's Convention rights. This explains the scarcity of case law in the first category. The analysis identified two strands of case law.

Chilling effect stemming from national legislation, which is not applied to the applicant's detriment

In the absence of concrete implementation of the legislation, the applicant is normally not able to convince the Court to consider him or her to be a victim in the sense of Article 34 of the Convention. "Victim status" requirement in principle requires that only those who have suffered a direct prejudice to their Convention rights ("direct victims") can reach the Court. Individuals cannot "complain against a law *in abstracto* simply because they feel that it contravenes the Convention", as there is no *actio popularis* before the Court. In principle, the applicant therefore cannot successfully claim that "the mere existence of a law violates his rights under the Convention". The law must be applied to his or her detriment.[27] Nevertheless, in some cases, the applicants were successful in claiming to be victims because the law itself worked as an effective constraint on their actions protected by the Convention. In such cases, the applicants often relied on the chilling effect to claim that the national legislation, not entailing any immediate consequences, made them afraid of being punished. They argued that the fear of future negative repercussions affected their behaviour, making them a victim of interference, even though no tangible sanction had been imposed.[28] However, the very purpose of the law is to influence the behaviour of legal subjects. This is why the Court used this exception only in cases in which the applicants were able to show that the national legislation strikes at the very heart of their personal identity, hollows out the protection of a certain Convention right, or substantially compromises the role a certain group plays in a democratic society. For example *Dudgeon*[29] and *Norris*,[30] the first and third case in which one of the Convention bodies

26 Compare to the Court of Justice of the EU (for example, case C-204/21 *Commission v Poland* (GC), 5 June 2023, paras 101, 158–159).

27 *Klass and others v Germany* App No. 5029/71 (ECHR, 6 September 1978), para 33; *Burden v the United Kingdom* (GC) App No. 13378/05 (ECHR, 29 April 2008), para 33.

28 In such cases, the Court has explicitly recognised the connection between victim status and the existence of interference (*Altuğ Taner Akçam v Turkey*, App No. 27520/07 (ECHR, 25 October 2011), paras 51, 65, 82–83; *Döner and Others v Turkey*, App No. 29994/02 (ECHR, 7 March 2017), para 81; *Metis Yayincilik Limited Sirketi and Sökmen v Turkey*, App No. 4751/07 (ECHR, 20 June 2017), paras 35–36; *Schweizerische Radio- und Fernsehgesellschaft and Others v Switzerland*, App No. 68995/13 (ECHR, 12 November 2019), para 68; *Ayuso Torres v Spain* (n 7), paras 30, 41–45).

29 *Dudgeon* v *the United Kingdom*, App No. 7525/76 (EComHR, 13 March 1980).

30 *Norris v. Ireland* App No. 10581/83 (EComHR 12 March 1987).

relied on the chilling effect,[31] concerned homosexual men who complained about Irish and British legislation criminalising homosexual conduct. Even though no criminal procedure was initiated, the Commission recognised them as victims since they ran a risk of being prosecuted as there was no official policy not to prosecute for homosexual behaviour. The impugned legislation had not been applied against the applicants, yet it affected their right to private life from Article 8 of the Convention as they had to choose between accommodating their behaviour and risking punishment. The chilling effect therefore bestowed on them the victim status.[32] Similarly, in *S.A.S. v France*,[33] the applicant, a female Muslim, complained about the prohibition of wearing a headscarf in public places. In *Michaud v France*,[34] attorneys had to report to the authorities if they suspected their clients to be involved in money laundering. A failure to do so could have exposed them to a disciplinary sanction.

The underlying premise of this strand of case law is that the applicants are directly affected by the national legislation, even if no measures are taken against them, since they are required to submit to the legislation or live in constant fear of punishment. This is why the Court does not require the applicants to wait to be sanctioned to get access to the Strasbourg Court. Again, it is chilling effect – the fear of punishment, affecting such applicant's behaviour – that opens the door to the Palace of Human Rights.[35]

However, the Court has made sure that the door was not wide open, but rather left ajar. In *Akdeniz and Others v Turkey*, for example, the Court was faced with a ban on dissemination through any channels of practically any information on a parliamentary inquiry for a month and a half. Relying on the chilling effect of such an overbroad prior restraint, it only granted victim status to a journalist, but not to two university professors of law, even though one of them was the head of an NGO and the other the director of a human rights centre at his university, and both were active social media and internet users, running

31 Albeit in a non-explicit manner. In *X. v Federal Republic of Germany*, the European Commission for Human Rights explicitly mentioned the "chilling effect" for the first time. It served as one of the important arguments that led the European Commission to find that there had been an interference with the freedom of expression of a college lecturer, who was dismissed for being a prominent member of a far-right political party, which pursued anti-constitutional aims (Ó Fathaigh (n 2), pp. 23–26).

32 In contrast to Dudgeon, whom the police questioned for four hours regarding his sexual activities after incriminating material was found in a house search aiming at drugs, Norris was never even questioned by the police.

33 *S.A.S. v France* (GC) App No. 43835/11 (ECHR, 1 July 2014).

34 *Michaud v France* App No. 12323/11 (ECHR, 6 December 2012).

35 Both in *S.A.S.* and *Michaud*, the Court relied on the logic of chilling effect, without explicitly mentioning the term. However, in *Dilipak v Turkey*, App No. 29680/05 (ECHR, 15 September 2015), para 46, the Court explicitly invoked explicitly the chilling effect when making a reference to these judgments.

an online platform for the promotion of human rights.[36] The strict approach requires even the most suitable applicants to show a real and not merely a hypothetical chilling effect stemming from the legislation personally affects them.[37]

Chilling effect of national legislation applied to the applicant's detriment

In cases from the first strand of case law, chilling effect works as a gatekeeper to Convention protection. In contrast, when the law has been applied against the applicant, the issue is no longer so much the victim status, but rather the "prescribed by law" requirement and the function of gatekeeping of the chilling effect argument is abandoned. This explains why the Court seems to be at least slightly more willing to recognise chilling effect stemming from the legislation in such cases. Still, the case law remains scarce, since the chilling effect argument would lead the Court to implicitly strike down national legislation, an action that the Court carefully tries to avoid.

In the context of freedom of expression of judges, *Panioglu v Romania* and *Kozan v Turkey* indicate the low standard currently in place for the quality of domestic legislation in Strasbourg. Even though the lack of precision and foreseeability of the provision, which was used against Mrs Panioglu in a code-of-conduct proceeding, was later confirmed by the Romanian Court of Cassation in a similar case, the Court found the provision complied with the Convention standards. The Court seems to have considered the chilling effect created by the legislation to be entirely irrelevant, despite implicitly recognising it by declaring that if "she had doubts about the exact scope of the provision in question, she could have refrained from publishing the article".[38] In *Kozan v Turkey*, a judge was reprimanded for sharing a Facebook post. The applicant relied on the Opinion of the Venice Commission, which found that the provision allowing the imposition of a reprimand for "improper conduct, harming respect and trust required by the official position" was vague and too broad and thus capable of being abused for sanctioning judges whose decisions were not favourable to the authorities.[39] The Court acknowledged the

36 *Akdeniz and Others v Turkey* App Nos. 41139/15 and 41146/15 (ECHR, 4 May 2021), paras 62–63, 78. Judge Kūris was critical of such an approach by the court in his partly dissenting opinion.

37 See also *A.M. and A.K. v Hungary* App Nos. 21320/15 and 35837/15 (ECHR, 4 April 2017), in which the Court found that the applicants, patients suffering from chronic diseases, failed to show that they had discussed the use of cannabis-based medication with their doctors or tried to procure such medication following the legal procedure in place in Hungary. As a result, the Court ruled it could not infer that the Hungarian legislation, which criminalised possession, acquisition, and importation of narcotic drugs, was "formulated in such a way as to create a chilling effect on doctors wishing to prescribe such medications".

38 *Panioglu* v *Romania* App No. 33794/14 (ECHR, 8 December 2020), para 106.

39 Venice Commission, Opinion 610/2011, Draft opinion on the Law on Judges and Prosecutors of Turkey, 8 March 2011, CDL(2011)003, https://www.venice.coe.int/webforms/documents/?pdf=CDL(2011)003-e, para 60.

Opinion, but simply continued its assessment under the presumption that the provision was prescribed by law.[40] However, in *Tuleya v Poland*, which should be considered an exception to the otherwise reserved approach, the Court found the Polish legislation was in breach of the prescribed by law requirement, after recognising it created a chilling effect on the freedom of expression of judges, since it essentially gave a carte blanche to the disciplinary prosecutor to initiate preliminary inquiries against judges at his will.[41]

Chilling effect of individualised threats

Whereas national legislation is rarely found to create a meaningful chilling effect in Strasbourg, the Court is more likely to recognise the chilling effect of threats aimed at an identified or identifiable person or entity. This is consistent with a recent study that has shown an increased "chilling" potential of individualised threats compared to unapplied legislation.[42] Unfortunately, the inquiry did not identify cases in which the Court had to distinguish between the legally relevant and legally irrelevant chilling effect stemming from a threat. Nevertheless, the cases in which the Court recognised threats as a source of chilling effect can illustrate situations capable of creating a legally relevant chilling effect. This part focuses on cases concerning threats from public officials.[43] These cases are particularly worth exploring as they tie closely to cases in which the Court acknowledged the chilling effect stemming from accountability proceedings with no sanctions imposed (see section Chilling effect of legal accountability procedures with no sanctions).

40 *Kozan v Turkey*, App No. 16695/19 (ECHR, 1 March 2022) paras 53–57. The same approach was taken in *Eminağaoğlu* v *Turkey*, App No. 76521/12 (ECHR, 9 March 2021), para 130, in which the legal basis for a disciplinary offence allowing the transfer of a judge was defined equally vaguely and broadly: "inappropriate conduct incompatible with the honour and dignity of judicial office or [leading to] loss of personal dignity and honour".

41 *Tuleya v Poland* App Nos. 21181/19 and 51751/20 (ECHR, 6 July 2023) paras. 534–537. Beyond judicial free speech cases, the Court seems to stick to a similar approach. It mostly avoids the question of the quality of the law. There are only a handful of cases in which the chilling effect stemming from deficient legislation was recognised as legally relevant (Altuğ Taner Akçam v Turkey (n 28), para 93; *Karastelev and Others v Russia* App No. 16435/10 (ECHR, 6 October 2020), para 90; *Vajnai v Hungary* App No. 33629/06 (ECHR, 8 July 2008) paras 54, 56).

42 Penney (n 24).

43 The Court is also willing to recognise threats emanating from private parties as a source of chilling effect (*Gaši and Others v Serbia* App No. 24738/19 (ECHR, 6 September 2022, para 78); *Dink v Turkey,* App Nos. 2668/07, 6102/08, 30079/08, 7072/09 and 7124/09 (ECHR 14 September 2010), para 137; *Khadija Ismayilova v Azerbaijan*, App Nos. 65286/13 and 57270/14, (ECHR, 10 January 2019), para 158). However, these cases are less relevant for this chapter since the Court assesses them under the doctrine of positive obligations. A thorough analysis of the Court's approach in these cases is beyond the scope of this chapter.

A famous example is the already mentioned *Wille v Liechtenstein*. A similar case comes from the domain of freedom of assembly and association. In *Trade Union of the Police in the Slovak Republic and others v Slovakia*, police officers demonstrated against poor social security and low salaries of Slovak policemen, and even called for the government to resign. In reaction, the Slovak Minister of the Interior publicly stated that calling for the resignation of the government was a "slogan ... completely contrary to the ethical code" since the police "must remain strictly apolitical". He threatened to dismiss the police officers behaving in such a way in the future and explained that he had already demoted the president of the trade union and might adopt stricter sanctions for others. The Court found an interference with the freedom of assembly and association from Article 11 of the Convention, after establishing that "the applicants were intimidated by the Minister's statements, a situation which could have thus had a chilling effect and discouraged them from pursuing activities within the first applicant trade union, including organising or taking part in similar meetings".[44] With five votes to two, the Court later found no violation of Article 11. In a separate Opinion, two dissenting judges relied heavily on chilling effect and criticised the majority's nonchalant attitude to the Minister's statements and actions that effectively "muzzle[d] the trade union's leadership [and] undermined the very essence of the trade union's rights".[45]

Chilling effect of legal accountability procedures with no sanctions

When criminal, civil, administrative, or disciplinary procedures result in sanctions, they in principle[46] create a chilling effect. This is so even in cases where the sanction is imposed but is not implemented,[47] or when amnesty or extraordinary legal remedies ultimately lift the sanction. Instead of analysing these two categories, this section focuses on cases where legal accountability procedures were initiated but no sanctions were imposed. As case law from the previous section shows, such cases could also be qualified as threats that did not amount to sanctions. However, separate examination is merited since legal

44 *Trade Union of the Police in The Slovak Republic and Others v Slovakia*, App No. 11828/08 (ECHR, 25 September 2012), paras 12, 59–61.

45 *Trade Union of the Police in The Slovak Republic and Others v Slovakia*, App No. 11828/08 (ECHR, 25 September 2012), dissenting opinion of Judge Myjer joined by Judge Gyulumyan, para 7.

46 The analysis identified cases where a lenient sanction was imposed, but the Court nevertheless found no chilling effect and declared the applications inadmissible. See, for example, *Skiba v Poland* App No. 10659/03 (ECHR, 7 July 2009) and *Artemenko v Ukraine* App No. 54574/10 (ECHR, 14 May 2019). Nevertheless, these cases should be regarded as exceptional due to the unique circumstances that led the Court to find no chilling effect.

47 *Financial Times Ltd and Others v the United Kingdom* App No. 821/03 (ECHR, 15 December 2009), para 56.

accountability proceedings carry a more tangible threat and normally entail additional inconvenience for the person at hand.

When the authorities react to exercising freedom of expression, assembly, or another fundamental right with criminal procedures combined with the detention of the applicants, even if no sanction is eventually imposed, the Court normally has no trouble in finding that such measures create a chilling effect.[48] When the applicants are not detained, the matters become more complicated.

The Court has ruled on various occasions that

> [w]here criminal prosecutions based on specific criminal legislation are discontinued for procedural reasons, but the risk remains that the party concerned will be found guilty and punished, that party may validly claim to be the victim of a violation of the Convention.

By their nature, criminal procedures carry the threat of the strongest sanction, which is why the Court is particularly attentive when authorities use the criminal justice system against individuals who exercise their Convention rights.

In *Bowman v the United Kingdom*, the applicant was a pro-life activist who distributed leaflets with information on candidates' positions on abortion. She was charged under legislation prohibiting unauthorised persons from spending more than five pounds on promoting or procuring information on candidates for election in a period before elections. Criminal procedure was initiated, but the applicant was acquitted since the criminal prosecution was found to be time-barred. The Court found that the initiation of the procedure "was, at the very least, a strong indication to her that, unless she modified her behaviour during future elections, she would run the risk of being prosecuted again and possibly convicted and punished".[49] Similarly, the Court warned against the chilling effect of criminal procedures in numerous cases from Turkey, where starker penalties than those in Bowman[50] were at stake, and in which the prosecutions lasted for considerable time before being discontinued on procedural grounds.[51]

48 *Kandzhov v Bulgaria* App No. 68294/01 (ECHR, 6 November 2008); *Yaşar Kaplan v Turkey* App No. 56566/00 (ECHR, 24 January 2006), para 35; Mehmet Hasan Altan v Turkey, App No. 13237/17 (ECHR, 20 March 2018), para 212. Compare with *Döner and others v Turkey* (n 28), outlined in footnote no. 51 and in the main text in section Chilling effect: a hostage of admissibility requirements and rationales.

49 *Bowman v the United Kingdom* App No. 24839/94 (ECHR 19 February 1998), paras 12, 21, 29. See also *Lyashko v Ukraine* App No. 21040/02 (ECHR, 10 August 2006), paras 32–33.

50 In *Bowman*, the offence was punishable by a maximum sentence of one year's imprisonment and/or a fine of up to 5000 pounds, in addition to the potential loss of active and passive rights to vote to the House of Commons for up to five years.

51 *Kaboğlu and Oran v Turkey (no. 2)* App No. 36944/07 (ECHR, 20 October 2020), paras 113–115 (criminal procedures lasting more than three years, initiated by third parties in response to an official report the applicants authored on cultural and minority rights); *Selahattin Demirtaş v Turkey (no. 3)* App No. 8732/1 (ECHR, 9 July 2019), paras 25–26 (crimi-

As in the case of criminal sanctions, disciplinary sanctions for publicly expressing an opinion regularly create chilling effect and thus interfere with freedom of expression. In cases concerning judges and lawyers, the Court continuously finds that a mere reprimand is sufficient to grant the applicants victim status.[52] As we have seen with criminal proceedings, which do not result in a sanction, disciplinary proceedings without sanctions can also be a source of chilling effect. In *Steur v the Netherlands*, a lawyer argued in a civil case that incriminating statements his client made during an investigation for social security fraud could not have been obtained without unacceptable pressure. The social security investigation officer, offended by this remark, filed a disciplinary complaint to the local Bar Association, which partially upheld his complaint, without, however, imposing a sanction. The Court nevertheless found that

> the threat of an ex post facto review of his criticism with respect to the manner in which evidence was taken from his client is difficult to reconcile with his duty as an advocate to defend the interests of his clients and could have a "chilling effect" on the practice of his profession.[53]

Disciplinary proceedings can also create a chilling effect when they are discontinued on procedural grounds, but the risk remains that the person will be punished in the future. The Court recognised a potential chilling effect of the procedure that could lead to the dismissal of the President of the Slovak Supreme Court.[54] In *Ayuso Torres v Spain*, a professor of constitutional law, who was at the same time a member of the military legal corps, appeared on a televised debate where he discussed the Spanish transition and described

---

nal proceedings lasting for five years on charges of propaganda of a terrorist organisation); *Dilipak v Turkey* (n 34) (criminal proceedings lasting over six years, where a sentence from six months to three years threatened a journalist for insulting two generals of the Turkish army); *Ali Gürbüz v Turkey* App No. 52497/08 (ECHR, 12 March 2019), paras 63–64 (seven sets of criminal procedures, lasting up to seven years, initiated against an owner of a daily newspaper for publishing statements, irrespective of their content, of organisations designated as terrorist by the Turkish authorities); *Döner and Others v Turkey* (n 28), paras 87–89 (house search, arrest, detention, and criminal procedure for alleged support of terrorism; procedure lasting a year and four months, initiated against parents, who had written petitions for the use of the Kurdish language in public schools).

52 *Kozan v Turkey* (n 39); *Guz v Poland* App No. 965/12 (ECHR, 15 October 2020), para 73; *Di Giovanni* v *Italy* App No. 51160/06 (ECHR, 9 July 2013); *Ottan v France* App No. 41841/12 (ECHR, 19 April 2018), paras 25, 49. See also a case concerning a university professor (*Kula v Turkey* App No. 20233/06 (ECHR, 19 June 2018), para 39) and a case concerning a physician (*Frankowicz v Poland* App No. 53025/99 (ECHR, 16 December 2008), para 51).

53 *Steur v the Netherlands* App No. 39657/98 (ECHR, 28 October 2003) paras 15, 44. See also *Ottan v France* (n 52) (warning imposed on a lawyer in disciplinary proceedings).

54 ECtHR, No., *Harabin* v *Slovakia* App No. 62584/00 (ECHR 29 June 2004). The motion later failed to secure the required parliamentary majority.

the Spanish constitution as a "pseudo-constitution" with "spurious and bastardised" origins, ideas that he had previously also expressed in his academic articles. As a result, he was charged with a serious offence in military disciplinary proceedings, which were terminated after four months since they became time-barred. The Military Court did not find that the statements constituted a minor offence as the military general proposed. Instead, in an *obiter dictum*, the disciplinary decision stated that despite the academic context, the applicant had exceeded the contours of freedom of expression and that a restriction of the said right would be justified. The Court ruled that such a "conclusion could be deemed a *de facto* warning or admonition addressed to the applicant, which could have a chilling effect, preventing him from expressing in the future similar opinions since fresh disciplinary proceedings might be brought". The Court underlined the relatively serious nature of sanctions that could be imposed – "a maximum penalty of one month's house arrest if the facts had been found to amount to a minor offence and two months' committal to a disciplinary unit if they had been found to amount to a serious offence".[55]

The Court distinguished the case from *M.D. and Others v Spain*, discussed in the introduction of this chapter, where 20 Catalan judges wrote a manifesto supporting the right of the Catalan people to self-determination. In this case, the Court held that no chilling effect stemmed from the fact that disciplinary proceedings took place.[56] The Court found it significant that the disciplinary action was brought by a legitimate third party and not the state, that the Spanish authorities closed all the disciplinary proceedings in a relatively short time (less than a year) after finding that the manifesto was a "legitimate exercise of their freedom of expression and therefore no sanctions should be imposed", and that "the applicants continued their professional careers and were promoted under usual procedure by the General Council of the Judiciary without any prejudice resulting from their participation in the aforementioned manifesto".[57]

As can be seen from the above, the Court's approach to chilling effect is similar in disciplinary and criminal cases. The central question for the Court is whether the proceedings can be regarded as genuine and effective restrictions *per se*, or as comprising purely hypothetical risks to the applicant.[58] Since no other tangible sanction has been imposed, the existence of chilling effect determines the dividing line in such cases. The factors that the Court uses to distinguish between legally relevant and irrelevant chilling effect are the following. The first factor is the nature of accountability proceedings. Criminal proceedings, of course, carry the strongest weight. An interconnected factor

55 *Ayuso Torres v Spain* (n 28), paras 5–7, 10, 12, 44–45.
56 *M.D. and Others v Spain* (n 7), para 90.
57 *M.D. and Others v Spain* (n 7), paras 85–90.
58 See, for example, *Ali Gürbüz v Turkey* (n 49), para 68.

is the severity of the sanction that can be imposed.[59] When no (meaningful) sanction can be imposed, the Court will be inclined to rule that the risks to the applicant's Convention rights are purely hypothetical.[60] The Court also consistently considers the length and number of proceedings as well as the quality of the legal basis for triggering the accountability procedure. When the legal basis leaves too much discretion to the authorities, this increases the chilling potential. Another element is whether the applicant suffered any other inconvenience as part of the proceedings, such as hearings by the police or public prosecutors, detentions, or house searches. Perhaps the most important factor is the reason for terminating the procedure. If it is merely procedural, but the risk to the Convention right remains, the Court will, in principle, recognise the chilling effect. If the national authorities terminated the procedure by declaring that the applicant had exercised his freedom of expression or another Convention right, this will constitute a very important element normally leading the Court to find that no chilling effect occurred.[61] Whether a legitimate private party or the state is responsible for the initiation of the proceedings and whether the rights of others or the public interest are at stake, are also relevant factors.[62]

The Court does not require the applicants to prove the existence of chilling effect. However, they have to adduce sufficient elements to convince the Court that the risk to their Convention right is not purely hypothetical.[63] The fact that the applicant continued to exercise the Convention right after being subjected to an accountability procedure does not necessarily mean that the chilling effect had not occurred, but can also support such a conclusion, depending on the circumstances of the case.[64] All the factors presented above are always assessed against each other and all the other relevant circumstances

59 Ali Gürbüz v Turkey (n 49), paras 63–64; *Fatih Taş v Turkey (no. 5)* App No. 6810/09 (ECHR 4 September 2018) paras 29, 37; *Ayuso Torres v Spain* (n 28), para 45, *Dilipak v Turkey* (n 35) paras 48, 50; *Selahattin Demirtaş v Turkey* (n 50), para 25.

60 *Schweizerische Radio- und Fernsehgesellschaft and Others v Switzerland* (n 28), paras 45–46, 72–80.

61 *M.D. and others v Spain* (n 7), para 86; *Erkem v Turkey* App No. 38193/08 (ECHR, 2 October 2018), para 27; *Hanbayat and Others v Turkey* App No. 6940/07 (ECHR, 6 February 2018), paras 11, 41–42; *Metis Yayincilik Limited Sirketi and Sökmen v Turkey* (n 28), para 34.

62 *M.D. and others v Spain* (n 7), paras 85, 88; *Metis Yayincilik Limited Sirketi and Sökmen v Turkey* (n 28). See also footnote no. 46.

63 *Akdeniz and Others v Turkey* (n 36), paras 71–74; *A.M. and A.K. v Hungary* (n 37), paras 48–51; *Schweizerische Radio- und Fernsehgesellschaft and Others v Switzerland* (n 28), paras 72–80; *Hanbayat and Others v Turkey* (n 60), paras 41–42; *Erkem v Turkey* (n 61), paras 29–30; *M.D. and others v Spain* (n 7), para 82.

64 In *Tuleya v Poland* (n 41), Poland argued that no chilling effect occurred since the applicant did not cease criticising the attempts to reform the justice system despite the measures taken against him. The applicant and the Court disagreed (see paras 464, 481, 488, and 544). See also *Schweizerische Radio- und Fernsehgesellschaft and Others v Switzerland* (n 28), paras 72–80.

on a case-by-case basis. The cases referred to in this paragraph may be studied as examples of how the Court makes this assessment.

Chilling effect: a hostage of admissibility requirements and rationales

The analysis showed that the assessment of chilling effect is not an autonomous exercise, detached from the stage of review at which it is conducted. The Court does not seek to determine whether the chilling effect as a behavioural phenomenon exists and how strong it is in the real world, to then draw conclusions on whether the applicant can be deemed a victim of a genuine interference with a Convention right. Instead, the opposite seems to be the case. The Court includes the chilling effect in the landscape of legal criteria it employs for determining the victim status and the existence of interference. The actual chilling effect is only one of the relevant considerations. However, to avoid an internally contradictory situation in which the Court would recognise the chilling effect but nevertheless find no victim status and no interference, the Court decides to omit any reference to the chilling effect or rules that the measure entails no chilling effect.

The chilling effect therefore currently seems to be a hostage of admissibility requirements and their underlying practical and socio-political considerations. To illustrate, the Court interprets the chilling effect strictly when it appears in the determination of victim status requirement to prevent being flooded by applications. In *Akdeniz and Others*, it has denied that the chilling effect affected the work of two university professors, despite their active civic engagement in the field of human rights. When the chilling effect is not performing the gatekeeping function, the Court's approach seems slightly more lenient. The Court still very rarely rules that the national legislation is creating the chilling effect, as it tries to avoid performing constitutional review of national legislation.

A similar approach concerning the no significant disadvantage rule from Article 35 (3) (b) of the Convention is visible in *Artemenko v Ukraine*, a case concerning a journalist who published an article in a local newspaper allegedly defaming a politician. She described how the politician tried to sponsor an agreement between a local university and the city, under which the city would invest in the university's football stadium in return for allowing the local football club to use it. After one year, the agreement was not signed, since, as she wrote, the MP "has received a new toy – almost his own stadium in the city park". The MP lodged a civil action against the journalist for defamation and won: the applicant was ordered to pay court expenses (around 6 EUR) and to publish a clarification of the above-quoted statement. The Court relied on the fact that no "real" sanction was imposed, that the applicant's statement was not important for the main idea of the article, and that, perhaps most unconvincingly, Ukraine had a pluralistic political and media landscape. The Court might be right that there was no violation of Article 10 in this case. However, a careful reader cannot ignore the impression that the Court simply wanted to dismiss the case on the grounds of no significant disadvantage. However, to do so, the judges had to find no chilling effect. It seems that this is what they did not want to proclaim. As a result, they ruled that the applicant could hardly be said to have suffered any chilling effect and thus no significant disadvantage occurred.[65] This phrase seems like a declaration of "no chilling effect" through gritted teeth.

The principle of subsidiarity, albeit not explicitly mentioned, also strongly influences the assessment of the chilling effect. When the national courts terminate the proceedings with a conclusion that the applicant's actions are protected by freedom of expression, the Court generally concludes that the chilling effect did not arise. This leads to a questionable level of protection of freedom of expression, at least in some cases. In *Erkem v Turkey*, for example, the Court ruled that no chilling effect occurred in a case in which the Turkish authorities had initiated a criminal procedure against a lawyer, who, in her capacity as head of the Bar Association's Commission for the Prevention of Torture, had made a public statement about the riots in a juvenile prison, claiming that the uprising was provoked by violence and ill-treatment of minors in the prison facilities, and accusing the guards of having beaten the minors to repress the insurrection, left them without proper medical assistance, and obstructed their communication with lawyers. The lawyer was charged with abuse of office, insult through the press, and slanderous denunciation. At the first hearing, the first instance court acquitted her, relying on her right to freedom of expression after an 18-month-long criminal procedure.[66] Comparison between this case and *Steur v the Netherlands*, described above, is revealing the strength of the subsidiarity principle in the assessment of the chilling effect.[67] Even though the criminal procedure lasting 18 months seems to have a stronger chilling potential than a mere disciplinary pronouncement with no sanctions,

65 *Artemenko v Ukraine* (n 46), paras 33–34.

66 *Erkem v Turkey* (n 61).

67 A similar conclusion can be drawn from *Metis Yayincilik Limited Sirketi and Sökmen v Turkey* (n 28), where an ultra-nationalist attorney brought the criminal complaint under the infamous Article 301 of the Turkish Criminal Code, which the Court found to be contrary to the Convention in the already mentioned *Altuğ Taner Akçam v Turkey* case, claiming that certain passages from the book *The Bastard of Istanbul* constituted "denigration of Turkishness". The Court underlined that the applicant and the author of the book were never arrested or placed in detention, and that the first instance court acquitted the author after five months as it found that her work was covered by freedom of expression. Despite the police having twice entered the publishing house and questioned the applicant, and that at least prima facie, the procedure was of an abusive nature, the court ruled that the "*criminal prosecution in this case could not have constituted a chilling effect*" Compare this to *Macatė v Lithuania* (GC) App No. 61435/19 (ECHR 23 January 2023), para. 182, in which the Court recognised the chilling effect on freedom of expression of a writer, whose book was first temporarily suspended and later labelled as harmful to minors under the age of 14.

the Court found no chilling effect in the first case because the Turkish authorities ultimately recognised the lawyer's freedom of expression.

The characterisation of the chilling effect as a hostage of admissibility requirements and their underlying premises explains very well the inconsistencies occurring in the jurisprudence. The Court is fairly consistent in drawing the line between legally relevant and legally irrelevant chilling effect within each category of case law, since the chilling effect is evaluated in the same legal context. However, when cases from different categories are compared, the different legal "environment" leads to some striking inconsistencies. Note, for example, the above-mentioned comparison between *Steur* and *Erkem*, *Wille* and *M.D. and Others* from the introduction, or *Ayuso Torres* described above, and *Döner and Others v Turkey*, in which a parent who was suspected of having submitted a petition for the use of the Kurdish language in public schools suffered a house search, arrest and four-day detention for alleged support of terrorism. The Court ignored the chilling effect and ruled that there was no interference with his freedom of expression, as it turned out the applicant had not submitted the petition.[68]

Conclusion

Whenever the applicant suffered no tangible harm but claims to be a victim of the chilling effect, the Court is faced with a situation it is ill-equipped to solve. It lacks the required scientific knowledge to assess the actual existence and strength of chilling effect. According to Schauer, the courts, facing such a "dilemma of ignorance", in essence have three different solutions. They can try to completely avoid taking such decisions, they can seek to bridge the knowledge gap, or they can decide the case despite the lack of expertise. The Court adopted the latter approach, picturesquely referred to as "muddling through".[69]

The legal analysis this chapter provides cannot help the Court to bridge the scientific knowledge gap. Nevertheless, it sheds important light on an obscure area of case law, providing an opportunity to reflect on the ways in which the Court currently handles such situations. Consciously or unconsciously, the Court seems to have adopted a pragmatic approach. It leans on the rules governing the determination of the admissibility criteria, which, therefore, govern the evaluation of chilling effect. As a result, the chilling effect's great potential to increase the general level of protection of Convention rights,[70] is left dormant. A more determined approach, freeing the chilling effect from the

68 *Döner and Others v Turkey* (n 28), para 80. See the partly dissenting opinion of judge Turković, who disagreed on this aspect and heavily relied on the chilling effect.

69 Schauer (n 10), p. 288–295.

70 Pech (n 2); Mohor Fajdiga, 'Chilling effect: Turning the Poison into an Antidote for Fundamental Rights in Europe' (2024) 31(1) Maastricht Journal of European and Comparative Law 9.

abduction of admissibility requirements, could prove to be an avenue worth exploring if the Court wants to avoid becoming a bystander in the era of new human rights challenges. Applying such an approach in cases concerning judges – guardians of Convention rights for us all – could be a modest, yet crucial first step towards spelling a more confident "to be" for the freedom of expression of judges and other applicants.

Acknowledgements

The research for this article would not be possible without the "TRust, Independence, Impartiality and Accountability of Legal professionals under the EU Charter – part 2" (TRIIAL 2) project, which is funded by the European Union under the Justice Programme (Project no. 101089737). This research was also supported by the Slovenian Research and Innovation Agency (ARIS) under the research project J5-4583 "Judicial Selection Under Scrutiny: Judicial Independence, Lawfulness and Merit".

4 What standards should be applied to judges exercising freedom of expression on social networks?

Pierpaolo Gori and Oreste Pollicino

Judges' free speech on social media, an initial assessment

According to estimates, social media users worldwide reached 4.89 billion in 2023, and the number is expected to rise to almost 6 billion by 2027.[1] The percentages are impressive, not only among young people but also among adults. For those with a public image, social media has provided a valuable opportunity to connect more effectively with a community: not only people working in show business but also many politicians[2] and public servants have their professional profiles, which in some cases are mixed with and in others separate from their personal profiles.

Members of the judiciary may comprise a particular case. In October 2023, a senior judge at the Court of Catania in Sicily came under fire from the Italian government and the mass media for having decided on 29 September 2023 to disapply the government's decree on the detention of asylum seekers in "detention and repatriation centres", finding that it violated EU law. As a result of the ruling, the detention of several Tunisian citizens in similar situations, who landed on the island of Lampedusa on 20 September 2023 and were subsequently transferred to one of these centres, was ruled unlawful. As a further result, the financial bond of 4,938 euros that asylum seekers must pay to avoid being detained at such centres under the terms of recently adopted Italian regulations on landings was cancelled in those specific cases. On 2 October, the conservative newspaper *Il Giornale*[3] published an article based on a review of the judge's Facebook profile and wrote that, in July 2018, she had allegedly shared (albeit without any comment) a petition on her private

1 Statista Research Department, 'Social Media: Worldwide Penetration Rate 2024' (Statista) <https://www.statista.com/statistics/269615/social-network-penetration-by-region/>, accessed 2 April 2024.

2 On the consequences of platform power, see Giovanni De Gregorio and Oreste Pollicino, 'The European Constitutional Road to Address Platform Power' (Verfassungsblog, 31 August 2021) <https://verfassungsblog.de/power-dsa-dma-03/> accessed 2 April 2024.

3 Francesca Galici, 'Firme anti-Salvini e post pro migranti. Ecco chi è la giudice che sfida il governo' (Il Giornale, 2 October 2023) <https://www.ilgiornale.it/news/politica/firme-anti-salvini-e-post-pro-migranti-ecco-chi-giudice-che-2219534.html>, accessed 2 April 2024.

DOI: 10.4324/9781003470779-5

Facebook profile calling for a "motion of no confidence" against a prominent conservative political leader. In June 2018, she also reportedly posted a newspaper article featuring cases involving the migrant-rescue non-governmental organisations "Open Arms" and "Sea Watch" as well as a request by Palermo public prosecutors to close a criminal file opened against them. In addition, she had allegedly "liked", amongst others, the two organisations' Facebook pages alongside those of minor left-wing parties and the profile of a trade unionist who represented migrant farmworkers and is now a member of parliament. In 2016, she reportedly shared another petition urging EU institutions to save migrant lives and to host them using funds designated for Turkish and Northern African authorities to stop cross-border movements. Finally, she had allegedly also "liked" posts published by "Permanent No Borders Unit – Ventimiglia" as well as photographs taken in May 2011 when a ferry carried 1,300 migrants to Catania, captioned "modern deportation, support to no-border networks". Although she did not have to face any disciplinary proceedings, the judge's Facebook profile was nevertheless closed immediately after the publication of the article in *Il Giornale* due to its significant mediatic echo.

This case helps us to outline how freedom of expression on social media platforms differs from other traditional media or, more generally, in public. This is especially true when the person exercising their freedom of expression is a public official or, even more, a judge. All the values and fundamental rights underpinning the model of free speech on classic media, such as the press, are still relevant. However, the critical difference is the technological context within which we try to guarantee free speech on social networks.[4] First, opinions or comments expressed on social networks may have more far-reaching effects than on other media because a post can typically be seen/read worldwide. Second, the consequences are often lasting, given that the information shared on social media is not only recorded but is often also available on the web several years after being initially shared. Third, after information has been disseminated worldwide, the enforcement of an individual's "right to be forgotten" and, therefore, the delisting of that content face significant issues in practical terms and may, therefore, lead to unsatisfactory results when such a right is invoked before a national court.[5] Fourth, the author may not be fully aware of the consequences of their speech (which are also not entirely foreseeable). Moreover, the speech can be shared at any time, including when at home or during time off work, and therefore may not be sufficiently meditated. Fifth, a "like," a "friendship," or sharing an image or document on social media, even without any comment, are characteristic forms of communication on digital platforms. They differ from expressions in traditional media, such as

4 Jack Balkin, 'The Future of Free Expression in a Digital Age' (2012) 36 Pepperdine Law Review <https://digitalcommons.pepperdine.edu/plr/vol36/iss2/9>.

5 See, among others, Paul Lambert, *The Right to Be Forgotten* (2nd edn, Bloomsbury 2022) 145–154.

in an interview released to the press, but must not, as such, be disregarded as irrelevant. Finally, platforms are easily exposed to data collection in bad faith ("*doxing*"),[6] which involves searching for and publishing private or identifying personal information selected over a significant period. Whereas individual instances of communication on social networks may not be particularly relevant, the online disclosure of bulk details associated with a personal profile may have a distorting effect, as it may involve self-serving cherry-picking of specific pieces of information and the presentation only of the content that reflects the bias of the person who carried out the search. Sophisticated and relatively accessible software may be used extensively (e.g. facial recognition scanners in conjunction with artificial intelligence) to search and select frames captured in private videos spontaneously or unthinkingly posted on social networks years before. Although these technologies have been developed only recently, they can draw on considerable digital archives, in many cases created before the adoption of privacy guidelines, and may be purposely used to challenge and undermine the public credibility of the targeted victim.

Moving to the particular characteristic of free speech on social media involving members of the judiciary, this analysis covers both ordinary judges as well as public prosecutors, as both groups endorse, and should continue to endorse, a shared judicial culture of impartiality and independence to prevent and prosecute crime and protect citizens' rights.[7]

This chapter will specifically address individual judges' use of social media, given that communication by courts as a whole is a separate issue.[8]

As far as methodology is concerned, it must be accepted that, due to a lack of sufficient case law on the specific topic primarily addressed (judges' freedom of expression on social networks), the reasoning used here will need to be developed starting from a broader perspective on freedom in general, then moving step-by-step through the free speech of judges as a particular category of civil servant, and finally focusing on the consequences of the use or rejection of social media.

For the same reason, given the lack of extensive specific statutory regulation of a newly expanding phenomenon, this article aims to analyse the legal framework by considering the case law, especially that of the European Court

6 "*Doxing*" can be defined as the practice of "releasing private information … online to the wider public without the user's consent", including "information that may put users at risk of harm, especially names, addresses, employment details, medical or financial records, and names of family members". Rob Cover, 'What Is Doxing, and How Can You Protect Yourself?' (The Conversation, 13 February 2024) <http://theconversation.com/what-is-doxing-and-how-can-you-protect-yourself-223428>, accessed 2 April 2024.

7 *Kayasu v Turkey* App No. 64119/00 and 76292/01 (ECtHR, 13 November 2008).

8 Press releases are often published on institutional web pages, where the courts announce and summarise, *inter alia*, important decisions informing the public. This information may well also be released on digital networks; however, it is not analysed here as it cannot be regarded as individual communication by judges.

of Human Rights (ECtHR) and the Court of Justice of the European Union (CJEU), as well as soft law rules, mainly from the Council of Europe and the United Nations, seeking to identify viable international standards.

We shall consider whether, in the digital era, there is scope for a specific type of freedom of expression for individual judges, whether it can be classified as a "right" for them to intervene in the media, and, finally, whether it matters in terms of the proper administration of justice. There may be conceptual difficulties in identifying a right of free speech from a classical point of view because, at first sight, communication on social media by judges may seem not natural at all. Indeed, those in whose name justice is administered have the right to know how this is achieved and how judges, who are subject only to the law, exercise their judicial power. However, this right is traditionally meant to be satisfied by providing reasons for rulings and establishing rules on access to case documents.

For sure, the right of the public to be adequately informed in this area entails a duty on judges to state reasons for their judgments. Nonetheless, it could also be essential to strengthen the system's antibodies, thus enabling it to avoid – or at least limit – the risks associated with the so-called "spectacularisation" of justice. Indeed, it is widely accepted that media accounts of judicial action may end up presenting to the public at large a distorted image of how justice is administered.[9] With the appropriate content and in a measured tone, judges can help limit such a phenomenon by providing good quality sources of information concerning legal issues relevant to public debate, which is increasingly shaped by general and often inaccurate information gathered on social networks. Just as the media has the task of imparting reliable information and spreading ideas, the public also has a right to receive them.[10]

The inherent risks connected to judges' use of the internet must be balanced against the freedom enjoyed by them precisely because their assessment commits not only the respective author but also, due to the often evident nature of online communication, to some extent, the entire judicial system. During the inauguration of the 2019 judicial year in Florence, Italian President Sergio Mattarella called on judges to exercise restraint and use social networks with discretion, as he saw a risk that their impartiality might be questioned.[11]

9 European Network of Councils for the Judiciary, 'Report on Public Confidence and the Image of Justice 2019–2020: Communication with Other Branches of Power' (*ENCJ*, 10 June 2020) <https://www.encj.eu/index.php/node/480> accessed 2 April 2024.

10 *Bédat v Switzerland* App No. 56925/08 (ECtHR, GC, 29 March 2016), para 51.

11 Concetto Vecchio, 'Giustizia, Mattarella: "Uso Social Magistrati Può Offuscare Credibilità" – La Repubblica' (La Repubblica, 5 April 2019) <https://www.repubblica.it/politica/2019/04/05/news/giustizia_mattarella_magistrati_siano_sobri_nei_comportamenti_-223350476/>, accessed 2 April 2024; Vito Tenore, 'La Libertà Di Pensiero Tra Riconoscimento Costituzionale e Limiti Impliciti Ed Espliciti: I Limiti Normativi e Giurisprudenziali per Giornalisti, Dipendenti Pubblici e Privati Nei Social Media' (2019) 2 Il lavoro nelle pubbliche amministrazioni 83.

Hence, insofar as judiciary members are called upon to have a say in exercising democratic freedoms, including, in particular, freedom of expression in the digital society,[12] they must also balance and minimise their own use of those tools.

Judges must not disregard the need for reasonable self-restraint to guarantee their dignity, integrity, impartiality, and independence as individuals and uphold the image of impartiality of the judicial system as a whole[13] and of colleagues, even when expressing sharp criticism.[14] However, judges who are "anodyne" to the values, issues, and ideals of the society in which they live and operate may be so detached as not to be able to guarantee effective service in applying the law and protecting citizens' fundamental rights.

The imposition of clear limits on judges' online "footprint" would help to meet these goals whilst also ensuring freedom to participate in public debate. The Council of Europe also felt a similar need when its Commission for the Efficiency of Justice adopted the "Guide on Communication with the Media and the Public for Courts and Prosecution Authorities".[15] Its main objective is to offer guidance to members of the judiciary in managing communications with the media. Moreover, its introductory part clarifies how important it is to use instruments of this type,[16] not only in the context of judges' public roles but also in their private lives.[17]

This chapter will distinguish between judges' individual use of social networks in their official capacity, usage directly related to judicial functions, and their private communication, since the three scenarios raise different questions.

Finally, the issue of whether the standards that are called for differ from those applicable to other forms of expression will be assessed by considering criminal law alongside disciplinary liability rules, coupled with a comparative analysis and a consideration of soft law international standards as possible sources of homogeneous regulation, which may strike a fair balance between the different human and fundamental rights at stake.

12 For further references, see Oreste Pollicino, *Judicial Protection of Fundamental Rights on the Internet: A Road Towards Digital Constitutionalism?* (Hart 2021).

13 *Olujić v Croatia* App No. 22330/05 (ECtHR, 5 February 2009).

14 *Di Giovanni v Italy* App No. 51160/06 (ECtHR, 9 July 2013).

15 European Commission for the Efficiency of Justice (CEPEJ), 'Guide on Communication with the Media and the Public for Courts and Prosecution Authorities' (CEPEJ 2018) CEPEJ(2018)15 <https://rm.coe.int/cepej-2018-15-en-communication-manual-with-media/16809025fe>, accessed 2 April 2024.

16 See Article 1.3 of the document.

17 The CEPEJ points out that judicial offices should be ready to communicate in three different situations: first in relation to ordinary activity, second, in situations in which public debate raises questions about the functioning of the judicial system or specific processes, and third, in emergency situations where a judge or a judicial institution has been publicly attacked in a case involving suspected or proven judicial error.

Restrictions on free speech, public authorities, and members of the judiciary in particular

Freedom of expression is one of the core fundamental rights on which modern democratic states are based. Moreover, this freedom provides a matrix to which a whole "constellation" of other fundamental rights can be linked. These include, *inter alia*, the right to disseminate and receive information, the right not to be harassed because of one's opinions, the right to freely profess one's religion or political beliefs, and freedom of association. To a certain extent, even the ability to receive free and independent information is protected as a precondition for exercising truly free expression of thought.[18] Since the European Communities initially pursued aims of a purely economic nature, the right to freedom of expression has only been positively recognised within EU law in recent times through the reference made by the Treaty of Maastricht to the rights secured by the European Convention on Human Rights (Article F).[19] Subsequently, since the proclamation of the Charter of Fundamental Rights of the European Union,[20] the rules contained in it have had the same status as the Treaties (Article 6 of the Treaty on EU). The right to freedom of speech is expressly enshrined in Article 11 of the Charter, the wording of which is almost identical to Article 10 of the Convention. Articles 6, 8, and 17 of the Convention, as well as Articles 7, 47, and 54 of the Charter, are also significant as paradigms for international case law and European law frameworks when dealing with freedom of expression, including freedom of expression for the judiciary. As is the case for all other relative rights,[21] freedom of expression can be limited,[22] although not all forms of interference are tolerated. Interference with the right to free speech may entail various measures, generally a "formality, condition, restriction or penalty".[23] Hence, when interpreting the Convention, the Strasbourg Court carries out a case-by-case review of situations that may have a restrictive impact on freedom

18 Pierpaolo Gori, *ECHR Article 10: How Does the Protection Work?* (Aracne 2014). For general principles in relation to the duties of internet providers of news, see the landmark case *Delfi AS v Estonia* App No, 64569/09 (ECtHR, 16 June 2015).

19 Convention for the Protection of Human Rights and Fundamental Freedoms, ECHR, Rome, 4 November 1950.

20 Charter of Fundamental Rights of the European Union OJ C 364/1 2000.

21 By contrast, "absolute rights", like the prohibition of torture or inhuman or degrading treatment (Article 3 of the Convention), do not tolerate any interference in principle.

22 According to the framework set out above, it is possible to identify a pattern of internal and external limitations of the exercise of freedom of expression as follows: internal limitations, enshrined by Article 10(2) ECHR and Article 52(3) of the Charter; external limitations, set by other human rights/fundamental rights protected by the Charter and the ECHR that need to be balanced with Articles 10 ECHR and 52 Charter, as typical "relative" human and fundamental rights, namely Articles 6,18, and 17 ECHR, and Articles 7 and 47 of the Charter.

23 *Wille v Liechtenstein* App No. 28396/95 (ECtHR, 28 October 1999), para 43.

of expression[24] and applies a proportionality test[25] in the form of a "three-step analysis" that takes into consideration the proportionality of the measure adopted and the necessity of the limitation within the democratic sphere.[26]

Within this scenario, sectoral public authorities' freedom of speech may manifest in two ways: it may be exercised privately or in an official capacity.[27] It is essential to distinguish between situations in which freedom is significantly restricted due to the speaker's status as a civil servant and ordinary personal communications, bearing in mind that even the latter may be subject to more constraints than those applicable to the speech of ordinary citizens.

Regarding private communication, judges are treated in a similar but not identical manner to other public figures, such as members of the Parliament.[28] First, they are bound by professional duties, which prevent them from disseminating information about the functions performed within trials.[29] Second, as is inevitable within a democratic society, politicians knowingly expose themselves to close scrutiny by the public at large; consequently, they must display a greater degree of tolerance, especially when making public statements open to criticism.[30] This principle of increased tolerance does not apply in the same way to all persons employed by the state,[31] and it is not accepted[32] that a government-appointed expert can be equated with a politician.

24 An example may be found in *Schweizerische Radio- und Fernsehgesellschaft and Others v Switzerland* App No. 41723/14 (ECtHR, 22 December 2020), para 72.

25 Gehan Gunatilleke, 'Justifying Limitations on the Freedom of Expression' (2021) 22 Human Rights Review 91.

26 The first step requires verification as to whether the interference by the responsible government is prescribed by law. If the first condition is satisfied, the second stage of the analysis involves ascertaining whether the legal interference is pursuing a legitimate aim as defined by Article 10(2) ECHR and Article 52(3) of the Charter. If the second condition is also fulfilled, then a final requirement must be met, namely the proportionality of the measure as needed in a democratic society. See Pierpaolo Gori, 'La Libertà Di Manifestazione Del Pensiero, Negazionismo, *Hate Speech*' in Francesco Buffa and Maria Giuliana Civinini (eds), *La Corte di Strasburgo* (Key Editore 2019).

27 On this aspect, as well as the consequences for the application of limits and counter-limits to Article 10 ECHR, it is important to recall Judge Wojtyczek's dissenting opinion in *Baka v Hungary* App No. 20261/12 (ECtHR, 23 June 2016).

28 An example is to be found in Article 68(1) of the Italian Constitution, which provides: "members of parliament cannot be held accountable for the opinions expressed or votes cast in the performance of their function".

29 On this issue, the resolution published by the Italian Consiglio Superiore della Magistratura (CSM), 'Linee-guida per l'organizzazione degli uffici giudiziari ai fini di una corretta comunicazione istituzionale – dettaglio' (CSM, 11 July 2018) <https://www.csm.it/web/csm-internet/-/linee-guida-per-l-organizzazione-degli-uffici-giudiziari-ai-fini-di-una-corretta-comunicazione-istituzionale>, accessed 2 April 2024.

30 *Mladina d.d. Ljubljana v Slovenia* App No. 20981/10 (ECtHR, 17 April 2014), para 40.

31 *Busuioc v Moldova* App No. 61513/00 (ECtHR, 21 December 2004), para 64.

32 *Nilsen and Johnsen v Norway* App No. 23118/93 (ECtHR, GC, 25 November 1999).

Members of the judiciary occupy a unique position,[33] which needs to be further distinguished from that of other civil servants, since judges form part of a fundamental institution of the state, which is a prominent guarantor in a democratic society,[34] and therefore the judiciary is not considered to be part of the ordinary civil service.[35]

As far as official communications are concerned, when acting in their official capacity, public prosecutors and judges may thus be subject to stricter limits in terms of what is regarded as acceptable criticism than ordinary citizens.[36] Judges have an obligation and a duty of discretion falling under Article 10(2) of the Convention, which usually prevents them from replying even when provoked.[37] However, they may still be subject to personal criticism, within permissible limits, and not only in a theoretical and generic manner.[38] This threshold is reached when comments made against judges turn into destructive attacks that are essentially unfounded.[39] The overriding interest here is the need to maintain the proper functioning of the judicial system, which would be impossible without relations based on consideration and mutual respect among its various protagonists and without retaining the judiciary's authority.[40]

Against this backdrop, since an individual judge who has been criticised in the media is subject to a duty of discretion that in principle prevents them from responding in person,[41] there is a question as to who, among the members of the judiciary, can express themselves in an official capacity to ensure that correct information is given concerning a particular matter.

The heads of courts and public prosecutors' offices are certainly under a legal duty to engage in public debate to correct fake news through the media, including on social networks, in accordance with Council of Europe recommendation Rec(2003)13. Any such communications must be made in a measured and precise manner to avoid unintended misinterpretations and must take into account any risk of prejudicing ongoing legal proceedings, the rights of the parties involved, and the presumption of innocence.

33 This aspect was previously examined by the Italian Constitutional Court in Judgment No. 100/1981, which states as follows: "judges must enjoy the same rights of liberty as are guaranteed to every other citizen, but it must also be admitted that the functions exercised and the qualifications they hold are not indifferent and without effect for the constitutional order".

34 *Prager and Oberschlick v Austria* App No. 15974/90 (ECtHR, 26 April 1995), para 34.

35 *Albayrak v Turkey* App No. 38406/97 (ECtHR, 31 January 2008), para 42.

36 *Do Carmo de Portugal e Castro Câmara v Portugal* App No. 53139/11 (ECtHR, 4 October 2016), para 40.

37 *Buscemi v Italy* App No. 29569/95 (ECtHR, 16 September 1999).

38 *Morice v France* App No. 29369/10 (ECtHR, GC, 23 April 2015).

39 *Prager* (n 34) para 34.

40 *Morice* (n 38) para 170.

41 Ibid., para 128; *Kudeshkina v Russia* App No. 29492/05 (ECtHR, 26 February 2009), para 86.

The ECtHR specifically considered implementing Article 10 in the case of *Baka v Hungary*.[42] Although this case did not involve any social networks, since the applicant had not used them to express his disputed opinion, it is nonetheless interesting how the Court interpreted the violation of Article 10 of the Convention, which was specifically applicable to the matter. In fact, the Court reiterated that Mr Baka not only had a right but was also under a duty as the President of the National Council of Justice to state his opinion on any legislative reform that affected the judiciary. His removal and the premature termination of his contract were found to amount to a disproportionate attack on the independence not only of the individual judge but also of the judiciary as a whole.[43]

The Court held that this measure was not necessary or proportionate in a democratic society and that it could potentially create a chilling effect,[44] specifically by discouraging judges from publicly expressing their opinions and participating in the debate on issues concerning the judiciary, whereas it is crucial to ensure better and more open engagement between the judiciary and the general public.[45] Hence, according to the interpretation endorsed by the Grand Chamber, Article 10 applies not only to personal speech but also to individual speech in an official capacity.[46]

Since *Baka* concerned the court's president, one might ask whether a distinction should be drawn between ordinary judges and heads of courts in situations involving free speech in the media. The answer to this may depend,

42 *Baka v Hungary* (n 27). In contrast to several previous rulings adopted *inter alia* by the Inter-American Court of Human Rights, which are quoted within the judgment itself, the ECtHR did not consider the independence of the judiciary itself as part of the guarantee of a fair trial under Article 6 of the Convention as a key issue in resolving the case, given that the case was examined principally under Article 10.

43 At para 172 of the ruling, the Grand Chamber mentioned the principles relating to the irremovability of judges apparent within the Court's case law on Article 6(1): *Fruni v Slovakia* App No. 8014/07 (ECtHR, 21 June 2011), para 145; *Henryk Urban and Ryszard Urban v Poland* App No. 23614/08 (ECtHR, 30 November 2010), para 53.

44 On this aspect, see 'The Chilling Effect in Constitutional Law' (1969) 69 Columbia Law Review 808.

45 See para 101 of the ruling: the Court held that the fear of sanction had a "chilling effect" on the exercise of freedom of expression and could risk discouraging judges from making critical remarks about public institutions or policies, for fear of losing their judicial office. See, *mutatis mutandis*, also *Wille v Liechtenstein* (n 21) para 50, and *Kudeshkina v Russia* (n 41), paras 98–100. This effect, which operates to the detriment of society, is also a factor relevant for the proportionality of, and thus the justification for, the sanction imposed on the applicant. See the chapter by Mohor Fajdiga in this volume.

46 It is indeed interesting to read Judge Wojtyczek's opinion, which seeks to distinguish between the public and private role of the judge making the communication. See, in particular, para 4 of his opinion attached to the judgment. The Polish judge criticises the findings of the Grand Chamber based on the application of Article 10 guarantees to the official speech, as, in his opinion, "it would mean that the manner in which a state organ speaks is to be considered a matter of personal freedom".

amongst other things, on the constitutional model of the judiciary adopted by the relevant national constitutional framework.[47] This question may be easier to answer in the affirmative in countries where a hierarchical model shapes the distribution of judicial power. On the other hand, in states where each judge is fully empowered by the Constitution[48] and embodies the entire judicial function, the answer may be less straightforward, depending on the specific circumstances.[49]

In any case, on account of their public roles, ordinary judges certainly enjoy some individual freedom of speech in an active sense, as they have the right to inform the public properly concerning issues relating to the functioning of the judicial system. Such speech falls within the public interest as it is essential in a democratic society.[50] It is also widely accepted that ordinary judges are subject to a professional duty to intervene in public debate when judicial independence is threatened by other branches of state or legislative or constitutional reforms.[51]

However, information that is sensitive within ongoing proceedings must not be made publicly available, and in many states judges as individuals are prosecuted if they unduly reveal or publish case documents or details concerning the facts of a case.[52]

It is also important to mention a further specific aspect of freedom of speech of the judiciary: communication by an individual in their capacity as a speaker for an association of members of the judiciary, as a council member,

47 *Harabin v Slovakia* App No. 58688/11 (ECtHR, dec, 20 November 2012).

48 Article 107 of the Italian Constitution states that: "Judges may not be removed from office; they may not be dismissed or suspended from office or assigned to other courts or functions unless by a decision of the High Council of the Judiciary, taken either for the reasons and with the guarantees of defence established by the provisions concerning the organisation of the Judiciary or with the consent of the judges themselves. The Minister of Justice has the power to originate disciplinary action. Judges are distinguished only by their different functions. The state prosecutor enjoys the guarantees established in the prosecutor's favour by the provisions concerning the organization of the Judiciary".

49 See *Buscemi v Italy* (n 37), paras 67–68.

50 *July and SARL Libération v France* App No. 20893/03 (ECtHR, 14 February 2008), para 67.

51 See Rafael Bustos Gisbert, 'Judicial Independence in European Constitutional Law' (2022) 18 European Constitutional Law Review 591, 620.

52 This is the case in Italy, for instance, where Article 2(2)(u) of Legislative Decree no. 109/2006 establishes criminal liability for judges. The offence may be committed by various breaches of the duty of confidentiality, which is particularly serious in cases where it is carried out through the mass media (newspapers, television networks, websites). Germany is an interesting case, where a specific provision of the Criminal Code, Article 24, punishes the use of social media by judges in cases of apprehension of bias. In this regard, see Jannika Jahn, 'Extrajudicial Use of Social Media by Judges in Germany' in Anja Schoeller-Schletter (ed), *Impartiality of Judges and Social Media: Approaches, Regulations and Results* (Konrad Adenauer Stiftung e V 2020). Another example can be found in a decision of the French Superior Judicial Council, Disciplinary Council, case p077, Prosecution, 29 April 2014.

or a trade union official.[53] Such internal bodies play a pivotal role in ensuring judicial independence and, within the national judicial systems of many but not all member states of the Council of Europe, operate independently of their respective jurisdictions to guarantee, *inter alia*, respect for the rule of law and protection for individual rights.[54]

Given their collective representative capacity and status, resulting from their established activity of preserving the role of the judiciary *vis-à-vis* other branches of the democratic state and society, the freedom of expression enjoyed by them may in some specific cases be broader than that guaranteed to individual ordinary magistrates: they act as public watchdogs, e.g. in issuing interviews or press releases concerning judicial reforms or other external initiatives that may have a potential impact on the independence of the judiciary.[55] From this perspective, since it furthers the public debate on the rule of law itself, the freedom of expression of speakers from judicial associations deserves to be protected according to standards very close to those initially developed for the press. Indeed, professional organisations of judges are central actors within civil societies, and their statements must benefit from a high level of protection since they are part of a debate on questions of public interest, particularly regarding the separation of powers and the independence of the judiciary.[56].

A similar approach underpins whistleblowing by public servants, as considered in the landmark case of *Guja*[57] in which the ECtHR ruled that Moldova had breached Article 10 of the Convention when it dismissed a civil servant who had revealed information of public interest regarding attempts by high-ranking politicians to influence the judiciary. The Court therefore recognised that Article 10 applied to civil servants in general, including those who are not

53 See, recently, *Miroslava Todorova v Bulgaria* App No. 40072/13 (ECtHR, 19 October 2021), regarding sanctions imposed on the applicant, a judge and president of the Bulgarian Union of judges.

54 See ECJ 27 February 2018; Cases C-83/19 and C-896/19 *Associaçao Sindical dos Juízes Portugueses (ASJP)* [2018]: the case involved a preliminary ruling concerning the temporary reduction in the remuneration paid to the members of that court, in the context of Portugal's budgetary policy guidelines; Case C-896/19, *Repubblika v Il-Prim Ministru* [2021] concerned a preliminary ruling on the conformity with EU law of the provisions of the Constitution of Malta governing the procedure for the appointment of members of the judiciary. See also Case C-83/19, *Asociaţia 'Forumul Judecătorilor Din România'* [2021], Case C-127/19, *Asociaţia 'Forumul Judecătorilor Din România' and Asociaţia 'Mişcarea Pentru Apărarea Statutului Procurorilor'* [2021] and Case C-195/19 *PJ* v *QK*, Cases C-291/19 *SO* v *TP and Others*, Case C-355/19 *Asociaţia 'Forumul Judecătorilor din România', Asociaţia 'Mişcarea Pentru Apărarea Statutului Procurorilor' and OL* [2021] and Case C-397/19 *AXE* v *Statul Român – Ministerul Finanţelor Publice* [2021]: they are all preliminary rulings regarding proceedings between legal persons or natural persons and authorities or bodies such as the Romanian Judicial Inspectorate, the Supreme Council of the Judiciary and the prosecutor's office attached to the high court of cassation and justice.

55 *Eminağaoğlu v Turkey* App No. 76521/12 (ECtHR, 9 March 2021), para 134.

56 *Sarisu Pehlivan v Turkey* App No. 63029/19 (ECtHR, 6 June 2023) paras 41, 46.

57 *Guja v Moldova* App No. 14277/04 (ECtHR, 12 February 2008).

members of the judiciary,[58] according to a case-by-case approach, and found that there is little scope under Article 10(2) of the Convention for restrictions on debate concerning questions of public interest.[59] Indeed, in a democratic system, the acts or omissions of the government must be subject to close scrutiny not only by the legislative and judicial authorities but also by the media and public opinion. The public's interest in obtaining qualified information can sometimes be so strong that it can override even a duty of confidentiality imposed by law.[60]

No binding regulation applicable to the freedom of expression of judges on social networks

The individual activity carried out by members of the judiciary on social networks is not, generally, subject to any specific domestic regulation in most countries.[61] A distinction should be drawn between, on the one hand, communication on electronic networks such as blogs that are shared among members of a restricted community to exchange their respective views on professional, legal, and organisational issues and rulings (where the risks of inappropriate communication are low) and, on the other hand, general commercial networks, such as Facebook, YouTube, WhatsApp, Instagram, Snapchat, Telegram, Twitter (X), LinkedIn, and TikTok, where several sensitive issues may arise. It is essential, where possible, to identify specific boundaries to judges' activities on broadly available social networks, and the regulatory tools adopted in pursuing this task have a massive influence on the final outcome.

New restrictions may be established both at the national level within legislation governing disciplinary liabilities[62] or criminal offences[63] and within

58 See *Wille v Liechtenstein* (n 23), paras 41–42 and the ECtHR decision *Harabin v Slovakia* (n 47).

59 See in part. § 74 of the *Guja v Moldova* (n 57), and, among other authorities, *Sürek v Turkey (no. 1)* App No. 26682/95 (ECtHR, 8 July 1999), para 61 and Directive (EU) 2019/1937 of the European Parliament and of the Council of 23 October 2019 on the protection of persons who report breaches of Union law.

60 See *Fressoz and Roire v France* App No. 29183/95 (ECtHR, 21 January 1999); *Radio Twist, a.s. v Slovakia* App No. 62202/00 (ECtHR, 19 December 2006).

61 See respectively the chapters by Federica Casarosa on Italy and Jarosław Gwizdak on Poland in this volume.

62 See, for instance, the guidelines relevant to disciplinary cases adopted for all Italian administrative judges (who are not members of the ordinary judiciary but rather of a special judiciary) by the *Consiglio di Presidenza della Giustizia Amministrativa*: Consiglio di Presidenza della Giustizia Amministrativa, 'Delibera sull'uso dei mezzi di comunicazione elettronica e dei social media da parte dei magistrati amministrativi' (giustizia.amministrativa, 25 March 2021) <https://www.giustizia-amministrativa.it/-/delibera-sull-uso-dei-mezzi-di-comunicazione-elettronica-e-dei-social-media-da-parte-dei-magistrati-amministrativi-consiglio-di-presidenza-della-giust>, accessed 2 April 2024.

63 Even national law, which differs from country to country, may be read in the light of international law in order to achieve a more harmonised understanding and interpretation: see, *ex*

international judicial decisions.[64] These include supranational legal sources that pursue the same task and aim to guide judges' actions in line with the dictates of decency and restraint, in a manner that protects the dignity of people involved in judicial proceedings.

It must be considered that the usage of punitive "criminal" rules in the area of free speech is often disproportionate regarding the legitimate aim pursued, as it may generate a chilling effect.[65] Moreover, criminal law emphasises for its scope and sanction the natural conflict between free expression, which deserves to be protected broadly in a democratic society, and other interests also protected by law. Therefore, the "civil" legal safeguard provided by balancing human and fundamental rights in accordance with the case law in Article 10 of ECHR and Article 11 of the Charter is more straightforward and effective in this specific domain.

Against this regulatory backdrop, alongside the "hard law" laid down by national criminal law and enforceable disciplinary liability codes, it is also important to refer to "soft law" measures[66] to identify the limits to freedom of expression. United Nations' legal sources are key in establishing their international legal status. Social media platforms did not yet exist when the 'Bangalore Principles of Judicial Conduct' and the related Commentary,[67] adopted in 2002, were first drafted; as a result, the documents do not make any reference to social networks. Nevertheless, several principles and paragraphs from the

multis, the Council Framework Decision 2008/913/JHA of 28 November 2008 on combating certain forms and expressions of racism and xenophobia by means of criminal law.

64 See, among *alia*, United Nations Office on Drugs and Crime (UNODC), 'Non-Binding Guidelines on the Use of Social Medias by Judges' <https://www.unodc.org/res/ji/import/international_standards/social_media_guidelines/social_media_guidelines_final.pdf>, accessed 2 April 2024; European Network of Councils for the Judiciary, 'Report on Public Confidence and the Image of Justice 2018–2019: Individual and Institutional Use of Social Media within the Judiciary' (ENCJ, 7 June 2019) <https://www.encj.eu/index.php/node/480>, accessed 2 April 2024.

65 See *Belpietro v Italy* App No. 43612/10 (ECtHR, 24 September 2013).

66 As is known, soft law is normally not considered to be made up of "rules" as it is not binding or enforceable before any court or authority. Soft law is comprised of principles, public declarations, and agreements that are not legally binding.

67 2002 Bangalore Principles of Judicial Conduct, as the universally recognised principles of judicial conduct, and the detailed 2007 Commentary on the Bangalore Principles. Further information concerning the Bangalore Principles and the Commentary on the Bangalore Principles is available at 'Commentary on the Bangalore Principles of Judicial Conduct' (*UNODC*) <//www.unodc.org/unodc/en/corruption/tools_and_publications/commentary-on-the-bangalore-principles.html>, accessed 2 April 2024. This document was adopted by the Judicial Group on Strengthening Judicial Integrity, within the scope of the United Nations. It develops the fundamental right to enjoy in full equality a fair and public hearing by an independent and impartial tribunal, in the determination of rights and obligations and of any criminal charge.

Commentary draw attention to judges' behaviour outside the courtroom and are highly relevant to this discussion[68] regarding the judiciary's integrity.

A more recent milestone is the "Doha Declaration" adopted by the UN Global Judicial Integrity Network entitled "The Risks and Benefits of Using Social Media by Judges".[69] Its purpose is to identify and address some of the fundamental ethical implications for judiciary members regarding their online presence or use of social media and to provide practical recommendations and guidelines for public prosecutors and judges on the daily ethical and responsible use of social media.[70] The aim of the 2020 Doha meeting was clearly not to discourage the use of this innovative communication medium: indeed, any such measure would have been disproportionate.[71] It is possible to recognise a two-pronged approach to the issue: on the one hand, judicial offices are encouraged to be more open towards the public,[72] whereas, on the other hand, each judge as an individual is required to comply with the above-mentioned limitations. In this regard, the United Nation's "Non-binding guidelines on the use of social media by Judges"[73] stress the need to build awareness among judges and public prosecutors concerning the use of social media,[74] with regard both to the content as well as the broad network used for disseminating news through digital platforms.[75]

The European Court of Human Rights followed a similar pattern in a specific internal resolution adopted in 2021, which stresses that judges, as individuals, shall proceed with the utmost care if using social media,[76] as well as in the 2021 "Guidelines on Ethical Usage of Social Media by Judges and Public Prosecutors" adopted by the joint European Union and Council of Europe

68 *Ex multis*, see Commentary, para 1.

69 The Global Judicial Integrity Network was established in April 2018 in Vienna, Austria. The Doha Declaration on Judicial Integrity was adopted in February 2020 in Doha, Qatar. Accordingly, the Spanish Ethical Commission CGPJ Opinion (Consultation 10/2018), dated 25 February 2019, point 5, states that it is necessary to preserve the independence and appearance of impartiality, as well as to manage the confidence of society in the administration of justice.

70 The Declaration engages with the ethical problems that may potentially arise from the use of social media by judges, including the possible creation of bias, prejudice, or conflict of interest, whether real or perceived, the current lack of formal guidance for judges, the need for general rules and guidelines on the use of social media by individual judges, and the need for specific recommendations on how judges should conduct themselves.

71 Session report template for substantive sessions, launch of the Global Judiciary Integrity Network (9–10 April 2018, United Nations Vienna), p. 8.

72 One example in this regard is the communication campaign launched during the presidency of the former Constitutional Judge, Marta Cartabia, within the context of the Italian Constitutional Court. Therefore, the guidelines adopted by the CEPEJ also focus on this very aspect.

73 United Nations Office on Drugs and Crime, implementation of the Doha Declaration.

74 See ibid., para 38, 'Training'.

75 An interesting analysis on the US approach is provided by John Browning, 'Why Can't We Be Friends? Judges' Use of Social Media' (2014) 68 University of Miami Law Review 487.

76 ECtHR, Resolution on Judicial Ethics, adopted by the Plenary on 21 June 2021, Point VI.

action, which aim to strengthen the independence and accountability of the judiciary.[77]

In light of these considerations, it is now necessary to explore some rulings that appear to be paradigmatic and may help draw a line by delimiting the exercise of this freedom by members of the judiciary online.

Social media and the judiciary in action: statements made in an official capacity or directly related to judicial functions

As regards the individual judge's freedom of expression within the context of the performance of institutional duties, or directly in relation to the exercise of judicial functions, the usage, place, and timing of language will establish whether or not the subject addressed in the communication is relevant for ongoing judicial activity. This will establish whether it falls outside the scope of or is protected under Article 6(1) read in the light of Article 10 of ECHR, given that not only judicial impartiality but also its perception amongst the general public is important.[78]

Judges typically make statements in judgments and hearings, ideally expressing themselves in these venues in a relevant, correct, clear, and understandable way. However, they could naturally feel driven to intervene outside of trials concerning issues they are currently dealing with or may deal with in the future within legal proceedings.[79] This type of information is broadly protected in the ECtHR case law where the relevant matter is in the public interest and concerns the proper and transparent operation of the judicial system itself.[80]

A distinction needs to be drawn between individual statements released in the context of a direct exercise of functions and the narrow – but not identical – situation where freedom of expression is exercised within an institutional setting, linked to the official scope of judicial activity. Both types of communication involve the judge as a public official and not as a private individual, although in different contexts.

The former scenario arises under specific circumstances where the judge is under a legal or ethical duty to disseminate information through social networks concerning legal reforms that may impact judicial independence or that concern procedures for establishing key facts that have been reported incompletely and inaccurately in the media.

77 See also the comparative work of the CoE Venice Commission on the Use of Social Media by Judges Discussion Guide for the Expert Group Meeting (5–7 November 2018, Vienna).

78 *Denisov v Ukraine* App No. 76639/11 (ECtHR, 25 September 2018), para 63.

79 Even if a matter of debate has political implications, this fact alone is not sufficient to prevent a judge from making a statement on the matter; see *Wille v Liechtenstein* (n 23), para 67.

80 See *Kudeshkina v Russia* (n 41): the applicant was deprived of status as a judge after making public statements concerning political interference within the Russian judicial system; the Court found by a majority that Article 10 had been violated.

The latter scenario may arise in a variety of situations and fora outside the scope of that duty and may involve, for instance, an interview given through a social network as an independent legal expert contributing to public debate, done prudently, or alternatively a post on digital social media that unduly discloses sensitive legal information.

In each member state of the Council of Europe, any communication made in an official capacity needs to be balanced against the rights of the defence and the requirement for secrecy of the investigation or inquiry.[81] As a matter of principle, from a professional ethics point of view, public communications in which a judge "pontificates" on topical issues that concern the fairness of the proceedings[82] are inappropriate and are often formally sanctioned,[83] even if the declarations concerned were made on social media anonymously or under a pseudonym.[84] Usually, the competent authority responsible for disciplining any such improper action is the judiciary's self-government body, which is thus required to ensure the guarantees of independence outlined in the Strasbourg Court's ruling of *Di Giovanni*.[85]

In the same way, it is inappropriate for a judge to express personal opinions concerning the parties or defendants within judicial proceedings that he or she is dealing with or has dealt with. For instance, in a disciplinary decision by the French *Conseil supérieur de la magistrature*, the Council ruled on the disciplinary relevance of remarks concerning the office of the public prosecutor made by a judge during a hearing. Interestingly, the judge who made the comments did not personally use social networks. However, the comments were published on social media on the blog of the defendant's lawyer and were also reported on Twitter (X).[86]

Statements may be punished by fines if they are not publicly shared or have limited reach on social networks, e.g. posted to closed WhatsApp groups only.

81 See, for instance, for France, Article 10 of the *Ordonnance* of 22 December 1958.

82 *Olujić v Croatia* App No. 22330/05 (ECtHR, 5 February 2009), para 59.

83 Luca Longhi, 'I magistrati e l'uso dei social. Appunti sulla deontologia professionale di categoria nell'era della comunicazione di massa' (2019) 10 Diritto Pubblico Europeo – Rassegna online 192; Consultative Council of European Judges (CCJE), 'Opinion No 7 on Justice and Society' (*CCJE*) pt C <https://www.coe.int/en/web/ccje/opinion-n-7-on-justice-and-society>, accessed 2 April 2024; Venice Commission, 'Use of Social Media by Judges Deontological Rules or Instruction/Relevant Case-Law: Contribution by the Venice Commission to the Guidelines on Judges' Use of Social Media Prepared by the UNODC Global Judicial Integrity Network' (Council of Europe 2019) CDL-PI(2019)003 <https://www.venice.coe.int/webforms/documents/?pdf=CDL-PI(2019)003-e>, accessed 2 April 2024.

84 Pseudonyms should never be used to enable unethical behaviour on social media. In addition, the use of aliases offers no guarantee that the real status will not become known; see UNODC, 'Non-Binding Guidelines on the Use of Social Media by Judges', <www.unodc.org>, accessed 10 October 2023.

85 This is the case for the Italian Consiglio Superiore della Magistratura; see *Di Giovanni v Italy* (n 14).

86 See French CSM, Case p082, decision of 13 October 2015.

Alternatively, they could constitute serious crimes if, for instance, a natural person is defamed on a widely used online medium such as Twitter (X), or if the statements concern specific matters protected by professional secrecy.[87]

While the Strasbourg Court has already ruled on several cases concerning the protection of human rights in the context of the usage of social networks, *Kozan*[88] was the first case decided on the use of social media by judges themselves. The facts concerned a disciplinary sanction imposed on the applicant, a serving Turkish judge, for having shared on Facebook a press article concerning a disciplinary procedure before the High Council of Judges and Prosecutors. It is interesting to note that the Facebook group concerned was closed, and all members were colleagues. Nonetheless, both the issue (an allegation of corruption) and the interference (a reprimand for sharing a press article on Facebook) were recognised by the Court to be matters of particular interest within public debate, since they were closely related to the independence of the judiciary *vis-à-vis* the government, with respect to events surrounding proceedings for suspected corruption and the executive's opposition to those proceedings.

The application, rooted in Articles 10 and 13 of ECHR, objected that freedom of speech on digital networks had been violated and that there was no effective domestic remedy to governmental interference. The Court ultimately held that the measure was not proportionate, as it was unnecessary in a democratic society. The disciplinary sanction exceeded the state's margin of appreciation given the magistrate's duties and responsibilities relating to his professional activity and judicial status. Indeed, disciplinary measures may entail severe consequences for the lives and careers of the members of the judiciary who are penalised and, as both the ECtHR and CJEU[89] have also pointed out, the review carried out in relation to the judge must thus be appropriate to the disciplinary nature of the decisions in question.

This case also provides explicit confirmation of the relevance of the ethical duty incumbent upon an individual ordinary judge (in this specific case, a judge specialising in criminal law) to become active on networks such as Facebook to inform and contribute to the debate on serious issues regarding the independence and effectiveness of the judicial system, and as result the rule of law, in the interest of all citizens. The ECtHR ruling in *Danileț v Romania*, delivered on 20 February 2024, recently intervened on the use of Facebook by a judge who had published two messages on his page and, for this reason, had been disciplinarily sanctioned. The Section Panel decided (four to three) for the violation of Article 10 of ECHR, with one concurring opinion attached

87 See French CSM, Case p077, decision of 29 April 2014, and Case s212, decision of 30 April 2014.

88 *Kozan v Turkey* App No. 16695/19 (ECtHR, 1 March 2022).

89 See Case C-791/19, *Commission v Poland* [2021], para 83, and the ECtHR case law mentioned therein.

and one dissenting opinion expressed by three judges. It is likely that the case will be accepted for further decision by the Grand Chamber. It is a significant confirmation that the matter is sensitive in several European countries and complex for the fundamental rights at stake, needing to be carefully balanced.

The other side of the coin: private communications by individual judges

If, on the other hand, communication by the individual judge is not related to or incidental to ongoing crucial judicial reforms or legal activities that may potentially impinge upon the future competence of the judge and is expressed in various social media fora, then the matter is likely to fall within the scope of "private life", protected under Article 8 of ECHR, read in conjunction with Article 10. From this perspective, discerning the limits to freedom of expression becomes even more delicate, and the case law on disciplinary liability is not homogeneous.[90] This is first because the phenomenon is not regulated in detail in most European countries, and indeed there is scant awareness of it; secondly, different ethical standards may apply, mainly depending upon the social context and on the different generations of magistrates involved in the use of social media.

The critical duality is reflected by a survey arranged by several European supreme courts, including the Italian Court of Cassation, which considered the use of social media more closely.[91] It addressed the issue of the specific usage of social media by judges by virtue of their active participation on social media platforms: this may be relevant in terms of the content they like and the groups they join, particularly those of a political nature. In most, but not all European countries,[92] actions of this nature could undermine public confidence in the judge's impartiality or the impartiality of the judiciary in general.[93]

90 See Mario Fresa, *La giustizia disciplinare: i magistrati ordinari: quali controlli sui controllori?* (Edizioni scientifiche italiane 2021); Mario Fresa, *Il Dibattito Pubblico Sui Processi e Sulle Questioni Di Giustizia. La Parola Dei Magistrati Tra Libertà Di Espressione, Obblighi Di Segreto e Dovere Di Riserbo* (Aracne 2019); Adriana Apostoli, *Implicazioni costituzionali della responsabilità disciplinare dei magistrati* (Giuffrè 2009).

91 Corte Suprema di Cassazione, 'Risposte Della Corte Suprema Di Cassazione al Questionario Proveniente Dalla Corte Suprema Della Repubblica Ceca Su Le Attività Secondarie e l'uso Dei Social Media Da Parte Dei Magistrati' (1 October 2021) <https://www.dirittodelrisparmio.it/wp-content/uploads/2021/10/CASSAZIONE_QUESTIONARIO_SULLE_ATTIVITA_SECONDARIE_DEI_GIUDICI_REPUBBLICA_CECA_.pdf>, accessed 2 April 2024.

92 In Germany, judges may be members of political parties but must—even during political activity – refrain from any action that could endanger public confidence in their independence. See Anne Sanders and Elisabeth Faltinat, 'Judges, Political Mandates and Judicial Independence in Germany: How to Deal with Radicalised Judges?' [2023] Verfassungsblog <https://verfassungsblog.de/judges-political-mandates-and-judicial-independence-in-germany/>, accessed 2 April 2024.

93 See UNODC (n 65), para 21.

It is accepted that a judge's duty to comply with standards of professional ethics may influence their private life to a certain extent.[94] Turning to the most common cases, the use of the "like" button on social networks such as Facebook or "emojis" on WhatsApp is covered by Article 10 of ECHR[95] as current and popular forms of the exercise of freedom of expression online to approve content published by a third person. A case currently pending before the Strasbourg Court concerns the issue of whether being "friends" with third parties on Facebook may directly affect a judge's appearance of impartiality, which should result in his or her recusal in a specific case.[96] However, according to the French CSM Guidelines, the "friending" on social media of different users is not sufficient to establish automatically that the judge who exercised that freedom of expression on a social network is biased.[97]

In general, the rule of sobriety in terms of behaviour requires that certain aspects of private life remain confidential and not be revealed to the public. Otherwise, there is a risk that the necessary seriousness, composure, and discretion that every magistrate, and therefore the judiciary as a whole, must respect *vis-à-vis* public opinion might be undermined.[98] Thus, even the failure to take prompt action to delete illegal comments posted by others on the "wall" of a Facebook account that is freely accessible to the public may be relevant. Recently, the Strasbourg Grand Chamber accepted[99] a referral against a Chamber judgment finding no violation of Article 10 of ECHR in a case involving the censure of a local councillor for having failed to take action in response to an abusive statement posted by a third party. It is important to be clear about the distinction between public and private profiles on social media and the fact that no protection is provided for "hate speech" according to Article 17 of ECHR.[100] This matter, along with the scope for positive obligations and hence the requirement of immediate action by internet providers, is analysed further in the landmark *Delfi* ruling of the Court.[101]

It cannot be excluded that any activity on Facebook by a judge's close family member – such as a spouse – might, in certain circumstances, adversely

94 *Özpınar v Turkey* App No. 20999/04 (ECtHR, 19 October 2010).

95 *Melike v Turkey* App No. 35786/19 (ECtHR, 15 September 2021), para 44.

96 *Chaves Fernandes Figueiredo v Switzerland* App No. 55603/18 (ECtHR, pending).

97 See Conseil Supérieur de la Magistrature, 'Compendium of the Judiciary's Ethical Obligations' <http://www.conseil-superieur-magistrature.fr/compendium-judiciarys-ethical-obligations>, accessed 2 April 2024.

98 *Panioglu v Romania* App No. 33794/14 (ECtHR, 8 December 2020); *Guz v Poland* App No. 965/12 (ECtHR, 15 October 2020).

99 *Sanchez v France* App No. 45581/15 (ECtHR, 2 September 2021); *Sanchez v France* App No. 45581/15 (ECtHR, GC, 15 May 2023), which found that there had been no violation of Article 10.

100 See *M'Bala M'Bala v France* App No. 25239/13 (ECtHR, 20 October 2015).

101 *Delfi AS v Estonia* (n 17).

affect the perception of the judge's impartiality.[102] The critical consideration, also in light of the UN Principles of Judicial Conduct referred to above, is that from the standpoint of an objective observer, the judges sufficiently distances themselves from statements made by close relatives on a social network.[103]

As this excursus has attempted to establish, it is still challenging to identify one single standard for all possible personal behaviour by judges on social networks, especially in situations involving conduct that is not explicitly related to professional matters but may have a potential impact on judicial impartiality and its perception by the public. However, some aspects appear to recur: the need to strike a fair balance between public and private figures, between speech and interactions, and between self-restraint and the need to use instruments that form part of the new digital *agora*.

Impartiality and independence of the courts are guaranteed by legal procedures and public scrutiny of decisions, not by the online screening of private life

Impartiality and independence are a duty and essential part of the status of a member of the judiciary. Due consideration for the ethical framework applicable to judges – the duties of impartiality, independence, discretion, and respect for the public image of justice – is a key aspect of the meaning of "impartial and independent judge" protected by the Convention and by the right to an effective remedy and a fair trial enshrined by the Charter. Its implementation is dependent first and foremost on the professional activity of the individual judge and prosecutor, as reflected by the reasons given in support of decisions and their content, but also on the person's behaviour in public and participation in social life, including when using social media for official and, to some extent, even private communications. However, the research suggests that asserting a general rule about what a judge can or should, or should not, do on social networks may be problematic. This is particularly the case with private communications as there may be significant generational differences in ethical values and social contexts.

The highly fragmented scenario described above does not take the judicious use of social networks for granted and suggests a need to specifically adapt the standards used for other forms of expression. The current uncertainty might mislead members of the judiciary into feeling free to make almost any public statement if it is made in a private capacity, or into considering that they do not need to use social media at all, thereby isolating themselves from an essential and transparent part of modern democratic society and ultimately impoverishing public debate on relevant legal issues.

102 *Rustavi 2 Broadcasting Company Ltd and Others v Georgia* App No. 16812/17 (ECtHR, 18 July 2019).

103 Ibid., para 344.

By contrast, a canon that defined once and for all (in)appropriate behaviour might interfere with the right to act freely and independently from outside influence. The greater the density of the rules applicable to judicial behaviour, the greater the risk that political players, other state bodies, or the judicial authorities may use them to discipline and exercise control over individual judges about their professional conduct.

According to established case law, criminal punishment within the area of freedom of expression proves in many cases to be disproportionate to the legitimate aim pursued by the government[104] and due to its nature and scope, often does not take complete account of the natural interaction between free speech (as a paramount liberty to be carefully protected in democratic societies) and other human and fundamental rights enshrined by the Convention and the Charter. Parallel criminal and disciplinary proceedings may also be launched in relation to the exercise of freedom of expression by judges and prosecutors, and this may be liable to enhance the "chilling effect", endangering public debate on critical legal reforms and issues regarding the judicial system:[105] even if the criminal conviction is suspended there may still be interference with freedom of expression.[106]

In the authors' view, soft law and codes of conduct based on an innovative international comparative approach, in conjunction with national provisions, can improve protection for the freedom of expression of judges and prosecutors. At the same time, they may help to strike a fair balance between judges' free speech on social networks and the human and fundamental rights of others enshrined by the Convention and the Charter.

This result may be secured in different ways: first, guidelines developed by means of comparative analysis and adopted by respected international organisations may effectively help to draw a clear dividing line between generally accepted standards and grey areas. Second, through its persuasive strength, soft law can effectively contribute to achieving recognition for a consensus among relatively homogeneous European countries, or at least underscore trends that may help interpret national regulations. Third, codes of conduct can in some cases even operate as an external source supplementing the relevant provisions on criminal or disciplinary liability, thus enabling a welcome balance to be struck between the rigidity of specific rules, which is necessary to ensure their foreseeability, and the need for some degree of elasticity. Rules need to be read in light of ethical standards that change considerably across generations and social contexts as well as the ongoing technological revolution.

104 See *Sallusti v Italy* App No. 22350/13 (ECtHR, 7 March 2019) and several judgments quoted therein.

105 *Żurek v Poland* App No. 39650/18 (ECtHR, 16 June 2022).

106 *Durukan and Birol v Turkey* Apps Nos. 14879/20 and 13440/21 (ECtHR, 3 October 2023).

It could represent a significant achievement because the findings of this study stress the current lack of a clear framework for the use of social media that takes into account the need to respect private life in conjunction with free speech, and this situation affects the democratic participation in the public debate of judges as citizens. Moreover, the current uncertainty does not appear to be fully compliant with foreseeability requirements in relation to the usage of online tools and respect for private life, as laid down in the case law of the European Court of Human Rights, nor with the awareness of the risks of online surveillance[107] and failures of data protection.[108] All such aspects are relevant for each citizen, although they may potentially undermine judges' status as impartial and independent authorities, resulting in long-standing consequences for democratic societies.

The publication online and even the collection of personal data regarding judges may appear to be a transparent instrument pursuing the legitimate aim of safeguarding the political neutrality and impartiality of judges themselves, as well as confidence in that impartiality, and of protecting the dignity of their duties. However, it should be regarded not only as an interference in the rights of those involved to respect their private lives and protect their personal data, but also as an action that does not comply with the principle of proportionality and thus infringes requirements arising under EU law. As the CJEU recently pointed out,[109] less intrusive means already exist for that purpose. These include specific procedures for recusal and the provision to the bodies responsible for ensuring compliance with professional rules, or for appointing benches of judges hearing individual cases, of information relating to certain activities carried out by judges outside their duties that might give rise to conflicts of interest.

The legal procedures established for recusal in advance of a judgment, and also for appeal against an existing judicial decision, coupled with scrutiny of the proceedings by media and public opinion, if relevant for democratic debate, cannot and must not be replaced with screening of a judge's private life based on a review of their use of social networks in the past, nor using the publication online of the results of "*doxing*" to challenge an undesired decision. The danger for judicial impartiality and independence lies not in ideas expressed publicly and indifferently but in almost invisible, opaque networks of interests.

107 See, for a detailed discussion of the principles of and case law on foreseeability and private life, *Big Brother Watch and Others v United Kingdom* Apps Nos. 58170/13, 62322/14, and 24960/15 (ECtHR, GC, 25 May 2021).

108 For instance, see *M.D. and Others v Spain* App No. 36584/17 (ECtHR, 28 June 2022), paras 61–64.

109 Case C-204/21, *Commission v Poland* [2023], paras 297–298.

Part 2

Lessons for Europe

National perspectives on freedom of expression of judges

5 All quiet in the judiciary

Low voice of Hungarian judges and the role of European courts

Gábor Halmai and Ágnes Kovács

Introduction

Hungary's transition from democracy to autocracy has drawn global attention. Neither domestic checks and balances, such as an independent judiciary, nor transnational institutions, such as the European Union and the Council of Europe, have been able to intercept the process, and by now autocratisation has reached a level where resistance is less and less effective. By resistance, we mean, in this chapter, any form of contestation to autocratisation from institutional or non-institutional actors in the domestic or transnational sphere which aims to prevent, stop, or minimise autocratic power. This can be manifested in judicial decisions and criticisms of the state of judicial independence by judges and other legal professionals.

Public support for changing the Orbán government's constitutional regime is limited, with the majority viewing it as democratic.[1] The presence of single-party dominance is also a sign of the lack of a constitutional moment, as argued in the case of other countries, such as India, Mexico, South Africa, and Japan,[2] or recently regarding the Israeli government's judicial overhaul.[3] Mass protests, as another characteristic of the constitutional moment, are also not present in Hungary.[4] Ever since the adoption of the "illiberal" Fundamental Law in 2011, there has been no "constitutional enthusiasm" to re-institute liberal democracy, which was introduced in 1989 without serious public involvement in a constitutional moment. This attitude of the people, including the

1 Laura Clancy, 'Hungarians Differ in Their Evaluations of Democracy Under Orbán's Leadership' (Pew Research Center, 3 August 2022) <https://www.pewresearch.org/short-reads/2022/08/03/hungarians-differ-in-their-evaluations-of-democracy-under-orbans-leadership/ > accessed 6 April 2024.

2 Rosalind Dixon and Guy Baldwin, 'Globalizing Constitutional Moments? Reflections on the Japanese Art 9 Debate?' (2019) 6 The American Journal of Comparative Law 145.

3 Lazar Berman, 'Why the Deepening Judicial Crisis Could be Israel's Constitutional Moment' (Times of Israel, 10 July 2023) <https://www.timesofisrael.com/why-the-deepening-judicial-crisis-could-be-israels-constitutional-moment/amp/> accessed 6 April 2024.

4 Juliano Zaiden Benvindo, 'The Seeds of Change: Popular Protests as Constitutional Moments' (2015), 99 Marquette Law Review 363.

DOI: 10.4324/9781003470779-7

intellectuals, which is, of course, determined by the democratic development of the country, explains the lack of resistance against illiberal constitutionalisation and the curtailment of judicial independence. Historically, in Hungary, as in almost all East-Central European countries, there were only some unexpected moments – quick flourishes of liberal democracy – followed by equally quick acts to delegitimise them.

In this chapter, we deal with the very weak domestic and transnational resistance against the Orbán government's efforts to dismantle judicial independence since 2010. Domestically, the focus will be on judges' resistance, while at the transnational level, we concentrate on the role of the Court of Justice of the European Union and the European Court of Human Rights. Our aim is limited to assessing judicial strategies in challenging authoritarian tendencies in Hungary. Consequently, we do not discuss the (lack of) strategies of other state organs and European actors and do not address the responses of extra-institutional actors, such as civil society organisations and citizens either.[5] But almost the same can be said of extra-institutional resistance as can be seen regarding institutional, particularly judicial resistance: it has been limited in scope, with the exception of the actions of some courageous lawyers, legal academics, and civil society organisations.

The low level of resistance in the Hungarian judiciary was clearly visible from the start of the rule of law backsliding, and judges rarely relied on their freedom of speech to speak up against such tendencies. This situation is certainly related to the fact that the Hungarian judiciary is traditionally apolitical, and the legislative framework reflects a highly restrictive approach to judicial free speech, which fundamentally shapes judges' understanding of the scope of their freedom of expression. We seek to determine the core of this understanding as we believe it presents a major obstacle to mobilising judges to defend judicial independence. Since 2010, the government has been putting constant political pressure on courts, and more recently even court executives have taken various steps to silence judges critical of some elements of the legal system or the current form of court administration.[6] All these seriously discourage judges from making extrajudicial statements in matters related to the rule of law and judicial independence.

This chapter deals with judges exercising their right to freedom of expression as a rare form of resistance against the autocratic government of Hungary. On the other hand, we also discuss the responsibility of the European institutions when responding to the violations of the freedom of expression of

5 See the differentiation of institutional and extra-institutional strategies in Laura Gamboa, *Resisting Backsliding. Opposition Strategies Against the Erosion of Democracy* (Cambridge University Press, 2022).

6 On this, see also Etienne Hanelt and Attila Vincze, 'A Hybrid Judiciary in a Hybrid Regime: A Case Study on Hungary' (2023) JUSTIN Working Paper Series <https://justin.law.muni.cz/media/3565890/hanelt-vincze_a-hybrid-judiciary-in-a-hybrid-regime-2023.pdf> accessed 25 November 2023.

judges and the dismantlement of judicial independence more generally. The European Court of Human Rights judgment in the *Baka* case,[7] together with the Council of Europe's failure to enforce it and the decision of the Court of Justice of the European Union on the early retirement age of judges[8] seem to demonstrate that the European courts often choose the simpler solution, which, besides national government's actions, also lower the voice of Hungarian judges.

This chapter is divided into three sections. First, we provide a very brief sketch of how the Hungarian government dismantled judicial independence step by step, starting in 2010. Then, we critically examine the mostly timid and inadequate responses of domestic and European courts to the systemic attacks against the judicial organisation. In the next part, we look at judges' freedom of expression as a possible tool to resist authoritarian tendencies and explore the relevant legal and institutional framework to better understand why Hungarian judges have remained largely silent when their own independence was put at risk. Although judicial resistance in Hungary can mostly be seen as a story of failure, we discuss the exceptional role of the National Judicial Council (NJC) in fighting for the independence of the judiciary. The operation of the NJC between 2018 and 2023 can provide both a model and hope for future collective actions.

Hungary's judicial overhaul after 2010

After the electoral victory of Fidesz in 2010, the country, according to Prime Minister Orbán's self-definition, became an "illiberal democracy", with a new constitution called Fundamental Law enacted with the exclusive votes of the governing party. Characterising the results of the 2010 elections as a "revolution of the ballot boxes", Orbán's intention with this revolution was to eliminate any checks and balances, as well as the institutional guarantees of fundamental rights, by dismantling the independence of the Constitutional Court and the ordinary judiciary.

Besides packing the Constitutional Court and curtailing its competencies to review legislation, one of the first steps of this autocratisation was to reform the judicial system. In late 2011, the government dismissed András Baka, the President of the Supreme Court, more than three years before the expiry of his mandate. The decision came after Baka publicly criticised the government's upcoming judicial reforms. In 2012, the previous model of judicial self-governance was replaced by a centralised form of court administration in which substantial powers were conferred on the President of the National Judicial Office (NJO), elected by the Parliament for nine years. The National Judicial Council (NJC) had only weak competencies to supervise the activity

7 *Baka v Hungary*, App No. 20261/12, 23 June 2016.
8 CJEU, Case C-286/12 *Commission v Hungary*, 6 November 2012, ECLI:EU:C:2012:687.

of the President of the NJO.[9] The new illiberal Fundamental Law reduced the retirement age for judges on ordinary courts from 70 to 62, starting on the day it went into effect. This change forced 274 judges into early retirement. In July 2012, the Constitutional Court declared that the suddenly lowered retirement age for judges was unconstitutional.[10] But by the time the Court ruled, the 274 judges had already been fired, and the Constitutional Court failed to order their reinstatement. The President of the Republic, János Áder, one of Fidesz's founders, said he would not withdraw the orders firing the judges. The President of the NJO did not encourage the judges to challenge the firings[11] and said that the newly hired and promoted judges would not be displaced even if the unconstitutionally fired judges were reinstated by order of the labour courts.

After direct attacks against courts, thereby causing a severe breakdown of judicial independence by 2012, the new Fidesz government has kept the courts under constant pressure. It has used various tools, from further legislative reforms and public criticism of individual judgments to putting administrative pressure on the everyday operation of the judiciary by court executives, who have served as transmission belts of the government. Some steps are worth highlighting here to illustrate the never-ending process of regime consolidation within the judiciary.

As part of its strategy to contain the judiciary, the government was determined to set up a separate system of administrative justice to transfer politically sensitive administrative lawsuits to specialised courts operating under the tighter control of the executive branch. However, in 2019, the government unexpectedly retreated from its plan, maintained the unified structure of the judicial organisation and took a different path to extend its influence over the administration of justice. It conferred significant powers on the Supreme Court (from 2012, officially called Kúria) while paving the way, by a series of *ad hominem* legislation, for electing a pro-government Supreme Court President, András Zs. Varga, for nine years. Court-packing continued in the top court, resulting also in the appointment of a former State Secretary, who secured a seat in the Kúria without any previous judicial experience.[12] In 2023, both apex courts were controlled by the government.

9 The NJC consists of 15 judges, of which 14 are elected by their peers. The President of the Kúria is an ex officio member of the body.

10 Decision 33/2012 (VII.17) of the CC.

11 'Kényszernyugdíjazás: Handó nem fordul Áderhez' *HVG* (Budapest, 26 July 2012) <https://hvg.hu/itthon/20120726_kenyszernyugdijazas_birak> accessed 6 April 2024.

12 Hungarian Helsinki Committee, 'Tribunal Established by Sleight of Hand' (Helsinki.hu, 4 September 2022) <https://helsinki.hu/en/tribunal-established-by-sleight-of-hand/> accessed 30 January 2024

Soft judicial voices resisting the dismantlement of independence

Resistance through judicial decisions

Judicial resistance to authoritarian tendencies has been rare since 2010; however, the Hungarian judiciary is not without tools and strategies to defend itself against political interference. Relevant scholarship revealed that the level and understanding of judicial autonomy considerably weigh in choosing the form of opposition against the political regime.[13] Hungarian judges understand autonomy narrowly, in a strictly professional sense, primarily related to their decision-making activity. Judges are seen as highly qualified, competent civil servants acting autonomously, without undue political interference within their professional capacity. Beyond that, individual autonomy is seriously constrained by a historically hierarchical organisational setting.[14] Given the latter understanding of judicial autonomy, reliance on formal judicial tools seems to be the most obvious avenue for judges to challenge the existing legal and political framework.

Judges can use their decision-making power to prevent, mitigate, neutralise, or invalidate government measures. However, in institutional settings where the ruling parties can amend the legal system by constitutional and legal means, resistance can be difficult through the traditional form of judicial decision-making. The Hungarian government, in office since 2010, gradually transformed the legal system to align with the interests of the authoritarian regime, occasionally legislating reactively in direct response to judicial decisions unfavourable to the ruling party.[15] As part of this process, it repealed the pre-2012 case law of the Constitutional Court[16] and continuously legislated to replace the previous jurisprudence of the Supreme Court that served as a basis for administering justice in compliance with the rule of law.[17] Nevertheless, judges still have discretion. As historical experience shows, they can, for instance, rely on the general principles of law to interpret new legislation in compliance with the rule of law, equality, and human rights for which the textual basis

13 Alexei Trochev and Rachel Ellett. 'Judges and their allies: rethinking judicial autonomy through the prism of off-bench resistance' (2014) 2 Journal of Law and Courts, 67, 80.

14 Mátyás Bencze, 'Judicial Populism and the Weberian Judge – The Strength of Judicial Resistance Against Governmental Influence in Hungary' (2021) 22 German Law Journal 1282.

15 This can be nicely illustrated by the changes in the Fundamental Law's text in the first years of the current regime and by the changes in the Hungarian electoral law, which regularly followed court decisions that were against the interests of the government. On the latter, see Viktor Z. Kazai and János Mécs, 'Local Elections in Hungary: the Results in Context' (Verfassungsblog, 14 October 2019) < https://verfassungsblog.de/local-elections-in-hungary-the-results-in-context/> accessed 2 February 2024.

16 The infamous Fourth Amendment of the Fundamental Law repealed the decisions of the Constitutional Court rendered before the new Fundamental Law entered into force.

17 In late 2019, this process culminated in establishing the so-called limited precedent system, requiring lower courts to follow the published decisions of the Kúria delivered after 2012. If lower courts seek to depart from the Kúria's decision, they must justify it.

has not been fully eradicated from the legal system.[18] András Sajó has recently argued that the concept of the militant rule of law provides ample interpretive tools for judges to respond to the abuse of power in "illiberal democracies".[19] According to Sajó, judges can engage in a legislative intent analysis or exercise a reasonableness review to defend the values of the rule of law.

In Hungary, collective judicial responses to the first comprehensive reforms were fully missing. The government first tamed the Constitutional Court by altering the system of nominating judges and expanding the size of the court from 11 to 15 judges, allowing the government to pack the court with government-friendly judges. In the meantime, the new Fundamental Law changed the review power of the Constitutional Court by restricting *ex-post* abstract norm control and abolishing *actio popularis*, one of the peculiarities of the Hungarian regime change in the 1990s. Also, it upheld the limited scope of constitutional review over budget-related laws, which the government first introduced in 2010 as a punishment for a decision unfavourable to the ruling majority.

The Constitutional Court failed to speak up against the changes in its composition and powers, which gradually turned the institution into an agent of the autocratic regime. Still, until April 2013, by the time the majority of judges were elected by Fidesz's parliamentary super-majority, the Constitutional Court, in certain cases, decided against the government. In 2010, it annulled a new supertax, a symbolic policy of the Orbán government, incurring a 98% tax rate on severance payments.[20] The government immediately responded and curtailed the power of the Constitutional Court to review tax-related laws; then, it reintroduced the annulled tax. However, the Constitutional Court stepped in again, and within its limited power, it annulled a substantial part of the law for the second time.[21]

In this short period, the small majority of still independent constitutional justices had to consider the possibility of the abolishment of the Constitutional Court and its merger into the Kúria, which certainly lowered the critical voice of those judges. This made the opposition of Constitutional Court judges cautious in its judgment of 28 December 2012 on the Transitional Provisions, an omnibus constitutional addendum to the Fundamental Law also passed at the very end of 2011. The Constitutional Court did not review the substance of the Transitional Provisions since the petition of the ombudsman had not requested it. Instead of requesting that the nullified provisions be reinserted into the Constitution as an amendment, the Court only said that if the Parliament wanted a provision to be part of the Constitution, it was

18 David Dyzenhaus, *Hard Cases in Wicked Legal Systems: Pathologies of Legality* (Oxford University Press 2010) 48.

19 András Sajó, 'Militant Rule of Law' (Verfassungsblog, 20 December 2023) <https://verfassungsblog.de/militant-rule-of-law/> accessed 2 January 2024.

20 Decision 184/2010. (X. 28) of the CC.

21 Decision 37/2011. (V. 10) of the CC.

not enough to declare that the Transitional Provisions had constitutional status. Instead, the Parliament had to use the formal procedure laid out in the Constitution to make a constitutional amendment.

The ruling on the Transitional Provisions made it possible for the Constitutional Court to review the substance of some of the cardinal laws that said the same thing as the corresponding parts of the Transitional Provisions. Most of the provisions struck down by the Constitutional Court when it reviewed the Transitional Provisions were also embedded in cardinal laws that the Parliament had passed earlier, and with these provisions now "demoted" from constitutional status by the Court's ruling, the Court then undertook to review the almost identical provisions in the cardinal laws.

The Fourth Amendment of the Fundamental Law and the final packing of the Constitutional Court at the same time was a tipping point in the constitutionalisation of the autocratic system in Hungary when the cautiously resistant Constitutional Court against Viktor Orbán's constitutional hardball became an enabler of unchecked executive power.[22]

The difficulties of judicial resistance through litigation are aggravated by rulers of new authoritarianism successfully capturing top courts, thereby blocking some well-established channels for lower courts to oppose important political actors. In Hungary, the Constitutional Court is no longer independent, so the low prospect of winning a case before a highly politicised court can discourage Hungarian judges from seeking the invalidation of legislative measures via constitutional complaints. Similarly, if apex courts deliberately limit the applicability of EU law in domestic proceedings,[23] and judges have to face repression for referring questions of EU law for a preliminary ruling, they are likely to choose risk-averse strategies and refrain from engaging in judicial dialogue with the CJEU. In contrast, Polish judges have referred many questions about the independence of the Polish judiciary to the CJEU, turning the preliminary reference procedure into a strategic tool to address the problems of political interference with the administration of justice.[24] While questions regarding the deficiencies of the Hungarian asylum system have been referred to the CJEU,[25] and these have touched upon some explicit rule of law problems,

22 In his book *The Specter of Dictatorship: Judicial Enabling of Presidential Power* (Stanford University Press, 2021), David M. Driesen compares the cases of Hungary, Poland, and Turkey with that of the US in how high courts enabled the unlimited power of the executive.

23 Decision 11/2020. (VI. 3.) of the CC. See also Viktor Z Kazai and Ágnes Kovács, 'The Last Days of the Independent Supreme Court of Hungary?' (Verfassungsblog, 13 October 2020) https://verfassungsblog.de/the-last-days-of-the-independent-supreme-court-of-hungary/ accessed 11 November 2023

24 Claudia-Y. Matthes, 'Judges as activists: how Polish judges mobilise to defend the rule of law' (2022) 38 East European Politics 468.

25 Alessandra Favi, 'Protecting Asylum Seekers and Migrants in the Context of the Rule of Law Crisis in EU Member States: The Recent Approach of the Court of Justice of the EU through the Lens of the Global Compacts on Refugees and Migration' (2022) Laws 37.

it was only one reference in the *IS* case[26] that boldly raised the question of whether the independence of Hungarian judges is guaranteed. Judge Vasvári, in his request for a preliminary ruling in a criminal case, addressed structural problems of judicial independence in Hungary. But the Kúria, on the motion of the Prosecutor General, found the request unlawful for being irrelevant to the outcome of the case at hand. The referring judge was also subject to disciplinary proceedings on the same grounds. The story of Judge Vasvári shows that judges could be exposed to retribution for turning to the CJEU on constitutional issues that challenge the fundamentals of the current political system. Moreover, a junior judge, Gabriella Szabó, was found unsuitable for judicial office and was dismissed after successfully challenging some elements of the Hungarian asylum legislation in her reference to the CJEU.[27]

Judicial resistance through extra-legal actions

As regards off-bench strategies, judges can rely on individual and collective measures. Individual resistance is particularly costly as it can trigger retaliatory measures, as happened with Supreme Court President Baka, the very first ordinary judge criticising the Fidesz government's efforts to dismantle judicial independence.[28]

The other way is collective resistance, which has many advantages compared to isolated, individual actions. Organised resistance provides greater visibility for judges while showing unity and solidarity within the judiciary. It might be more effective in framing the public debate according to the main interests of the judiciary and strengthening the social legitimacy and support of an otherwise unprecedented judicial behaviour.[29] Collective actions may take two major forms: judges can form alliances with their peers or seek cooperation with other actors capable of promoting the organisational interests of the judiciary under attack.

The beheading of ordinary courts by firing the most senior judges between 62 and 70 years of age, mostly those in leading positions, through the introduction of the aforementioned early retirement age was met with very little collective resistance. In the beginning, court presidents spoke out against the measure in an open letter, finding it discriminatory, contrary to international

26 CJEU, Case C-564/19, *IS*, 23 November 2021, ECLI:EU:C:2021:949.

27 Hungarian Helsinki Committee, 'Another Scandal at the Judiciary: No Effective Remedy for Judges Dismissed from the Bench' (Helsinki.hu, 12 September 2022) <https://helsinki.hu/en/another-scandal-at-the-judiciary-no-effective-remedy-for-judges-dismissed-from-the-bench/ >accessed 11 November 2023.

28 Katarína Šipulová, 'Under Pressure: Building Judicial Resistance to Political Interferences' in DJ Galligan (ed), *The Courts and the People: Friend or Foe? The Putney Debates* (Hart Publishing 2019) 153, 166.

29 Trochev and Ellett (n 13) 77.

standards of judicial independence, and politically motivated.[30] However, most of the judges accepted the offered retirement status and did not ask for reactivation, even though a new law adopted by the Parliament after the judgment of CJEU allowed them to do so without separate court proceedings. The lack of collective resistance was also reinforced through the institutional weakening of the previously strong judicial self-governance.[31] The head of the newly created NJO, who has been a close personal friend of the Prime Minister and is also married to the chief author of the Fundamental Law, got the power to exercise the "central responsibilities of the administration of the courts", including the power to appoint court executives and exert significant influence on judicial careers, primarily through court executives appointed under her discretionary power. Although the reform retained the NJC as part of the system, it had barely any power to exercise effective supervision over the NJO President.

In Poland, judges and their associations have started networking and made conscious use of several forms of off-bench strategies to challenge powerful political actors.[32] However, if potential allies are either captured (media, academia) or incapacitated (NGOs),[33] and the public perception of the justice system is considerably shaped by government manipulation, it is difficult to build a social network. The low internationalisation of Hungarian judges also reduces their capacity to extend their transnational network and rely on the help of international peer pressure.[34] This situation somewhat changed in 2018 when a new NJC was elected. The NJC has become a strategic actor off the bench by using public speaking[35] and actively engaging with transnational judicial networks to make the problems of the Hungarian judiciary more visible.[36] For these purposes, it set up its webpage and published the minutes of its meetings not only to make its operation fully transparent but also to reach out to the professional and general public with the main debates within court

30 'Bírósági vezetők tiltakoznak nyílt levélben a korhatárcsökkentés miatt' *HVG* (15 April 2011) <https://hvg.hu/itthon/20110414_fobiro_korhatar_biro_nyugdij_politika>, accessed 6 April 2024.

31 See in more detail Kriszta Kovács and Kim Lane Scheppele, 'The fragility of an independent judiciary: Lessons from Hungary and Poland – and the European Union' (2018) 51 Communist and Post-Communist Studies 189.

32 Matthes (n 28).

33 Gerő Márton and others, 'Strategies for Survival: Human Rights Organizations' Responses to the Closing of Political Opportunity Structures in Hungary' (2020) 27 Politologicky Casopis 119.

34 Trochev and Ellett (n 16) 80.

35 In December 2022, the NJC invited media representatives for a "press breakfast" to inform them about the current debates in court administration. <https://obt2018.hu/az-orszagos-biroi-tanacs-sajtoreggelivel-nyitotta-a-decemberi-ulesnapjat/>, accessed 6 April 2024.

36 The NJC has actively collaborated with the European Network of Councils for the Judiciary (ENCJ) since its election in 2018. It applied for membership in the Executive Board, which it held for two years between 2019 and 2021.

administration. It made several legislative proposals to strengthen judicial self-governance and the safeguards of judicial independence, keeping the need for a comprehensive reform of court administration on the agenda.[37] The NJC could mobilise the Hungarian Association of Judges (MABIE) to some extent, but as it will be presented below, it has remained the sole actor in domestic resistance.

Transnational resistance

European institutions, including transnational courts, had long ignored the fact that there is a non-democratic state within the EU, where the attacks against judicial independence have become systemic. This made international legal tools ineffective not only to stop but even to slow down the erosion of the rule of law.

In 2012, due to the submission of the European Commission, the CJEU could not provide an adequate framework for dealing with the issue of the forced retirement of judges. By focusing on the violation of age discrimination and failing to deal with the systemic nature of the infringement, it ignored the broader rule of law perspective of the case, namely the violation of judicial independence.[38]

Later, the ECtHR followed suit. In the *Baka* judgment, the ECtHR, concentrating on a narrow interpretation of both Article 6 and 10 of the ECHR, also missed the chance to raise the main structural rule of law problem behind Baka's dismissal.[39] The premature termination of the Supreme Court President's mandate was thus depicted as a single issue in judicial governance in Hungary. Nevertheless, the judgment catalysed significant doctrinal developments in the jurisprudence of the ECtHR concerning the freedom of expression of judges, interpreted primarily against the background of judicial independence. However, this approach alone lacks the potential to grasp the systemic nature of political interference with the functioning of courts. No less remarkably, the ECtHR could have also taken the road suggested by Judge Sicilianos in his concurring opinion. He argued that Article 6 could have been interpreted as guaranteeing not only a right for persons involved in court proceedings for an independent tribunal but also as "a subjective right for judges to have their individual independence safeguarded and respected by the State".[40] Under these circumstances, Article 6 could be directly invoked by judge applicants, and the ECtHR could frame these issues as they are:

37 See, for instance, decision 65/2022 (IX. 7.) NJC on an initiative for amending legislation.

38 Gábor Halmai, 'The Early Retirement of the Hungarian Judges', in Fernanda Nicola and Bill Davis (eds), *EU Law Stories: Contextual and Critical Histories of European Jurisprudence* (CUP, 2017).

39 David Kosař and Katarína Šipulová, 'The Strasbourg Court Meets Abusive Constitutionalism: *Baka v. Hungary* and the Rule of Law' (2018) 10 Hague Journal on the Rule of Law 83.

40 *Baka v Hungary* (n 7), Concurring Opinion of Judge Sicilianos, para 13.

restrictions of judicial independence. This approach could encourage judges' efforts at self-defence and make the judiciary more resilient against the systemic dismantling of judicial independence.[41]

The implementation of the *Baka* judgment is still pending, and the Committee of Ministers (CM) is trapped not only by the lack of real enforcement power of the Council of Europe *vis-à-vis* the defiant Contracting States but also by the approach taken by the ECtHR itself. General measures determined by the CM focus on providing judicial review against the possible impeachment of the Supreme Court's President by the Parliament and eliminating the chilling effect on judges' freedom of expression.[42] The CM has also established a link between the two requirements set out concerning the violations of Articles 6 and 10 of the Convention. It argues that providing effective judicial oversight against the Parliament's power to remove the President would be an important step towards redressing the chilling effect on judges' freedom of speech caused by the premature dismissal of former President András Baka. However, the incumbent Supreme Court President was appointed for nine years in 2021 in a highly politicised process and has been acting in the interest of the governing majority ever since, being also a major source of the chilling effect within the judiciary. So, fulfilling the first requirement would make no difference to the current state of judicial independence and would in no way alleviate the concerns about the freedom of speech of judges. Furthermore, the protection of the latter is considerably determined by traditions, judicial socialisation, and the general climate of courthouses, so formal legal changes promise little success on their own.

In 2018, the ECtHR again missed the opportunity to address the attacks on the judiciary as a systemic problem and to treat the removal of court executives as a manifest violation of the separation of powers principle. Many judges, forced into early retirement in 2012, filed lawsuits in Strasbourg. However, the ECtHR found all elements of their complaints inadmissible and failed to examine how the challenged measure had affected judicial independence in Hungary, even though the applicants argued about it.[43] The ECtHR endorsed the remedies the Hungarian government provided for the retired judges,[44]

41 While acknowledging the subjective right of judges to their independence can be seen as a form of judicial activism, the same applies to other approaches established by the ECtHR to provide stronger protection for judicial independence. See Mathieu Leloup, 'Who Safeguards the Guardians? A Subjective Right of Judges to Their Independence under Article 6 (1) ECHR'. (2021) 17 European Constitutional Law Review 394.

42 See the latest communication from the Committee of Ministers regarding the supervision of the execution of the *Baka* judgment, adopted at the 1483rd meeting, 5–7 December 2023 (DH), CM/Notes/1483/H46-17 (7 December 2023), available at https://search.coe.int/cm/Pages/result_details.aspx?ObjectID=0900001680ad3fd0#_ftnref12, accessed 30 January 2024.

43 *J.B. and Others v Hungary* App No. 45434/12, 27 November 2018, para 113.

44 The lump-sum compensation was found to be "adequate and sufficient" by the ECtHR to remedy the losses of the judges for their early removal, while judges who requested reinstate-

disregarding the substantial harm caused by the challenged legislation to the judiciary in general: as a result of the early retirement scheme, the top echelon of the Hungarian judiciary was significantly remade at a glance. The overhaul of judicial leadership is particularly damaging to judicial independence in a highly centralised career judiciary, where court executives enjoy broad administrative powers over rank-and-file judges. The ECtHR's reluctance is especially disappointing given the timing of the judgment amid clear declines in the rule of law in Hungary and Poland.[45] A more proactive approach by European courts could have empowered Hungarian judges to resist autocratic regimes leveraging legal professionals for autocratic legalism.[46]

Freedom of speech as a tool for judicial self-defence

Judicial independence has been elevated to a key component of the European legal order based on the values of the rule of law, democracy, and human rights. This is primarily owed to European courts, which have played a leading role in determining solid standards for organising domestic judiciaries across Europe. The process was not devoid of controversies as European tribunals developed new doctrines in this field, thereby extending their supervision over judicial issues that once belonged to the province of national governments.[47] The concept of freedom of expression is not an exception either. The ECtHR presumes that there is a link between judicial independence and the freedom of expression of judges.[48] While judges' public statements can be restricted to maintain the independence of the judiciary, judicial independence also serves as a ground for a high level of protection for the free speech of judges.

Our analysis builds on a similar assumption: we believe that efforts to restore judicial independence cannot be successful if judges' freedom to speak up is seriously curtailed. In countries like Hungary, where the authoritarian turn took place by constitutional and legal means, under the cloak of formal

ment could not substantiate the seriousness of the harm to their professional lives. Also, the ECtHR did not find it relevant that judges could not return to their previous administrative positions. ibid. para 136.

45 Renata Uitz, 'The Perils of Defending the Rule of Law Through Dialogue' (2019) 15 European Constitutional Law Review 1, 6–7.

46 Hungary is the main example of the concept of autocratic legalism, invented by Kim Lane Scheppele. See K. L. Scheppele, 'Autocratic Legalism' (2018) 85 The University of Chicago Law Review 545.

47 On these developments, see, for instance, Joost Sillen, 'The Concept of "Internal Judicial Independence" in the Case Law of the European Court of Human Rights' (2019) 15 European Constitutional Law Review 104; Aida Torres Pérez, 'From Portugal to Poland: The Court of Justice of the European Union as Watchdog of Judicial Independence' (2020) 27 Maastricht Journal of European and Comparative Law 105; Rafael Bustos Gisbert, 'Judicial Independence in European Constitutional Law' (2022) 18 European Constitutional Law Review 591. See also Leloup (n 41).

48 *Baka v Hungary* (n 7), para 165.

legality, off-bench resistance and the use of judicial free speech might figure more prominently within judicial strategies for fighting against the authoritarian backlash. So, the freedom of expression of judges is an essential prerequisite for safeguarding the independence of the judiciary. Consequently, we also claim that Hungarian judges' reluctance to bring judicial issues before the public further reduces the already low level of resistance within the judiciary.

The Hungarian legislative framework for judicial communication

The 2011 Fundamental Law and the Act on the Status of Judges prohibit judges from political affiliation or activities.[49] This provision was first introduced in the 1989 amendment to the 1972 Act on Courts, and the explanatory memorandum provided a broad understanding, including a ban on public statements on national or local issues of public affairs.

The Fundamental Law contains similar provisions for members of the Constitutional Court, the Commissioner for Fundamental Rights, prosecutors, and professional members of the police, the Defence Forces, and security services. The ECtHR reviewed these bans for civil servants in the case of *Rekvényi v. Hungary*. The petitioner, Mr Rekvényi, complained – ultimately unsuccessfully – against the ban on members of the police force joining political parties or engaging in political activities.[50] The majority decision did not find any violation of freedom of expression (Article 10 ECHR) or freedom of assembly (Article 11 ECHR) based on national security, public safety, and prevention of disorder as legitimate aims of the law. However, the reasoning of the judgment emphasised that these limitations of fundamental rights can be proportional, particularly in a period of transition into a fully democratic society as a sort of militant democracy measure.[51] Despite this opinion of the ECtHR, the Fundamental Law upheld all the limitations after more than two decades of the democratic transition, maybe as another sign of the undemocratic character of the new constitutional order introduced in 2011.

As the relevant laws fail to define the concept of the political, the scope of the ban is mostly determined by historical experiences and the norms of judicial socialisation, which, as we have argued above, favour a strict interpretation of judges' ability to address questions of the rule of law and judicial independence. However, the ECtHR has developed a more nuanced approach

49 These are Article 26(1) of the Fundamental Law of Hungary and Article 39(1) of the Act CLXII of 2011 on the Status and Remuneration of Judges.

50 *Rekvényi v Hungary*, App No. 25390/94, 20 May 1999.

51 Similar transitory limitations for the sake of political loyalty were considered by the ECtHR in the cases of *Glasenapp* and *Vogt* in the early years of the German Federal Republic, based on the bad experiences of the Weimar Republic regarding teachers who were members of the Communist Party. Judge Fisach, in his dissenting opinion to the Rekvényi case, found the curtailment of the right to join a political party, even in a transitional period, to be a limitation of democratic pluralism.

to judges' public engagement with societal and political issues. It provides a high degree of protection for expressions related to the justice system or the separation of powers, even if the statements have political implications.[52] This approach entails that broadly formulated domestic restrictions on the political activity of judges can hardly serve as legitimate limits to judges' right to join public debates.

This restrictive approach to judges' public appearances is backed by the relevant provisions on how Hungarian judges can make statements concerning individual court cases. Article 43 of the 2011 Act on the Status of Judges states that "A judge may not, outside his or her official capacity, publicly express an opinion on a case pending or formerly pending before a court, in particular with regard to cases which he or she has decided". Rules on making statements on particular court cases did not change compared to the previous law between 1997 and 2011. The explanatory memorandum of the 1997 law stated that judges could express their opinion about individual cases only in professional consultations held with their fellow judges in the courthouse, meaning the ban on forming an opinion ranges from friendly discussions to talking to the press.

The Hungarian rules restricting judges' commenting on particular court cases are also overbroad. The prohibition regarding judicial statements on ongoing cases can be justified, even based on international standards. The ECtHR requires maximum discretion from judges concerning the cases with which they deal to preserve their image as impartial judges.[53] Similarly, to uphold the authority of courts and public confidence in the functioning of the judiciary, judges should also show restraint in criticising the judicial handling of any ongoing cases. However, in the *Eminagaoglu v Turkey* case,[54] the ECtHR held that the duty of discretion does not automatically apply to already closed cases. Judges' freedom of expression can enjoy a high degree of protection even concerning already resolved cases if the comments concern issues of general interest and are incapable of undermining the dignity of the profession or do not contain destructive attacks against fellow judges. From the above, we can conclude that Hungarian laws go far beyond the restrictions determined in the ECtHR's jurisprudence by prima facie prohibiting judicial remarks on any cases the judiciary has ever dealt with.

These provisions that set out the scope of permissible public statements of judges envisage a highly restrictive legal framework and can be criticised based on the ECtHR's relevant standards. The two types of restrictions, one

52 See *Baka v Hungary* (n 9) para 165. The growing ECtHR jurisprudence on judges' free speech is discussed at length in the chapter by Sietske Dijkstra: The Freedom of Expression of Judges in Europe: An Analysis of the Case Law under Article 10 of the European Convention on Human Rights – The Rule of Law in the Leading Role.

53 *Olujić v Croatia*, App No. 22330/05, 5 February 2009, para 59.

54 *Eminağaoğlu v Turkey*, App No. 76521/12, 9 March 2021, paras 141–144.

regarding judges' political involvement in general and the other on expressing their opinions on particular cases, seem to be categorical and have a mutually reinforcing negative effect, resulting primarily in a chilling effect on judges' public statements.

The jurisprudence of Hungarian courts on the illicit political activity of judges

Hungarian laws ban the political activity of judges in general while failing to define the meaning of the term political. In the following part, we will examine the relevant Hungarian jurisprudence to reveal how judges, when sitting on the bench, think about the term political regarding extrajudicial activities.

In 2012, a Hungarian judge was removed from his office as a disciplinary sanction for publicly criticising particular judgments and the functioning of the judiciary.[55] The judge argued, among other things, that the deep crisis of the Hungarian judiciary can be attributed to the corrupt system of court administration and the lack of judicial independence, rooted in the 1997 reform which established a feudal system where judges, appointed and socialised within the Kádár era (in the pre-1989 communist regime),[56] occupied senior offices and served political and "other higher" interests.

Service courts hearing disciplinary cases against judges argued that he engaged in prohibited political activity by linking all negative developments and personalities within the organisation to a particular political system and ideology, namely to the Kádár era by characterising his peers' attitudes as "Kádárist", "neo-Kádárist", "communist", or "socialist". The first-instance decision held that these statements revealed the judge's political views to the outside world while the appeal court added that professional criticism does not allow such political labelling of fellow judges. Furthermore, as he called for the removal of Kádárist judges from senior offices, and some also from the judiciary in April 2011, when the forced retirement of judges sparked serious controversies, his statements could have been seen as a need for a politically motivated purge in the judiciary and as a justification for the government's policy.

We should note that most of the impugned statements concerned public issues related to the justice system, which should have enjoyed a high level of protection. While the statements went beyond the limits of professional criticism, particularly in style and tone, the judge's removal seemed to be

55 Decision SZF1/46/2011 of the First Instance Service Court attached to the Budapest-Capital Regional Court of Appeal and Decision Szf.F.II.1/2012/9 of the Second Instance Service Court attached to the Kúria.

56 János Kádár was the *de facto* leader of the Hungarian Socialist Workers' Party and the communist regime in Hungary between 1956 and 1988.

disproportionate, capable of discouraging judges from speaking out against the anomalies of court administration.[57]

In recent years, Hungarian courts adjudicated several lawsuits filed by judges against media outlets for attacks on their judicial activities and professional integrity. Typically, members of the NJC have faced smear campaigns by pro-government media seeking to discredit the NJC for its criticism of the NJO President and court administration in general. Some findings of these judgments are relevant to the debate about the scope of permissible extrajudicial activities.

Courts argued in one case that attending conferences and other professional events or participating as an expert in human rights NGOs' projects is incapable of compromising the independence of the judge or the authority of the judicial office.[58] Furthermore, they noted that public criticism of the NJO *per se* cannot be regarded as political activity against the government, considering the separation of powers principle. Besides, the social media activities of judges, such as liking some funny content on Facebook reflecting on issues of public interest, cannot be seen as political activity either.[59]

Similar issues were addressed when courts had to decide on the permissible scope of social media communication for prosecutors. In 2018, a prosecutor was removed from his office for undermining the prosecution service's authority and impartiality with his Facebook posts. The first post concerned an article from an online news outlet (*index.hu*) about a Fidesz MP involved in large-scale heritage fraud, which was shared and commented on by the prosecutor as follows: "Well, every 'accused' chooses his own defence; we laugh at him at most. Go … Oh, and April 8". (8 April might have been a reference to the date of the upcoming general elections in Hungary.) Then, on a national holiday, he shared a picture of a flock of sheep flock with the following comment: "This is what I will remember from today's celebration … Hopefully, this time next year, I'll feel like going out". In the third case, the prosecutor shared a post from an anti-Orbán site.

The Hungarian courts found that only the first of the three impugned Facebook posts violated the authority of the prosecution service, so the

57 Later, the removed judge challenged the decisions before the Constitutional Court and the ECtHR. The CC annulled the service courts' judgments because disciplinary proceedings failed to ensure the guarantees of a fair and impartial trial. See Decision 21/2014. (VII. 15.) CC. Consequently, the judge withdrew his complaint under Article 6 before the ECtHR, which found the rest of his complaint under Article 10 premature. *Ravasz v Hungary* App No. 64239/12, 7 October 2014.

58 Judgment 2.Pf.20.516/2019/4 of Budapest-Capital Regional Court of Appeal.

59 The judge posted likes, for instance, on a meme page "Szomszédok forever", dedicated to an old, famous Hungarian TV series called "Neighbours", which often reacts to issues of public interest. See the site here: https://www.facebook.com/Szomszedok.forever. Judgment 2.Pf.20.516/2019/4 of Budapest-Capital Regional Court of Appeal.

prosecutor's dismissal was disproportionate.[60] All court instances stressed that prosecutors have the right to freedom of expression protected by the Fundamental Law and are not prohibited from using Facebook. They agreed that personal communication between private individuals, even if it takes place in a Facebook group, cannot be considered political activity.[61] Political activity is an "intentional and active conduct with substantial political content which transcends the private sphere and reaches the public directly".[62] The Kúria noted that political activity, in the narrow sense, is the action of a political party to obtain or retain power. A broader concept covers the activity of expressing opposing views to government policy before the public at large while openly inviting or encouraging others to take action.[63] This case was built on a narrow definition of impermissible political activity, while the courts also emphasised the lack of professional guidelines for the ethical use of social media by prosecutors.

Overall, we can say that the removal of the judge for his public criticism of the justice system in 2012 could have a chilling effect on those judges who seek to engage in public debates over the problems of the justice system. However, recent findings of the Hungarian courts reflect a less stringent interpretation of the ban on the political activity of judges and prosecutors, capable of better protecting judges' freedom of expression and public appearances.

Soft instruments – the Code of Judicial Ethics

In 2022, the NJC adopted a new Code of Ethics to address concerns over judicial freedom of speech, partially in response to the ECtHR's *Baka* judgment, which the Hungarian government had failed to execute fully.[64] It also aimed to clarify rules for court executives and judges' social media use.

The Code sparked debate within the judiciary, with some advocating for broader speech rights and others for stricter limits,[65] resulting in a compromise banning political activity but allowing broader societal engagement.

While the final version of the Code maintained a general ban on political activity by stating that "the judge shall not engage in political activity and shall refrain from political statements in public", other provisions specified the above statements to provide broader protection for public statements and societal involvement of judges. While the previous Code prohibited judges from participating in "political rallies and events", the new Code envisages a

60 Judgment Mfv.X.10.015/2020/4. of the Kúria.

61 Judgment 70.M.1051/2018/36 of the Budapest Administrative and Labour Court.

62 Judgment 5.Mf.680.296/2019/14. of the Budapest-Capital Regional Court.

63 Judgment Mfv.X.10.015/2020/4. of the Kúria.

64 See the intervention of Viktor Vadász during the NJC meeting on 6 October 2021, pp. 34–35 < https://obt2018.hu/2021-10-06/>, accessed 6 April 2024.

65 The State Secretary and the President of the Kúria argued in tandem for a highly restrictive approach to judicial free speech.

more permissible understanding of social engagement by stating that "judges can attend public events organized in accordance with law", with the limitation that their participation does not create the perception of political commitment.[66] Furthermore, it contains a new Article titled "Publicity, Social Media", which declares that "*judges can freely express their views on the law, the legal system and court administration, and in particular, they can publish, give lectures and teach*".[67] This article also states that judges have the right to freedom of expression, conscience, and religion, as well as the right to freedom of assembly and association, which must be exercised to ensure the authority and dignity of the judicial office. However, no further guidelines have been drafted for judges' freedom of expression on social media, even though the revision of the previous Code officially aimed to "clarify ethical issues related to the use of social media".[68]

Besides, the drafters removed from the old text the passage that prohibited judges from supporting businesses, charities, or non-governmental organisations that can be linked to any political activity. This latter amendment must be welcomed in light of the government's commitment to stigmatise human rights NGOs as political agents serving foreign interests.[69]

The President of the Kúria challenged the new Code of Ethics before the Constitutional Court.[70] He argued that the new Code seeks to redefine and extend the scope of judicial free speech, contrary to the existing legal framework. In his submission, despite the growing respective jurisprudence of the ECtHR, he invoked only the *Panioglu v Romania* case, presumably to misrepresent the ECtHR's stance on this very complex issue and to emphasise the necessary limitations of extrajudicial activities.[71] By not deciding on the complaint since May 2022, the Constitutional Court contributes to maintaining the chilling effect on judges' public engagement regarding issues of judicial independence.

66 Article 2(1) of the Code of Judicial Ethics. < https://birosag.hu/sites/default/files/birak_etikai_kodexe_.pdf> accessed 17 November 2023.

67 Article 4(2) of the Code of Judicial Ethics.

68 Decision 52/2019. (XI.6) of NJC.

69 European Commission, 2023 Rule of Law Report: Country Chapter on the rule of law situation in Hungary, Brussels, 5 July 2023. < https://commission.europa.eu/system/files/2023-07/40_1_52623_coun_chap_hungary_en.pdf> pp. 35–36.

70 Case II/01285/2022. See the case file: <https://alkotmanybirosag.hu/ugyadatlap/?id=B1E83AFC8B10B1D2C125885B005B3B7E> accessed 6 April 2024.

71 *Panioglu v Romania* App No. 33794/14, 8 December 2020. In Panioglu, the ECtHR argued that judges must show restraint and moderation when publicly criticising their colleagues to maintain the judicial profession's authority and public confidence in the judiciary.

Approaches to the political by judicial bodies in court administration

No wonder the debates on the draft Code of Judicial Ethics primarily revolved around the concept of political activity. While political and judicial leadership joined their efforts to push for a restrictive interpretation capable of muzzling judges when government measures threaten judicial independence and the rule of law, the NJC, together with MABIE, supported an approach empowering judges to speak up freely for the interests of the judiciary. Such debates permeate the daily operation of court administration and reflect the power relations within the Hungarian judiciary. While collective bodies, such as the NJC and MABIE, are committed to promoting international standards, the approach endorsed by high-ranking court executives is not only doctrinally problematic but also used in an abusive way to discredit competing interpretations and their proponents.

For instance, the President of the Kúria argued that the activity of the NJC, including those instances when the NJC exercises its power, is political, even if it is within the scope of permissible political activity due to constitutional authorisation. Contrary to that, MABIE denounced the views that public statements made by judges are often seen in public discourse and within the judiciary as politicisation. MABIE warned that owing to this failed approach, judges are often reluctant to speak up regarding their status, remuneration, and administrative and organisational issues, and they fail to react to attacks against their personal and professional integrity. MABIE stressed that judges and their representative bodies could and should engage in dialogue with political branches, which is not by itself a political discourse and, therefore, cannot be forbidden.[72]

In 2020, the Vice-President of the MABIE argued in an opinion piece published on the association's website that only a narrow concept of political activity could serve as a legitimate ground for limiting judges' free speech.[73] Accordingly, judges are only forbidden to engage in a "sustained, continuous, systematic action in relation to a set of ideas or aims of a social group, class or party". Public statements regarding social phenomena and legal institutions, especially those based on professional knowledge, cannot be prohibited. Such statements do not undermine the impartiality of adjudication; instead, they promote the common good.

In 2022, the NJC refused to send its spokesperson to a panel discussion of the Budapest International Documentary Festival on the Polish documentary

72 'A bírókkal kapcsolatos sajtóban megjelenő vélemények margójára' (Mabie.hu, 2 September 2022) <https://mabie.hu/index.php/1661-a-birokkal-kapcsolatos-sajtoban-megjeleno-velemenyek-margojara> accessed 6 April 2024.

73 Orsolya Szántai, 'A véleménynyilvánítás szabadsága és a bírák számára tilalmazott politikai tevékenység összefüggései' 29 April 2020 <http://mabie.hu/index.php/1537-dr-szantai-orsolya-a-velemenynyilvanitas-szabadsaga-es-a-birak-szamara-tilalmazott-politikai-tevekenyseg-osszefuggesei%20(2020 >, accessed 6 April 2024.

"Judges under Pressure". Before voting, the President of the Kúria intervened by indicating that participation could be considered a political activity, given the documentary's content. This approach was also suggested by the State Secretary and the President of the NJO during their intervention. Finally, nobody in the NJC dared to vote to accept the invitation.[74]

When two members of the NJC met the new US Ambassador to Hungary for an introductory discussion as representatives of the NJC, they immediately became the target of a smear campaign launched by pro-government media outlets. The event made headlines in pro-government media, including public service media, where the judges were even called to resign.[75] Soon, government officials and court leadership joined the campaign against the respective judges. The President of the Kúria characterised the conduct of the NJC members as one "giving rise to public outcry", while the President of the NJO emphasised that the meeting could be the subject of reasonable and well-founded criticism in terms of its legality and justifiability.[76] The latter stressed that NJC members must bear a high level of tolerance for public criticism, and court executives should react only to the political assault on judicial independence; however, the respective criticism was expressed only by the press. These reactions of the highest judicial officials were not only harmful to the integrity of the NJC but were based on a false characterisation of the event and the scope of free speech of judges, capable of intensifying the chilling effect on any extrajudicial activities.

The catch-22: why has the NJC remained alone in resistance?

In 2018, the renewed NJC started a new course in representing the interests of the judiciary to resist the further erosion of judicial independence. This shift was directed towards a more permissible approach to judicial free speech, promoted by the NJC in public statements, professional discussions, and the new Code of Judicial Ethics. Also, since 2018, it has mainly been the NJC that has spoken up against political attacks regarding individual cases and against judges as high-ranking court executives had failed to do so. However, the NJC's heroic role has opened new frontiers for attacks: a steady confrontation with the government can be strategically used to question the independence

74 See the minutes of the meeting of the NJC on 5 January 2022 <https://obt2018.hu/2022-01-05/>, accessed 6 April 2024.

75 According to the Hungarian Helsinki Committee, within a month, discrediting materials about the meeting featured in 411 different publications in pro-government media. Presshelsinki, 'Így gondozd lejárató kampányodat!' (helsinkifigyelo.444.hu, 15 February 2023) <https://helsinkifigyelo.444.hu/2023/02/15/igy-gondozd-lejarato-kampanyodat> accessed 30 January 2024.

76 Public statement of the President of the National Judicial Office, 4 November 2022, https://birosag.hu/hirek/kategoria/birosagokrol/az-orszagos-birosagi-hivatal-elnokenek-kozlemenye

and legitimacy of the NJC, resulting in a catch-22 situation.[77] From then on, criticism from the government and smear campaigns against the NJC and its members in pro-government media have amplified. Judicial leadership took the government's side in attacking the NJC when the latter started to exercise effective supervision over the activity of central court administration.

The incumbent President of the Kúria, who took office in 2021 after a highly controversial election procedure,[78] repeatedly accuses the NJC of politicisation, which can discourage their peers from publicly addressing the threats to judicial independence. Under these circumstances, without a clearly defined concept of the political, the judiciary has remained without shields. Courts are exposed to politically motivated attacks by the government and judicial leadership while being silenced by the fear of engaging in impermissible political activity.

Conclusions

Going public and making the threats to judicial independence visible to a large audience can be an effective strategy for judicial self-defence in autocracies, drawing heavily on the formal legitimacy of the law. Despite systemic attacks on judicial independence and limits on free speech since 2010, the Hungarian judiciary has made only modest efforts to reconsider strict speech regulations. A radical change in judicial politics should have triggered a similarly determined shift in the approach to judicial free speech. The causes of the failure are manifold and largely determined by power relations within the judiciary.

The old blanket ban on judges' public engagement is no longer sustainable. The laws on the judiciary prohibit party membership and the political activity of judges in broad terms, but the argument on the historical experience with a politicised judiciary no longer holds. On the contrary, nowadays, it serves the very opposite goal: the further encroachment of the political branches in the sphere of the judicial branch. The NJC, elected in 2018, was a pioneer in advocating broader protection for extrajudicial activities, not least by revising the relevant provisions of the Code of Judicial Ethics.[79] However,

77 Martin Shapiro, 'Courts in Authoritarian Regimes' in Tom Ginsburg and Tamir Moustafa (eds), *Rule by Law: The Politics of Courts in Authoritarian Regimes* (CUP 2008) 326, 334–335. Shapiro uses the catch-22 metaphor, known from Joseph Heller's famous fictitious war novel, to describe the dilemma courts typically face in authoritarian regimes: challenging the regime could push the courts into the political arena, while being friendly with the government can serve a regime-legitimising function.

78 The election of András Zs. Varga was made possible by two legislative amendments tailored to him, as he lacked any previous professional experience as a judge in the ordinary judiciary. For these reasons, the NJC overwhelmingly rejected his nomination as President of the Kúria. See Decision 120/2020 (X. 9.) of NJC English: <https://obt2018.hu/2020-10-09/>, accessed 6 April 2024.

79 For similar developments, see Joan Solanes Mullor, 'Spain, Judicial Independence, and Judges' Freedom of Expression: Missing an Opportunity to Leverage the European Constitutional Shift?' 19 (2023) European Constitutional Law Review 271, 289–291.

their approach did not find sufficient support within the judiciary, and court executives deliberately hindered the emergence of a new concept, either by echoing the old views or accusing the NJC of politicisation. The President of the Kúria has questioned the legitimacy of the new standards by filing a constitutional complaint against the Code of Judicial Ethics, and by delaying the decision, the CC seems to be a partner in maintaining the uncertainty around the limits of judicial free speech. This situation also enables court executives to silence judges willing to criticise any action threatening judicial independence. The case law concerning judges' freedom of expression is scarce. Lately, courts have established progressive understandings, but these have not been reflected in public statements of the judiciary.

The problem of weak domestic mobilisation was not counterbalanced by a solid transnational approach to defending judicial independence in Hungary by European courts. The CJEU and the ECtHR failed to recognise the real stakes of the Hungarian cases, and the responses were typically badly construed or simply missing. The *Baka* case can be seen as the only exception, but, as we discussed above, its doctrinal contribution to the protection of judges' freedom of expression far exceeds its practical relevance regarding Hungary. Smear campaigns against judges intensified, and the chilling effect has not been mitigated. While the European Union has achieved significant developments in strengthening the position of the NJC by linking access to funds to judicial reform, the real impact of this cannot yet be seen. More visibility and public exposure could have benefitted the judiciary itself and enhanced the capacity of judges to be mobilised for their own interests.

But as the limitation of judges' free speech is only one of the many reasons for the weak resistance of courts against the dismantlement of judicial independence, the lack of judicial resilience is only one cause of the gradual loss of constitutional democracy in Hungary ever since 2010.

6 Speech is silver. Is silence *golden*?

Raluca Bercea

Introduction

"Speech is silver, but silence is golden"[1] is a saying of the mid-19th century, meaning that discretion can be more valuable than the most eloquent words. However, such a conclusion may not be accurate regarding national judges' freedom of expression. Hence, the interrogation proposed by the present contribution focuses on four sets of references for a preliminary ruling stemming from two different Central and Eastern European jurisdictions partaking to different extents in the rule of law regional crisis. While it primarily assesses whether the national courts have given the Court of Justice of the European Union (CJEU) the opportunity to advance its case law on the mechanism of Article 267 TFEU, this contribution also offers a human rights perspective on the national judges' referrals as an exercise of their right to freedom of expression.

Before the CJEU there is no jurisprudence on the freedom of expression of judges proper, if one understands it in a limited sense. The reason is twofold. First, the Charter of Fundamental Rights of the European Union ("Charter") is generally not applicable in such cases, as the European Union does not have the competence to enact standards for extrajudicial conduct of national judges. Second, the Court has not yet relied on the interconnected character of the freedom of expression of judges and judicial independence. Arguably, Article 19 TEU – effective judicial protection requirement – could serve as a legal basis in cases where a violation of freedom of expression would also represent a violation of judicial independence. But no case law confirms this approach for the moment such approach.

However, in certain jurisdictions, expressing opinions in public could expose national judges to disciplinary proceedings. Judges have therefore used the preliminary ruling mechanism as a means to seek change within their national legal orders, without openly exposing themselves. Could this be considered

1 See Oxford Reference at: https://www.oxfordreference.com/display/10.1093/acref/9780198609810.001.0001/acref-9780198609810-e-6666.

DOI: 10.4324/9781003470779-8

"an expression" in the sense of Article 10 of the European Convention on Human Rights (ECHR)? In light of the recent case law of the European Court of Human Rights (ECtHR), the response could be affirmative, for two reasons: first, traditionally the ECHR envisages expression very broadly. In the legal context, it may cover, for instance, petitions, a lawyer's pleadings, as well as criminal complaints. Second, the ECtHR has already ruled that magistrates who had expressed themselves in an official capacity and had the obligation to issue public statements enjoy guarantees of freedom of expression.

Against this background, the chapter contemplates the potential understanding of Article 267 TFEU requests in light of the freedom to receive information, which is covered by Article 10 ECHR. The particular context in which the national judges referred to the CJEU is first described, as neither the choice of cases nor their association within the same analysis are accidental. Moreover, the context of the referrals is also a key element in understanding the stakes of using the mechanism of Article 267 TFEU as a form of expression. The extent to which this type of reference has challenged the limits of Article 267 itself is then evaluated as the premise to underline the human rights dimension of the preliminary ruling mechanism operating in the very particular "rule of law" cases. A conclusion is finally drawn on the interplay between the specific case law of the two European courts concerning the freedom of expression of judges as an element of the rule of law.

The context

Context is never unimportant in law, and, all the more so, in references to a preliminary ruling.[2] This section focuses on a combination of several Romanian cases and a Hungarian one, associated for more than one reason, that can explain the connection between judges and freedom of expression.

First, the cases selected raise issues about the independence and accountability of the national judiciary. The first wave of Romanian rule of law cases is represented by the joined Cases C-83/19, C-127/19, C-195/19, C-291/19, C-355/19, and C-397/19 – *Asociația "Forumul Judecătorilor din România"* ("AFJR").[3] The second one consists of the joined Cases C-357/19,

2 "In other contexts, the same meaning may or may not be the right one", as states a common law judgment. In the practice of the European courts, the emphasis on context is noticeable, particularly in the judicial independence and impartiality case law, both in Strasbourg, where it connects with the "doctrine of appearances" and in Luxembourg (for an analysis of the latter, see Raluca Bercea, Op-Ed: 'It's All About (the Romanian) Context. The Judgment in Case C-817/21', EULawLive blog, 26 May 2023). Moreover, the very mechanism of Article 267 TFEU requires that context not only be accurately described by the referring court, but also relevantly relied on by the Court of Justice, whose judgments cannot offer a mere theoretical and abstract interpretation of EU law.

3 CJEU 18 May 2021, Joined Cases C-83/19, C-127/19, C-195/19, C-291/19, C-355/19, C-397/19, ECLI:EU:C:2021:393.

C-379/19, C-547/19, C-811/19, and C-840/19 ("the second wave of rule of law Romanian cases")[4] and the third one of Case C-430/21 – *RS*[5] ("the third wave of rule of law Romanian cases"). The Hungarian case under scrutiny is Case C-564/19 – *IS*.[6] While the questions addressed by the Romanian courts concern, in general, the rule of law, the fight against corruption, the disciplinary liability of magistrates, as well as the principle of the primacy of EU law in relation to the Romanian Constitutional Court's decisions,[7] the Hungarian case represents the first instance when a national judge stays proceedings to ask the CJEU preliminary questions about the independence of Hungarian courts.[8]

Second, both the Romanian waves of preliminary references and the *IS* case belong to broader national contexts of public concern. In Romania, the measures referred to by the judges were part of a reform affecting the justice and criminal systems so deeply that it was described as challenging the rule of law.[9] In Hungary, the referral was qualified as a form of protection sought by ordinary judges caught in a constitutional crisis.[10]

Third, both in Romania and Hungary, the referrals determined further resistance of the national higher courts reluctant to EU law to the judicial dialogue

4 CJEU 21 December 2021, Joined cases C-357/19, *Euro Box Promotion and others*, C-379/19, *DNA- Serviciul Teritorial Oradea*, C-547/19 *Asociația 'Forumul Judecătorilor din România'*, C-811/19 *FQ and others* and C-840/19 *NC and others*. ECLI:EU:C:2021:1034.

5 CJEU 22 February 2022, Case C-430/21, *RS*, ECLI:EU:C:2022:9. Also, Case C-817/21, *Judicial Inspection*, ECLI:EU:C:2023:391.

6 CJEU 23 November 2021, Case C-564/19, *IS*, ECLI:EU:C:2021:949.

7 For an analysis on the first wave of cases, see M. B. Moraru, R. Bercea, (2022), 'The First Episode in the Romanian Rule of Law Saga: Joined Cases C-83/19, C-127/19, C-195/19, C-291/19, C-355/19C-355/19, and C-397/19', Asociația 'Forumul Judecătorilor din România, and Their Follow-up at the National Level', in European Constitutional Law Review, vol. 18, nr. 1, 2022, pp. 82–113, doi:10.1017/S1574019622000074. For an extensive up-to-date analysis of the Romanian rule of law context, see the Romanian report in R. Aspetti, R. Bercea, A. Brás, F. Casarosa, M. Catanzariti, S. Doroga, M. Fajdiga, M. Ferri, Z. Fleck, R. Gião Hanek, J. Gwizdak, G. Grasso, T. T. Koncewicz, Á. Kovács, N. Lazzerini, D. M. Galera, M. Michalak, M. B. Moraru, A. Podolska, K. Podstawa, J. Solanes Mullor, 'TRIIAL National Reports Belgium, Hungary, Italy, Poland, Portugal, Romania, Slovenia, Spain, The Netherlands', EUI RSC, 2022/52, Centre for Judicial Cooperation – http://hdl.handle.net/1814/74814 [accessed 1 August 2022].

8 D. G. Szabó, 'A Hungarian Judge Seeks Protection from the CJEU – Part I', VerfBlog, 28 July 2019, available at: https://verfassungsblog.de/a-hungarian-judge-seeks-protection-from-the-cjeu-part-i/, DOI: 10.17176/20190728-200951-0 [accessed 1 August 2022].

9 S. E. Tănăsescu, 'The Independence of Justice as Proxy for the Rule of Law in the EU Case Study – Romania' (2021) 3 Nuovi Autoritarismi e Democrazie: Diritto, Istituzioni, Società (NAD-DIS), available at https://riviste.unimi.it/index.php/NAD/article/view/15826 https://verfassungsblog.de/goat-cabbage-and-wolf/?fbclid=IwAR1QyGLE6RiCxIs33DVx1ckofytU15DN8kMqiO8tQE9NUD_rtheQvGNqAkY, accessed 1 August 2022.

10 V. Vadász, A Hungarian Judge Seeks Protection from the CJEU – Part II, in *VerfBlog*, 7 August 2019, available at https://verfassungsblog.de/a-hungarian-judge-seeks-protection-from-the-cjeu-part-ii/, accessed 1 August 2022.

and to the primacy of EU law, and led to individual retaliation measures against the lower courts that sought the CJEU's empowerment. In Hungary, the Prosecutor General requested Hungary's Supreme Court ("*Kúria*") to review the preliminary reference order.[11] In the final judgment, the Kúria declared the order unlawful, finding that the questions raised were not relevant to deciding the main case, while the first question did not concern the interpretation of EU law but sought a finding that the applicable Hungarian law did not comply with the principles protected by EU law. Subsequently, the President of Budapest High Court brought disciplinary proceedings against the referring judge, reproducing verbatim the grounds of the Kúria's judgment.

In Romania, the Constitutional Court (RCC) refused to uphold the CJEU judgement in the *AFJR* case,[12] preventing the national courts, under disciplinary sanctions,[13] from applying the solutions thereon in cases pending at the national level. The RCC reaffirmed the supremacy of the Constitution over EU law based on the constitutional identity and estimated that the CJEU had overstepped the mechanism set in Article 267 TFEU while proposing criteria to assess the independence of national judicial bodies. It also reaffirmed that the judiciary partakes in the exclusive competence of the Member State,[14] and stressed that EU law priority could not disregard the national constitutional identity. Although the RCC did not clarify the scope and content of the constitutional identity, it generally prohibited national courts from applying EU law once it had qualified it as lacking a basis in the Romanian Constitution. The RCC also denied the obligation of the national courts to set aside any national statute or practice contrary to EU law, requiring the formal revision of the national Constitution for that purpose.

This decision triggered disciplinary proceedings against the ordinary court magistrates who had assessed the national law establishing the SIOJ as contrary to EU law, a fact that was found concerning by the European Commission.[15] In the Commission's view, the RCC prevented the national ordinary courts from fulfilling their EU law mandate.

11 For details see D. G. Szabó (n 9).

12 Decision 390 of 8 June 2021, published in the Official Gazette of Romania 612 of 22 June 2021.

13 Pursuant to Article 99(ş) of Law 303/2004, non-compliance with the Constitutional Court's decisions constitutes a disciplinary offence.

14 Decision 390/2021, para. 79 (n 15).

15 The Commission asked for clarifications on the impact of the RCC Decision on 20 October 2021 (https://www.juridice.ro/755091/comisia-europeana-solicita-clarificari-romaniei-ref-decizia-nr-390-a-ccr-care-pune-sub-semnul-intrebarii-constatarile-cjue.html, accessed 1 August 2022).

Irrespective of the national specificities, in both Romania and Hungary the authorities' reactions triggered a general chilling effect on the dialogue between the national courts and the CJEU.[16]

Fourth, and most importantly, both in the Romanian and the Hungarian cases, the national judges strategically offered the CJEU the opportunity to reflect on the mechanism provided by Article 267 TFEU in the context of the European rule of law crisis.

In the *IS* case, after the Prosecutor General's initiative and the Kúria's decision, the national judge decided to refer supplementary questions for a preliminary ruling. The CJEU was thus expressly invited to answer whether Article 267 TFEU may be interpreted as precluding a national practice whereby the court of last instance, in proceedings meant to harmonise the case law of the Member State, declared as unlawful a decision by which a lower court made a request for a preliminary ruling. The judge further enquired if, in the affirmative, Article 267 TFEU must be interpreted as meaning that the referring court must disregard contrary decisions of the superior courts and their positions of principle adopted in the interest of harmonising the law.[17]

All referring Romanian courts foresaw a potentially conflicting situation at the national level. In particular, the RCC Decision 390/2021 has determined several of them to refer back to the CJEU, which granted expedited procedure to remove serious uncertainties affecting fundamental issues of national constitutional law and EU law. In Case C-357/19, the referring judge warns about the serious risk that the CJEU answers to the questions referred would be inapplicable in the national legal order on account of the RCC Decision 104/2018, which denies the prevalence of EU law over national constitutional law in case of conflict.[18] Similarly, in Case C-379/19, the referring court explicitly asks whether, in exercising their judicial competence, national judges might disregard the effects of the RCC Decisions, should the latter overpass its powers, without risking disciplinary sanctions.[19] Finally, in Case C-811/19 and in Case C-840/19, the CJEU is asked to explicitly establish the obligation

16 Case C-564/19 (n 4), para 49: "However, the referring judge also stated that he did not intend to amend in that regard the supplementary request for a preliminary ruling, given that his concern stems not from the fact that he himself is the subject of disciplinary proceedings, but rather from the fact that such proceedings may be commenced in such circumstances". Also para 75: "Furthermore, that decision of the *Kúria* (Supreme Court) is likely to prompt the Hungarian courts to refrain from referring questions for a preliminary ruling to the Court, in order to preclude their requests for a preliminary ruling from being challenged by one of the parties on the basis of the Kúria decision or from being the subject of an appeal in the interests of the law". In Romania, the European Commission noted the chilling effect of the RCC Decision (n 16).

17 Case C-564/19 (n 6), paras 51, 24.

18 CJEU, 21 December 2021 (n. 4), para 67.

19 Idem, para 78.

of national courts to leave unapplied decisions of the RCC in order to grant full efficiency to European Union law.[20]

To sum up, no issue on the freedom of expression of judges stemming from their use of Article 267 could be raised in the absence of these particular very similar national contexts, and should the questions addressed by the national judges have been differently framed.

CJEU on Article 267 TFEU. The old and the new

Both Article 267 TFEU itself and a well-settled case law of the CJEU regard the referral as the national judges' discretionary prerogative to determine both the need for a preliminary ruling and the relevance of the questions referred. The Court is, in principle, bound to respond whenever the questions concern the interpretation of EU law provisions.[21] The rule of law referrals stemming from different Central and East European countries indicate a regional democracy crisis also acknowledged by other institutions of the European Union,[22] and, by their object, represent a novelty in the dialogue between the CJEU and the national courts.

The request for preliminary ruling as an expression of the principle of primacy

The first element in which resides the added value of the cases under analysis is that the right of ordinary courts to interact with the CJEU under Article 267 without any substantial or procedural limitations set out in national laws, constitutions, or internal judicial hierarchy is qualified as an expression of EU law primacy. Moreover, this prerogative is interpreted here as the possibility to discretionarily refer questions to the CJEU, without the risk of being subjected to disciplinary sanctions even in hypotheses of vertical conflict with superior ordinary courts or the Constitutional Court.

The CJEU reaffirms its exclusive competence in interpreting the principle of primacy, whose scope could not depend on the interpretation of either national or EU law provisions by national courts that would infringe the Court's judgments. The Grand Chamber refers in this context to the mechanism set by Article 267 TFEU as "the vault key" of the judiciary system established by the Treaties, which enshrines the possibility of a dialogue between the Member States' judges and the Court itself, ensuring that EU law remains coherent,

20 Idem, paras 101, 111.

21 Idem, para 139.

22 See the infringement procedures lodged by the European Commission to protect the right of Polish courts to vertical judicial interaction: European Commission, 'European Commission refers Poland to the European Court of Justice to protect independence of Polish judges and asks for interim measures', 31 March 2021, at https://ec.europa.eu/commission/presscorner/detail/en/IP_21_1524, accessed 1 August 2022.

fully efficient, and autonomous, preserving its particular nature.[23] The Court will therefore interpret the primacy of EU law as precluding a national regulation or practice according to which national ordinary courts are bound by decisions of the national constitutional court and may not, under penalty of committing a disciplinary fault, leave unapplied, of their own authority, the case law resulting from these decisions when they consider, in the light of an interpretative judgment of the CJEU, that such case law is contrary to binding EU law.[24] Consistently, in the *IS* case, the Court decides that the primacy of EU law requires a lower court to disregard a decision of the supreme court if it considers it prejudicial to the prerogatives granted by Article 267 TFEU and to the effective dialogue between the CJEU and the national court and tribunals.[25] In other words, no restriction on the freedom of national judges to seek assistance from the CJEU can be envisaged.

The request for preliminary ruling as a means of consolidating the CJEU competence on "rule of law" matters

The rule of law referrals under analysis allow the CJEU to consolidate its competence to adjudicate in matters such as the national organisation of the judiciary, the hierarchical relations between the national ordinary courts, or between the national ordinary courts and the Constitutional Court. The exceptions commonly raised by the national governments reside in the argument that such matters would fall within the exclusive competence of the Member States and, accordingly, would remain outside the scope of EU law and the Court's jurisdiction. The Court took the opportunity to hold that although the organisation of justice in the Member States falls within their competence, the Member States are nonetheless required, when exercising it, to comply with their obligations deriving from EU law. With specific reference to the preliminary ruling mechanism, the Court reaffirms that while it is not competent to state on the conformity to EU law of a national practice or rule, it is, however, fully competent to provide the national court with guidance in solving such matters.[26] The CJEU is therefore competent to provide the national courts with the required information.

The request for preliminary ruling – an additional approach to the need to refer in order to give judgement

Article 267 TFEU establishes a relationship of close cooperation between the national courts and the CJEU based on the assignment to each of different

23 Idem, para 254. Also, ECJ, 23 November 2021, paras 60, 61 and 67 (n 4).

24 CJEU, 21 December 2021 (n 2), point 4 in the operative part of the judgment; CJEU21 December 2021, point 1 and 2 in the operative part of the judgment.

25 CJEU23 November 2021 (n 4), para 81 and point 1 in the operative part of the judgment.

26 Idem, paras 131, 139.

functions. However, such a relationship knows boundaries. On the one hand, given the principle of the Member States' procedural autonomy, Article 267 TFEU could not *per se* exempt an order for reference from being subject to a judicial remedy under national law – however, within the strict limits of the principle of sincere cooperation. Nor can the mere reference made by the national judge to EU law justify *per se* the referral. The fine-tuning of these boundaries will be explored in the section to come. On the other hand, the preliminary ruling mechanism is inherently orientated by the adjudicatory context where it occurs. Thus, the reference made must be necessary to enable the referring court to give judgment in the case before it. The Court has thus repeatedly held that

> a national court or tribunal is not empowered to bring a matter before the Court by way of a request for a preliminary ruling unless, *inter alia*, a case is pending before it in which it is called upon to give a decision which is capable of taking account of the preliminary ruling.[27]

A connecting factor is required between the dispute at the national level and the provisions of EU law whose interpretation is sought.

As AG Pikamäe notes in the very first paragraph of his Opinion in the *IS* case, the rule of law questions referred by the national courts "are appeals for assistance from national judges concerned by or even subject to disciplinary proceedings". Although such requests must be answered in compliance with the conventions of the reference for a preliminary ruling, the connecting element, closely associated with the concept of "*res judicata*", may have here "a dimension other than strictly legal".[28] The national judges mainly need the Court's guidance to adjudicate, but, in addition, without the fear of national constraints. The preliminary ruling mechanism also fulfils here an auto-reflexive function allowing the conclusion that the dialogue, as the word *dialogue* itself suggests, does not take place within a triangular relationship, in the sense that it excludes the alleged prerequisite approval of any superior national court.[29] This does not exclude implicit third parties within the domestic system of courts or outside of it – in the Romanian saga, the response provided by the CJEU to the requests of the ordinary courts triggers the reaction of the constitutional court whose position is to be feared as it risks triggering a systemic chilling effect.

27 Opinion of AG Pikamäe delivered on 15 April 2021 in Case C-564/19.
28 Idem, para 2.
29 Idem, para 47.

The human rights dimension of the preliminary ruling mechanism in the "rule of law" cases

From the EU law perspective, the national follow-ups of the referrals made by the ordinary judges both in the *IS* case and the Romanian first, second, and third waves of requests for preliminary rulings are practices incompatible with the mechanism set up by Article 267 TFEU.

On the one hand, the European Commission indicated that the RCC Decision 390/2021 violated the principle of sincere cooperation, having a negative impact on the effectiveness of the preliminary reference procedure.

On the other hand, commenting on the legal ground put forward by the Kúria, namely that the ordinary judge aimed to establish that the applicable Hungarian law was not consistent with the principles protected by EU law, AG Pikamäe concluded as follows:

> That ground, relating to an assessment of the purpose of the questions referred for a preliminary ruling, reflects the application of the settled case-law of the highest Hungarian national court, with the circumstance – in this case, aggravating – that the judgment delivered concerns the order for reference itself and not the decision by the trial judge to refuse to grant a party's application for a reference for a preliminary ruling, infringes Article 267 TFEU, as interpreted by the Court.[30]

Although Article 267 TFEU may enshrine a cooperation mechanism between the CJEU and the "courts or tribunals" of a Member State, its efficiency depends in fact on the national judges. Would that allow the assumption that national judges trigger rights from the essentially procedural provisions of the said article? Such a conclusion seems to be indeed embraced in the *IS* case by AG Pikamäe, who appreciated that the Kúria's judgment undermined "the referring judge's right to refer questions to the Court for a preliminary ruling".[31] However, since judges hold public offices and are entitled to refer to the CJEU only in an official, not in a private capacity, could the state interference with this right – ***a fortiori*** if it takes the form of ***individual*** disciplinary sanctions – be qualified as a violation of an individual human right? It is noteworthy that relevant synergies between the two European supranational courts have already occurred in situations in which the mechanism of Article 267 TFEU was at stake, so far from the perspective of the parties in the main national proceedings.[32]

30 Paras 43–44.

31 Para 44.

32 ECtHR, 8 April 2014, 17120/09, *Dhahbi v Italy*; ECtHR, 21 October 2015, 38369/09, *Schipani and others v* Italy; ECtHR, 16 April 2019, 55092/16, *Baltic Master Ltd v Lithuania*; ECtHR, 13 February 2020, 25137/16, *Sanofi Pasteur v France*, where the Court held that there had been a violation of Article 6 § 1 of the Convention given the national courts'

Courts or tribunals are made of judges. Are there individual human rights involved in "rule of law" applications?

The recent Member States' rule of law crisis has challenged the competence of both supranational European courts. While, as previously noted, through these referrals the CJEU crystallised its undisputed competence to adjudicate, the ECtHR has also already had the opportunity to adjudicate rule of law cases as individual applications of magistrates in high-ranking national positions, under Article 34 of the ECHR. Relevantly, the leading cases in this respect also stemmed from Hungary and Romania, with a very recent Polish illustration as well. Thus, in *Baka v Hungary*,[33] *Kövesi v Romania*,[34] and *Żurek v Poland*,[35] the applicants, Mr András Baka, Ms Laura-Codruța Kövesi, and Mr Waldermar Żurek, complained about the premature and arbitrary termination of their mandates as President of the Supreme Court of Hungary, chief prosecutor of the National Anticorruption Directorate of Romania, and, respectively, member of the Polish National Council of the Judiciary (NCJ). The measures were the consequences of the views that the first two applicants had expressed publicly (also) in their capacity as President of the Hungarian Supreme Court or Romanian chief prosecutor, concerning national legislative reforms affecting the judiciary; similarly, Judge Żurek, a symbolic figure of the Polish judicial community, one of the judges most engaged in the public debate concerning the independence of the judiciary, primarily expressed his views as an NCJ member and as the Cracow Regional Court's spokesperson. All three applicants successfully invoked Article 10 of the ECHR before the Court.

The preceding section of this chapter argued that in the context of the rule of law crisis, the preliminary ruling mechanism has been strategically used by national courts to preserve their voices within the domestic legal systems. Similarly, the rule of law dimension of individual complaints reaching the ECtHR has raised difficulties, although Article 10 of the ECHR had been previously applied to civil servants in general and, most importantly to members of the judiciary.[36]

failure to provide reasons for their decisions not to refer to the ECJ for a preliminary ruling. Although neither the Convention guarantees the right to have a case referred by a domestic court to the CJEU, nor could the ECtHR assess the conformity of such a refusal to EU law, Article 6 § 1 requires the domestic courts to give reasons for their decisions. A finding of violation is to be made on a case-by-case basis. Thus, in other situations, the ECtHR found that the national courts' refusal to refer could not be considered arbitrary and, therefore, rejected the applications on the merits (ECtHR, 28 August 2018, 60934/13, *Somorjal v Hungary*; ECtHR, 11 April, 50053/16, *Harisch v Germany*).

33 ECtHR, 23 June 2016, 20261/12, *Baka v Hungary*.

34 ECtHR, 5 May 2020, 3594/19, *Kövesi v Romania*.

35 ECtHR, 16 June 2022, 39650/18, *Żurek v Poland*.

36 In cases such as ECtHR, 26 September 1995, 17851/91, *Vogt v Germany*; ECtHR, 28 October 1999, 28396/95, *Wille v Liechtenstein*; ECtHR, 12 February 2008, 14277/04, *Guja v*

First, both in *Baka v Hungary* and in *Kövesi v Romania* a reversed argument pertaining to the rule of law was made. While the ECtHR concluded that the violation of Article 10 of the ECHR with respect with both applicants was detrimental to the said value, the national authorities insisted, on the contrary, that, on account of the public offices the two held, the restrictions on their freedom of speech were necessary to preserve the very rule of law. Thus, in *Baka v Hungary*, the government argued that the termination of the applicant's mandate was aimed at maintaining the authority and impartiality of the judiciary within the meaning of Article 10(2), as his office was of an administrative and governmental nature.[37] In *Kövesi v Romania*, the argument of the national interest was also made in the Report of the Ministry of Justice, explaining the restrictive measure by the applicant having created a rule of law crisis "without precedent in the recent history of this country", requiring active measures for the "protection of the national interest".[38]

Second, the unprecedented rule of law situation has injected tensions into ECtHR judgments, most visible in *Baka v Hungary*, the first leading case adjudicated by the Court, where concurring and dissenting opinions respond to one another. In their joint concurring Opinion, Judges Pinto de Albuquerque and Dedov refer to the ECHR as today's European *jus constitutionale commune*, supporting both a claim of institutional and functional independence of the judiciary in Hungary and the applicant's individual right that the respondent State could not circumvent by relying on the principle of subsidiarity or the doctrine of the margin of appreciation.[39] Also, in his concurring Opinion, Judge Sicilianos considers that a subjective right to judicial independence is inherent in the safeguards of the Convention.[40] On the contrary, Judge Wojtyczek questions the very possibility for judges acting in their official capacity to claim that they are exercising their individual human rights. From this perspective, the *Baka v Hungary* judgment would unwarrantedly interpret legal rules pertaining to judicial independence in a manner that transforms them into special human rights granted to judges, with the consequence for the Court to extend its jurisdiction to public-law disputes between State organs, qualified as human rights disputes. Conceding that the case concerns

---

Moldova; ECtHR, 13 November 2008, 64119/00 and 76292/01, *Kayasu v Turkey*; ECtHR, 7 December 2010, 15966/06, *Poyraz v Turkey*; ECtHR, 20 November 2012, 58688/11, *Harabin v Slovakia*.

37 *Baka v Hungary* (n 49), para 155.

38 *Kövesi v Romania*, n. 50, para 31.

39 *Baka v Hungary* (n 49), Opinion of Judges Pinto de Albuquerque and Dedov, para 25. The reference made by the CJEU to the EU treaties as the constitutional charter of a community of law, in the Romanian second wave cases, is not accidental either. ECJ, 21 December 2021 (n 2), para 247.

40 Idem, Opinion of Judge Sicilianos, para 15: "In my opinion, however, the rule of law is hardly imaginable without an obligation on the State to offer safeguards for the protection of judicial independence and, hence, without the corresponding right of judges themselves to independence".

fundamental questions of the rule of law in general and judicial independence in particular, Judge Wojtyczek concludes, however, that it remains outside the scope of the jurisdiction of the European Court of Human Rights.[41] Similarly to Judge Wojtyczek's reasoning, in ***Żurek v Poland***, a strict division was made by the government – but not followed by the Court – between official and individual speech[42] for the purpose of excluding the individual complaint from the scope of Article 10. Thus, the Government maintained that the applicant's dismissal from the position of spokesperson of the court would, at most, limit his ability to represent that institution publicly, which was not a right guaranteed in Article 10, while he was able to continue to express his views in the public debate on judicial reform in Poland at the meetings of judicial associations, through his interviews, statements, and other activities in the public debate.[43] Here again, in a partly dissenting, partly concurring Opinion, Judge Wojtyczek opposes the extension of the scope of applicability of Article 10 to official speech of public power holders.

Third (however), in the specific context of rule of law challenges at the national level,[44] in both *Baka v Hungary* and *Kövesi v Romania*, an important element in finding a violation of the applicants' rights as protected by Article 10 of the Convention (and implicitly for the admissibility of the applications) resided in the fact that the exercise of the right, albeit in an official capacity, represented an institutional obligation.[45] Also, in *Żurek v Poland*, the Court found that the audit of the applicant's financial declarations, the inspection of his work at the Cracow Regional Court, and the declassification of his financial declaration ordered by the Minister of Justice were prompted by the views and criticisms that he had publicly expressed in his professional capacity as member of a body constitutionally mandated to safeguard the independence of the courts and judges.[46] The offices held by each of the three applicants implied functions and duties to express their views on the national legislative

41 Idem, Dissenting Opinion of Judge Wojtyczek, *passim*.

42 For a contribution on the same distinction, see Sietske DiThe Freedom of the Judge to Express his Personal Opinions and Convictions under the ECHR, Utrecht Law Review, available at: https://utrechtlawreview.org/articles/10.18352/ulr.371, accessed 27 March 2023.

43 *Żurek v Poland* (n 51), paras 169–170.

44 *Mutatis mutandis* for the Polish context, see ECtHR, *Grzęda v Poland*, 15 March 2022, 43572/18, where the Court, finding a violation of Article 6 § 1, noted that in Poland, as a result of successive reforms, the judiciary – an autonomous branch of State power – was exposed to interference by the executive and legislative powers and thus substantially weakened (para 348).

45 *Kövesi v Romania* (n 50), para 31: "The Court attaches particular importance to the office held by the applicant (chief of the national anticorruption prosecutor's office), whose functions and duties included expressing her opinion on the legislative reforms"; *Baka v Hungary* (n 49), para 125: "It had been not only the applicant's right but also his duty as President of the National Council of Justice to express his opinion on legislative reforms affecting the judiciary".

46 *Żurek v Poland* (n 51), paras 211–213.

reforms objectively aimed at limiting judicial independence. Within this context, the question is whether a judge who would not hold such specific office would still be protected under Article 10 and to what extent. While providing an affirmative answer,[47] ***Żurek v Poland*** has established three progressive layers of interpretation: first, recalling that various Council of Europe instruments recognise that each judge is responsible for promoting and protecting judicial independence, the Court acknowledges the protection of Article 10 when a judge makes such statements in his or her personal capacity; second, such protection will be heightened when judges express themselves on behalf of a representative body of the judiciary; third, the general right to freedom of expression of judges to address matters concerning the functioning of the justice system may be transformed into a corresponding duty to speak out in defence of the rule of law and judicial independence when those values come under threat.[48]

Turning back to CJEU rule of law case law, one can wonder whether freedom of expression may receive a new dimension at the intersection with the ECtHR's recently developed standards. Is the exercise by the national judge of the right conferred under Article 267 TFEU to be qualified as falling within the scope of the individual right granted by Article 10 of the ECHR, as, through the procedure established by Article 267 TFEU, judges seek to receive information from the CJEU? Moreover, since, when referring to and following the CJEU judgments, the national judges are undisputedly fulfilling an obligation triggered by European Union law, will, in the future Article 11 of the Charter find its applicability?

The national judges' individual duty to speak out in defence of the rule of law and judicial independence recently established by the ECtHR could indeed open the way to acknowledge their individual right and duty to seize the CJEU for information when, given the national context, enforcing EU law requires the former's support. Such right and duty partly overlap with judges' institutional corresponding prerogatives; it is yet to be seen whether an individual disciplinary sanction incurred by them in the rule of law context conflicted within many Member States would be qualified as an interference with their individual rights within the scope of Article 10 of the ECHR as a ground norm or of Article 11 of the Charter as a special one.

47 On the contrary, the partly dissenting, partly concurring Opinion of Judge Wojtyczek, ***Żurek v Poland*** (n 51), para 3.1: "In my view, Article 10 does not apply to official speech of public office holders, it applies to utterances expressing the personal views of individuals. Official speech may be a matter of very broad discretionary power but does not constitute an exercise of a fundamental freedom."

48 ***Żurek v Poland*** (n 51), paras 221–222.

The freedom to receive information without interference by public authority

The right to freedom of expression (and information, in the system of the Charter), enshrined by both Article 10 ECHR and Article 11 of the Charter, undisputedly includes the freedom to receive information without interference by public authority.

As to the courts' need for this information, in the context of the rule of law challenges, the concept of "giving judgment", central to the preliminary ruling procedure, has acquired additional meanings,[49] in line with the CJEU findings on the institutional obligation of the national judges to refer and follow the interpretation thus provided to them, if necessary, by setting aside the contrary practice of the national superior ordinary courts or the decisions of the Constitutional Court.

Regarding the interference with such right, in the second wave of rule of law Romanian cases, the CJEU expressly stated that Article 267 TFEU precluded a national regulation or practice that would prevent national courts from either making use of their faculty or fulfilling their obligation to seize the Court, as enshrined in Article 267 TFEU. In addition, a national court that had exercised its option or fulfilled its obligation to seize the Court under Article 267 TFEU could not be prevented from putting into practice the European Union law pursuant to the Court's interpretation, without diminishing the efficiency of the referral mechanism that pertains, as shown above, to the principle of primacy.[50]

One can therefore conclude that, as a rule, the CJEU has established both the exclusive prerogative of the national judge to refer in order to receive the CJEU's guidance and the interdiction of other national authorities' interference: "it is an inherent guarantee of the independence of national judges that they will not be subject to disciplinary proceedings or sanctions because they have exercised the option to apply to the Court under Article 267 TFEU",[51] "an option which falls within their exclusive jurisdiction".[52]

However, a balance should be struck between the judges' exercise of their right and the normal boundaries thereof, mainly triggered by the principle of national procedural autonomy. Additionally, in the rule of law cases, ordinary courts adopt a critical position *vis-à-vis* the case law of the Constitutional Court or the superior courts, questioning either their jurisdiction or the binding character of their rulings. Thus, within the procedural autonomy framework, the specific issue of judicial disobedience must be addressed. By its nature, the speech of judges – and even more so their contribution to the conversation

49 Opinion of AG Pikamäe (n 39), para 1.

50 CJEU, 21 December 2021 (n 1), para 257, 260.

51 Idem, para 227. The Court also refers to the judgment of 5 July 2016, *Ognyanov*, C-614/14, EU:C:2016:514, paras 17, 25, and the Judgment of 26 March 2020, *Miasto Łowicz and Attorney General* (n 40), para 59.

52 CJEU, 23 November 2021, *IS* (n. 4), para 91.

initiated with the CJEU – is received as the expression of an objective assessment, which commits the entire justice system and may cast doubts on the legitimacy of the national superior courts in already difficult internal contexts. A tension occurs given that, as AG Bobek has pointed out, the very mechanism of Article 267 TFEU opens up a space for rational legal discourse about the correct interpretation of EU law for any national court, taking no account being taken of formal judicial hierarchy. On the one hand, according to AG Bobek, this means that any national court or tribunal must be allowed to apply EU law and to make a request for a preliminary ruling. On the other hand, however, provided that these minimum standards are met, by merely invoking EU law, a national judge does not completely break free from any constraints normally applicable to the exercise of the national judicial function, including national judicial hierarchy and discipline.[53]

Analysing these "constraints" as limitations to the judges' rights enshrined in Article 10 of the ECHR allowed by the Convention, which does not guarantee freedom of speech as an absolute right, it is noteworthy that, in general, the national authorities enjoy a certain margin of appreciation in determining the proportionality of the measures taken.[54]

Given the prominent place among state organs that the judiciary occupies in a democratic society, the national margin of appreciation also applies, therefore, in the event of restrictions on the freedom of expression of a judge in connection with the performance of their functions,[55] with two *caveats.* First, since the rule of law references made by the national judges occur within a debate on matters of great public interest, a high degree of protection for their freedom of expression and a strict scrutiny of any interference, with a correspondingly narrow margin of appreciation (and not "a certain" margin of appreciation) afforded to the authorities of the Member States, are required. Second, should a national judge be faced with disciplinary proceedings merely for having made a request for a preliminary ruling, implicitly or explicitly questioning the position of a national constitutional or ordinary superior court, not only, as AG Bobek points out, "any debate about the appropriate balance between the systemic requirements of national law and EU law is over",[56] but also, proportionality wise, the margin of appreciation granted to the state authorities is to be considered as largely abused. In EU law terms, while the procedural autonomy granted to Member States allows for the national review of a domestic court's referral, effectiveness and equivalence, as boundaries to such autonomy, require *mutatis mutandis* that the review should neither

53 AG Bobek in CJEU, 4 March 2021, C-379/19, *DNA – Serviciul Teritorial Oradea*, ECLI:EU:C:2021:174, para 93, also referring to his Opinion in *Euro Box Promotion*.

54 *Baka v Hungary* (n 47), para 162; *Vogt v Germany* (n 50), para 53; *Guja v Moldova* [GC] (n 50), para 70.

55 ECtHR, *Albayrak v Turkey*, 31 January 2008, 38406/97, para 42.

56 AG Bobek in *DNA – Serviciul Teritorial Oradea* (n 66), para 94.

render the dialogue with the CJEU ineffective nor give it less favourable protection than the protection afforded to similar (*here*: procedural) rights arising under domestic law.

Within such a background, the possibility of being the subject of disciplinary proceedings for submitting a request to the CJEU not only virtually undermines the mechanism of Article 267 TFEU and judicial independence in general, but it also potentially empties of content the right enshrined in Article 10 of the ECHR and Article 11 of the Charter.

Conclusion

That "speech is silver", yet that "silence is golden" may be true only outside today's intricate European rule of law context(s). Extolling the value of judges' silence over their speech is no longer a choice, despite the commonly admitted need that national courts should abide by the domestic rules on judicial hierarchies. Given the multileveled European constitutionalism, the rule of law crisis faced by several Member States has challenged the two European supranational courts that have had to face difficulties arising from both the limits of their own competence and the scope of the international instruments that they adjudicate on.

Thus, establishing the jurisdiction of the CJEU in rule of law cases has proven particularly difficult, given that, as a principle, the Member States retain competences over the organisation of their own justice systems. Stemming from the abundant dialogue with the Romanian courts (but also from the first Hungarian request for a preliminary ruling), the added value of the CJEU's recent case law resides mainly in consistently prohibiting the conditionality of vertical judicial dialogue on prior dialogue between national ordinary courts and supreme or constitutional courts. In addition, the CJEU has also prohibited retaliatory measures against the judges exercising their right to address preliminary questions or enforcing the preliminary rulings of the Court of Justice.

Likewise, beginning with the leading case of *Baka v Hungary*, the ECtHR has seemingly extended its competence *ratione materiae by* understanding the scope of Article 10 of the ECHR as covering the official speech of public power holders. Moreover, in the case of *Żurek v Poland*, while referring to the specific context of judicial independence, the ECtHR has acknowledged increased protection for judges expressing themselves on behalf of a representative body of the judiciary and, moreover, has noted the judges' duty to speak out in defence of the rule of law and judicial independence whenever those values may come under threat.

At the intersection of such bold sets of case law, one can inquire into the future developments of the European standards of human rights protection.

It is yet to be seen whether (or not) the request for a preliminary ruling will be interpreted as representing, in some particularly difficult contexts, (also) the exercise of an individual human right. Suffice it to say that for the purpose of protecting judicial independence at the national level, the two European courts have already decided to speak with one voice.

7 Judges' presence on Twitter in times of constitutional breakdown in Poland

Jarosław Gwizdak

Introductory remarks

Since the United Right took over the government in Poland in 2015, there has been a noticeable trend to limit the independence and impartiality of the courts.[1] The institutions that guarantee respect for the law[2] began to be taken over by people linked to the ruling party. Measures have been taken to silence legal professionals, especially judges, who informed the public about these actions.[3] The retreat from liberal democracy has also been reflected on social media. The judges felt that online social platforms could be a place where they could find an audience to communicate their views and objections to changes in the country's legal system.[4] Previously absent from this space, judges have begun to speak out on systemic, often political issues on digital platforms – Facebook, Instagram, and – mainly – Twitter (currently "X").[5]

On the one hand, judges speaking out on social media can be seen as an important step in bridging the gap between the judiciary and the public and as an element of civic education. A social media presence undoubtedly reduces the distance between sender and receiver and allows for much faster

1 Wojciech Sadurski, 'How Democracy Dies (in Poland): A Case Study of Anti-Constitutional Populist Backsliding' (17 January 2018). Sydney Law School Research Paper No. 18/01, < http://dx.doi.org/10.2139/ssrn.3103491 >, accessed 3 May 2024. Noah Waters, 'Democratic Backsliding in Poland', < https://www.democratic-erosion.com/2022/04/28/democratic-backsliding-in-poland/>, accessed 3 May 2024.

2 Ibidem and Christian Davies, 'Hostile Takeover: How Law and Justice Captured Polands Courts' <https://freedomhouse.org/report/analytical-brief/2018/hostile-takeover-how-law-and-justice-captured-polands-courts> accessed 3 May 2024.

3 The disciplinary actions were regularly reported by Helsinki Human Rights Foundation, latest report: <https://hfhr.pl/en/publications-7798/report-disciplinary-proceedings-against-judges-of-common-courts-in-poland-> accessed 3 May 2024.

4 Poland's largest association of judges, Iustitia, has been promoting legal knowledge and providing information on the activities of the courts through its information team since 2010: <https://iustitia.pl/zespol-informacyjny/> accessed 3 May 2024.

5 Ryan Mac, Tiffany Hsu, 'From Twitter to X: Elon Musk Begins Erasing An Iconic Internet Brand', 24 July 2023, <https://www.nytimes.com/2023/07/24/technology/twitter-x-elon-musk.html> accessed 3 May 2024.

DOI: 10.4324/9781003470779-9

communication. As a result, the public is better and more quickly informed. On the other hand, it offers the possibility for new reproaches against judges, who are accused of having politically biased opinions contrary to the prevailing understanding of the neutral role judges play in a democratic society. Especially pro-government media can often be characterised as vultures waiting for lapses in judges' social media communication, which are then (ab)used for advancing the government's political agenda of destroying the public trust in the judiciary.

Moreover, the new phenomenon of judges engaging in social media activity may prompt a transformation in the judiciary's communication paradigm: from the passive, "mouthpiece of the law" approach to spokespersons of the judiciary (or at least individual courts). Judges presenting their views, their interpretation of changes in court regulations, or their pro-European interpretation of laws on social media may be seen as communication innovators or advocates for a more open judiciary. The judges' use of social media – especially such a powerful tool as Twitter – has the potential to transform the judiciary's communication paradigm and opens new questions on what may be the consequences of this new communication method. For example, it seems that digital activity has become a pre-indicator for disciplinary proceedings, as the disciplinary commissioners have started to announce their intention to take disciplinary action against their colleagues on Twitter.

However, not every judge uses a social media account. Judges have approached this medium with caution, and to this day, most of them either do not have an account on social media platforms or have set one up solely to read messages and information posted by other people. Nevertheless, the phenomenon of social media affects the work and daily life of judges, even if they are not active on social media.[6] They cannot ignore the migration of debates focusing on the judiciary from the traditional media to the digital sphere.

In early 2017, the National Judicial Council in Poland acknowledged the presence of judges on social media, despite Facebook being in existence for nearly 13 years, and Twitter for 11 years. It is noteworthy that the debate on judges' use of social media has been ongoing since at least year 2013,[7] when Judge Judith Gibson asked a critical and provocative question: "Should judges use social media?".[8] Of course, the use of social media cannot be prohibited for

6 Judges have had to adjudicate cases, both civil and criminal, that originated with the posting of a particular piece of information on social networks. The first such cases came before the courts as early as 2009–2010, thus judges had to acquire a proper understanding of these situations as well.

7 Earlier, in 2012, Israeli judges started proceeding deontological rules on the public (including digital) presence of judges. See: 'The Use of Social Media by Judges in Israel', 2012, <https://www.venice.coe.int/files/un_social_media/isr.pdf.> accessed 3 May 2024.

8 Judith Gibson, 'Should Judges Use Social Media', 2013, <https://districtcourt.nsw.gov.au/documents/Should%20Judges%20use%20social%20media.pdf > accessed 3 May 2024. The author of the text also highlighted the lack of legal knowledge among judges in the 19th

judges. In the first decade of social networking, the main focus of researchers was on preserving the independence and impartiality of judges. It was pointed out that an online (Facebook) friendship between a judge and a defendant, or even his lawyer, could lead to a motion to recuse the judge.[9] After a period of relative stability and the establishment of certain rules for online presence, the attention shifted to the limits of judicial activism on platforms, especially in terms of communicating about the rule of law.[10]

To uncover the ways in which Polish judges communicate on social media and assess the implications of this shift to a new communication method, this chapter analyses the Twitter accounts of ten Polish judges[11] in the period of severe threats to independence (2018–2023), who represent both those opposing governmental activities and those who do not express such doubts and sometimes even benefit from the reforms implemented. Presence on Twitter is not a standard characteristic of Polish judges, nor is the language used there anything like typical. Nevertheless, "judicial" Twitter activity has had a more profound effect on the debates concerning the judiciary than other (traditional and social) media and thus merits special attention.

The Twitter interactions between the judges, commenting on each other's posts or forwarding them, were also extremely interesting. Often the polemical passion and the temperature of the dispute were higher here than in real space – e.g. at conferences or in the content of press releases or academic articles. In addition to commenting on the current situation, observing these activities in the digital space is extremely revealing. The judges' tweets sometimes uncover areas and considerations that should remain obscure to the wider public, for example, the political views of judges. Even though judges, by their very nature, are reluctant to reveal too much about their personal views and political sympathies.

---

century. It could be argued that some judges in 2023 lack "online behaviour" knowledge, particularly when it comes to navigating social media safely.

9 Shaziagh Singh, 'Friend Request Denied: Judicial Ethics and Social Media', Journal of Law, Technology & the Internet, Vol. 7, 2016 <https://scholarlycommons.law.case.edu/cgi/viewcontent.cgi?article=1099&context=jolti> accessed 3 May 2024 or https://lawreview.law.miami.edu/wp-content/uploads/2011/12/Why-Cant-We-Be-Friends-Judges-Use-of-Social-Media.pdf John G. Browning – 'Why Can't We Be Friends – Judges Use of Social Media', University of Miami Law Review, <https://lawreview.law.miami.edu/wp-content/uploads/2011/12/Why-Cant-We-Be-Friends-Judges-Use-of-Social-Media.pdf>, accessed 3 May 2024 – articles dealing mainly with the meaning of online "friendship".

10 Ibidem, also Jess Feyder, Lawyers Weekly, 14 November 2022, 'The rule of law is being undermined in the social media age, says WA Chief Justice'.
<https://www.lawyersweekly.com.au/biglaw/36045-the-rule-of-law-is-being-undermined-in-the-social-media-age-says-wa-chief-justice > accessed 3 May 2024.

11 The judges in alphabetical order: Olimpia Barańska-Małuszek, Piotr Gąciarek, Jakub Iwaniec, Jarosław Ochocki, Maciej Nawacki, Łukasz Piebiak, Bartłomiej Przymusiński, Przemysław W. Radzik, Paweł Strumiński, Dorota Zabłudowska.

The chapter starts with an overview of the regulatory framework for the use of social media by judges. In light of standards established by the domestic and international legislative framework and jurisprudence, the article then provides an analysis of judges' activities in the digital space from 2018 to 2023. An assessment and evaluation of the implications of the empirical analysis for the rapidly developing standards and guidelines for judicial speech concludes.

Regulatory framework for the presence of judges in social media

International human rights treaties and jurisprudence

According to both declarations of human rights in the European order – the Convention for the Protection of Human Rights and Fundamental Freedoms (the ECHR) and the Charter of Fundamental Rights of the European Union (the Charter),[12] everyone has the right to freedom of expression. Judges, as citizens, can also exercise this freedom, subject to some restrictions by virtue of their institutional role in democracy.[13] It is a universally accepted principle that a judge should show restraint while participating in public debate, regardless of the forum. Judges are not allowed to discuss the cases they hear, engage in purely political matters, or use extravagant words and expressions.[14]

International tribunals have already ruled on judges' speech in contexts similar to the Polish situation between 2018 and 2023. In *Lopez Lone and others v Honduras* the Inter-American Court of Human Rights (the IACtHR) heard a case concerning four judges who publicly expressed their opposition to the *coup d'etat* in Honduras. The court held that it is the duty of a judge to stand up for democratic values and to speak out in public debate.[15] The IACtHR defined judges as "guardians of the basic rights", obliged to defend them for society. The dismantling of democratic institutions in Poland, especially the judiciary, could not be characterised as a *coup d'etat.* However, the incremental autocratisation we witnessed in Poland can be regarded as calling for a similar approach to the one in *Lopez Lone.* When the independence of the judiciary is at stake (i.e. judges cannot fully exercise their duties because

12 Art 10 of ECHR, art 11 of the Charter of Fundamental Rights.

13 Bangalore Principles (The Bangalore Draft Code of Judicial Conduct 2001 adopted by the Judicial Group on Strengthening Judicial Integrity, as revised at the Round Table Meeting of Chief Justices held at the Peace Palace, The Hague, 25–26 November 2002), Articles. 4 and 6. <https://www.unodc.org/pdf/crime/corruption/judicial_group/> accessed 3 May 2024.

14 Bangalore Principles, especially Article 2.; Venice Commission recommendations – 'Use of Social Media by Judges – Discussion Guide for The Expert Group Meeting' (5–7 November 2018, Vienna) <https://www.venice.coe.int/files/un_social_media/unodc.pdf> accessed 3 May 2024.

15 *Lopez Lone and others v Honduras* – Inter-American Court of Human Rights, judgment from 5 October 2015; para 173 and following <https://www.corteidh.or.cr/docs/casos/articulos /seriec_302_ing.pdf>, accessed 3 May 2024.

they are at risk of, for example, disciplinary proceedings), they should be able to speak out about these violations through available means, including social media.

The jurisprudence of the ECtHR confirms such an approach. In its 2022 *Kozan v Turkey* judgment, the ECtHR indicated that

> The fact that a judge had shared with his colleagues certain views in the press about the independence of the justice system, and had allowed them to comment in response, had necessarily fallen within his freedom to impart or receive information in a crucial area for his professional life.[16]

For the Court, there was no doubt that a judge could publish content on Facebook and, moreover, that restricting his conduct constituted a violation of the Convention. The public activity of judges beyond the mere hearing of cases was also recently defined in the case of *Żurek v. Poland*.[17] In this judgment, the ECtHR confirmed that

> general right to freedom of expression of judges to address matters concerning the functioning of the justice system may be transformed into a corresponding duty to speak out in defence of the rule of law and judicial independence when those fundamental values come under threat.

National regulatory framework

In the Polish legal order, apart from individual disciplinary cases,[18] there is no jurisprudence concerning the judges' freedom of expression.

According to Article 178(3) of the Constitution of the Republic of Poland,[19] judges "shall not … perform public activities incompatible with the principles of independence of the courts and judges". Under Article 82(2) of the Law on ordinary courts,[20] "a judge should, on and off duty, uphold the dignity of the position of judge and avoid anything that would bring disrepute to the dignity of the judge or undermine confidence in his impartiality". The ethical

16 *Kozan v Turkey* 16695/19, <https://hudoc.echr.coe.int/eng?i=001-216271>, accessed 3 May 2024.

17 *Żurek v Poland* 39650/18, para 222 and following <https://hudoc.echr.coe.int/fre#{%22tabview%22:[%22document%22],%22itemid%22:[%22001-217705%22]}> accessed 3 May 2024 .

18 A separate issue here is whether such rulings by, for example, the Polish Disciplinary Chamber of the Supreme Court can be considered valid and binding. However, this issue is beyond the topic of this article.

19 Polish Constitution, official English translation <https://www.sejm.gov.pl/prawo/konst/angielski/kon1.htm> accessed 3 May 2024.

20 Law on Ordinary Courts (in Polish): <https://isap.sejm.gov.pl/isap.nsf/download.xsp/WDU20010981070/U/D20011070Lj.pdf> accessed 3 May 2024.

conduct of judges regarding their public presence and activities is regulated by the deontology of the office. The Polish National Council of the Judiciary (the KRS/NCJ) has enacted a set of ethical rules to guide judges in this regard.

In early 2017, the KRS/NCJ added a new Article 23[21] to the collection of ethical rules for judges. This article states that "judges must exercise restraint while using social media".[22] Judges who were responsible for communicating the work of the judiciary and the importance of the rule of law, including on social media, received this amendment with some disappointment. At the time, legislative work on the so-called justice reform was in progress, and disciplinary proceedings were being initiated. Also, politicians from the ruling party were censuring the judges for the inefficient state of the judiciary. As a rule, judges (rather than responsible politicians such as the Minister of Justice) were held responsible for any shortcomings or inadequacies in the work of the courts. In addition, any controversial judgment that was not in line with the alleged "will of the people" was repeatedly discussed in the public media, and in one case, a judge was screened, for example, for membership of associations or family connections. Judges, therefore, found themselves in a legal dilemma, akin to Heller's paragraph 22.[23] They had no other means (or very limited means) to oppose unfavourable changes in the organisation of the judiciary. While the top echelons of the judiciary were occupied by the government supporters who had the upper hand over judicial decisions, and the official channels of communication of the judiciary were concentrated in the hands of the pro-government judges, those who opposed the reforms were turning to social media to get their warnings across. If judges took such action, they exposed themselves to disciplinary responsibility and to accusations of engaging in political activities, undermining their independence. If they did not, they failed to pay tribute to their (moral) obligation to defend the rule of law and had to watch how the independence of the judiciary was undermined before their very eyes.

21 Pity it wasn't paragraph – "Catch" – 22, like in Joseph Heller's famous book of the same name – https://dictionary.cambridge.org/dictionary/english/catch-22, accessed 3 May 2024. "Collection of ethical rules for judges" (deontology) was an autonomous regulation adopted by NCJ. <https://www.krs.pl/pl/o-radzie/zbior-zasad-etyki-zawodowej-sedziow/591-uchwala-nr-25-2017-krajowej-rady-sadownictwa-z-dnia-13-stycznia-2017-r.html> accessed 3 May 2024. The previously elected council adopted a resolution regarding this matter in accordance with the provisions of the constitution before the revisions made after 2018.

22 Ibidem, https://www.krs.pl/pl/o-radzie/zbior-zasad-etyki-zawodowej-sedziow/591-uchwala-nr-25-2017-krajowej-rady-sadownictwa-z-dnia-13-stycznia-2017-r.html.

23 The judges were stuck in a situation similar to Heller's "Yossarian's dilemma" – by remaining silent, they were unable to communicate the detrimental changes to the judiciary in any way. Whenever they spoke out – they could be subject to disciplinary action as a consequence of the changes in the law.

Recommendation of CSO and soft law

Social media, as a part of the digital environment, is a relatively new marketplace of ideas. Thus, the issue of the presence and activity of judges on social media has also been addressed by NGOs. In 2019, the CEELI Institute published practical guidelines for judges on social media. The publication has an added value, as it deals with the activity of Central and Eastern European judges, who co-authored the guide.[24]

One of the more reasonable and easier-to-use tests for whether an opinion or graphic is acceptable online is the "front page of a newspaper" or "TV news" test. It is advisable to ask whether such a sentence or image could appear on the front page of a newspaper, linked to the author's name, without damaging the author's image or professional standing.[25]

In the recently published "Warsaw Recommendations" of the OSCE–ODIHR, only three sections are devoted to social media. The most important states that judges "should show particular caution in the exercise of [freedom of expression] when using social media".[26]

At the same time, the cited recommendations already assumed that judges simply use social media and not, as in the domestic recommendation (still binding) on Polish judges, to use it with restraint.

Examples of judges' activities in the digital space

This part presents a selection of statements made by Polish judges on Twitter, together with their context and implications. The choice of platform was based on a personal evaluation of the use of different social networking platforms by judges: for instance, Facebook was excluded as the activity of judges on this platform is, with some exceptions, typical behaviour.[27] Judges announce their participation in sports or cultural activities, wish each other happy birthdays, and exchange information about professional or life achievements. Facebook in Poland is also a rather "static" medium – the discussions that take place there attract few commentators, and the response time is sometimes a few days. Facebook's privacy settings also allow users not to appear in the portal's search engine.

24 'Practical Guidelines on Use of Social Media by Judges', Prague, November 2019, CEELI Insitute <https://ceeliinstitute.org/resource/practical-guidelines-on-use-of-social-media-by-judges> accessed 3 May 2024. Unfortunately, Polish judges were not involved in the preparation of the guide (author's note).

25 Ibidem, p. 14.

26 Recommendations on Judicial Independence and Accountability (Warsaw Recommendations), para 27–29 <https://www.osce.org/files/f/documents/c/5/552718.pdf> accessed 3 May 2024.

27 Andy Wu, 'The Facebook Trap', HBR, 19 October 2019, <https://hbr.org/2021/10/the-facebook-trap> accessed 3 May 2024. While judges are members of society, they do not differ a lot in using this platform.

A different situation appears on Twitter where the type of communication is different[28] and with different consequences.[29] Twitter is seen as a medium that is particularly effective in the face of crises.[30] Even more so – in view of the creeping crisis of the rule of law in some EU countries, an analysis of the entries on this platform provides an interesting picture. Moreover, the expectations regarding the privacy of communication are not applicable on this medium, as "[o]n Twitter, all messages were publicly available to those who are not members of that network, and a tweet can be copied and shared by email or other means without the knowledge of the person who wrote the tweet".[31] As active judges who have recently been the subject of disciplinary proceedings in Poland have sometimes expressed highly controversial opinions and have been used by the public media to stigmatise judges, actions on this platform deserve to be described.

In the first example, a judge made a social media entry that led to the opening of a case against the judge for insulting the head of state.[32] The following entries show the communication of the disciplinary commissioner on Twitter and the social media activity of a member of the NCJ in its new composition. Other examples include a former State Secretary at the Ministry of Justice and a judge seconded to the National School of Judges and Prosecutors. The statements as well as the accounts are public.

Despite all the recommendations, the activity of Polish judges on Twitter was quite expressive, controversial, and often went beyond the permitted forms of expression. The range and controversy surrounding the judges' posts mean that, despite the small number of active judges, the significance and scope of their activity is large. Not only did these judges disregard the recommendation of the judicial council, but they also dealt with communication in

28 "Twitter users have become notorious for taking advantage of the almost-direct communication channel with its more influential users", <https://www.socialmediatoday.com/content/how-twitter-has-changed-journalism-forever> accessed 3 May 2024.

29 See John H. Parmelee and Shannon L. Bichard, 'Politics and the Twitter Revolution: How Tweets Influence the Relationship between Political Leaders and the Public' (Lexington Books 2011), <https://books.google.com/books?hl=pl&lr=&id=ZcVxGdegAJ8C&oi=fnd&pg=PR5&ots=TN3GPRQOg2&sig=9Gywa0l8a0Iqt2E2IT3UH836skY> accessed 3 May 2024.

30 Michael Haman, 'The Use of Twitter by State Leaders and its Impact on the Public During the COVID-19 Pandemic', Heliyon, Volume 6, Issue 11, 2020, e05540, ISSN 2405-8440, <https://www.sciencedirect.com/science/article/pii/S2405844020323835> accessed 3 May 2024. Catherine M. Vera-Burgos, Donyale R. Griffin Padgett, 'Using Twitter for Crisis Communications in a Natural Disaster: Hurricane Harvey', Heliyon, Volume 6, Issue 9, 2020, e04804, ISSN 2405-8440, <https://www.sciencedirect.com/science/article/pii/S2405844020316479> accessed 3 May 2024.

31 See footnote 24 <https://ceeliinstitute.org/wp-content/uploads/2022/01/CEELI_SoMe_Guidelines_ENG_Upd2021.pdf> accessed 3 May 2024.

32 See also *Eon v France*, 26118/10, <https://hudoc.echr.coe.int/eng#{%22itemid%22:[%22002-7516%22]}>, accessed 3 May 2024.

a manner characteristic of internet personalities rather than legal professionals, let alone judges.

Alleged offence against the head of state

In order to understand the first case presented, it is necessary to begin by presenting the facts that occurred prior to it. Polish President Andrzej Duda, together with Prime Minister Mateusz Morawiecki, attended a "beer tavern"[33] organised by a trade union organisation in Katowice during the presidential election campaign on 18 January 2020. There, the President said, among other things, that:

> if we look at what has happened recently, how a certain part of the judiciary in Poland has unfortunately behaved, it is necessary to say clearly and unambiguously who judges are and what their role is. We may have various disputes in Poland, but in my opinion, it is indisputable that the judicial system needs to be repaired ***and judges need to understand what their role in the Polish state really is.*** It is a pity that many professors in the law faculties of Polish universities do not want to understand this. I am terribly sorry, but it is difficult. This is Poland and this is the state we have. I hope that we will be able to overcome it, just as we have overcome many other barriers that have blocked us, just as we once managed to overcome communism. In the same way, I believe that we will manage ***to clean our Polish home to the end***, so that it will be clean, tidy, and beautiful.[34]

This statement was almost immediately reported by the media, highlighting yet another attack by the executive against the independence of the judiciary. At around 18:00, the judge of the district court in Poznań – Jarosław Ochocki – commented on the president's pre-election activities. He tweeted: "Mr Duda, I write this with full responsibility. You are a bad man, a lousy president, spewing hate in the name of your immediate and party-political goals. You are damaging Poland! Judge Jarosław Ochocki".[35] Later the same day, at around 22:30, the deputy disciplinary ombudsman for magistrates,

33 It was a belated celebration of Saint Barbara's Day on 4 December each year – when coal miners celebrate their profession, more in Polish (Silesian, in fact) tradition <https://dmc.pwr.edu.pl/index.php/2020/12/04/saint-barbaras-day-barborka/> accessed 3 May 2024.

34 Based on 'Judge Critised President' <https://tvn24.pl/najnowsze/sedzia-jaroslaw-ochocki-skrytykowal-prezydenta-kilka-godzin-pozniej-zajal-sienim-zastepca-rzecznika-dyscyplinarnego-przemyslaw-radzik-3160496> accessed 3 May 2024. Emphasis by the author.

35 <https://twitter.com/jaroochocki> accessed 3 May 2024. The account was made private and, after 10 May 2020, remains inactive, although the original tweet can be found there <https://twitter.com/ZRDSSP_Radzik/status/1286277109040713728> accessed 3 May 2024.

Przemysław W. Radzik, wrote on Twitter that "the President of the Republic of Poland embodies the majesty of the Republic and is its highest representative". He went on affirming that "Insulting the president is a crime. It is unthinkable that this should be done by a judge who has sworn allegiance to his country. I have taken action in the case of Jarosław O". Radzik attached to his tweet an official communication from the Judicial Discipline Ombudsman, Piotr Schab, also dated Saturday, 18 January, informing him that Judge Radzik had

> decided to conduct an investigation regarding a justified suspicion of committing a disciplinary offence … consisting in an offence against the dignity of office by Jarosław O., a judge of the District Court in Poznań, acting as a division president in that court.[36]

More than six months later, on 23 July 2020, Przemysław W. Radzik, deputy disciplinary commissioner for common court judges, posted a tweet:

> Mr. Jarosław O. (Judge in Poznań) insulted the President of the Republic of Poland on Twitter with these words, which are undignified for anyone, especially for a judge. He has shown no restraint on social media. I have today opened disciplinary proceedings against him and filed a complaint against him.[37]

After the commissioner published his tweet, another judge, Judge Dorota Zabłudowska, commented, asking: "Why do you publish accusations against judges on Twitter instead of informing the accused? This violates all standards. Even a prosecutor presents an accusation to a suspect first and then informs the media".[38]

According to the press release: The Disciplinary Court of the Court of Appeal in Wroclaw has closed the case against Judge Ochocki with a non-final decision "due to the absence of a disciplinary offence". In its decision to close the case, the Disciplinary Tribunal clearly stated that the entry did not insult the President. "The expressions contained in the tweet in question are not so much an expression of contempt on the part of the defendant as a subjective assessment of the President made by him", it said. The court went on

36 <http://rzecznik.gov.pl/wp-content/uploads/2020/01/komunikat-Jaroslaw-O.pdf > accessed 3 May 2024.

37 <https://twitter.com/ZRDSSP_Radzik/status/1286277109040713728> accessed 3 May 2024.

38 <https://twitter.com/Zabudowska/status/1286291508581326848> accessed 3 May 2024. The way of informing the public (on Twitter) before official actions were taken became a common practice and a "signature" of the commissioners in a certain period.

to say that the entry was a comment on Duda's political activity and was not intended to insult him, but merely an assessment of his actions.[39]

Disciplinary commissioner – active (mainly) on Twitter

Recent examples show that the disciplinary commissioners have started to announce their actions on Twitter, often before official action was taken on the judges' cases, as the case presented in the previous section has also shown. As Judge Dorota Zabłudowska commented,[40] this has become a certain practice. The commissioner's actions announced via social media were thus able to reach a wider audience than on the official website, which was probably the intention. Such posts generated a lot of traffic and sometimes dozens of unfavourable, often rude comments against judges and the judiciary.

The question is whether, by communicating their work in this way, the ombudsmen were building or diminishing the authority and trust in the judiciary. Such actions can be seen in the work of one of the three ombudsmen, Przemysław W. Radzik.

Judge Radzik posted his first Twitter entry on the working day of 25 June 2019. In it, he said: "Good morning, this profile will be used to keep you updated on my activities as Deputy Disciplinary Ombudsman for Common Law Judges. I invite you to follow the accounts of @MichaLasota6 and @SchabPiotr.[41]

This was the beginning of the commissioner's social media activity. Since then, Mr Radzik's profile has generated 175 posts, mainly about disciplinary proceedings. The first post already received 80 replies on a wide range of issues. There have been denunciations of other judges related to their judicial and non-judicial activities, coming from ordinary users of the platform. One judge, also active on Twitter, Bartłomiej Starosta,[42] cynically asked whether the ombudsman would also answer questions via the platform or only publish statements.

The very next day (26 June 2019), Commissioner Radzik published information about the alleged false testimony of one of the judges, Ewa Maciejewska or Igor Tuleya.[43] He claimed that these judges had submitted an identical preliminary ruling reference to the ECJ. In the post, he pointed out that the

39 <https://www.newsweek.pl/polska/polityka/sedzia-jaroslaw-ochocki-napisal-ze-duda-jest-marnym-prezydentem-sad-umorzyl/22qt7y3> accessed 3 May 2024.

40 Supra (n. 38).

41 <https://twitter.com/ZRDSSP_Radzik/status/1143483708374212608> accessed 3 May 2024.

42 <https://twitter.com/Bartek_Star/status/1143492013020602368> accessed 3 May 2024.

43 <https://twitter.com/ZRDSSP_Radzik/status/1143892473489580032> accessed 3 May 2024.

judges interviewed in the case had denied that they had agreed on the content of their queries to the ECJ.

Radzik also stated: "It is untrue to report in the media that Mr Tuleya and Ms Maciejewska are being prosecuted for asking questions to the ECJ. I have checked whether anyone unlawfully influenced these judges to ask certain questions".[44]

The following day, the commissioner clarified his objections to the actions of Judges Maciejewska and Tuleya in another tweet:

> To answer your question – yes, the reasoning of judges Tuleya and Maciejewska is word for word identical. It is not the conclusions, but the literal wording of the orders and their reasons. Such papers would definitely not pass the anti-plagiarism system used at universities, for example.[45]

We can see here the dual role of the judge, who makes statements about the ongoing cases in addition to the judgments and actions taken.

On the profile of Przemysław W. Radzik, one can also find so-called "reposts" of information published in public media (public television) or in newspapers linked to the ruling party. Thus, on 9 July 2019, the judge invited people to read the material on public television, posting:

> I invite you to read the material of News TVP ("Wiadomosci TVP" – Polish public broadcaster – by author) on the case of the defendant[46] Krzysztof L., which includes, among other things, *my statements* as a response to the statement of the defendant Krzysztof L., published yesterday by the District Court in Poznan.[47]

Also in July 2019, the commissioner announced that some communications would be published in English. The first tweet responds to Amnesty International's report[48] on repressing Polish judges: "The publication of @ amnesty.pl about 'Polish judges standing for their independence' formulates glaringly erroneous conclusions. Below please find the English version of the

44 <https://twitter.com/ZRDSSP_Radzik/status/1143892142567362562> accessed 3 May 2024.

45 Ibid.

46 The defendant is obviously a judge, Krzysztof Lewandowski (author).

47 <https://twitter.com/ZRDSSP_Radzik/status/1148689625302654976> accessed 3 May 2024. Emphasis by the author.

48 Amnesty International report, 4 July 2019, EUR 37/0418/2019 'Free Courts, Free People, Judges Standing for their Independence'. <https://www.amnesty.org/en/documents/eur37/0418/2019/en/> accessed 3 May 2024.

official position of the Disciplinary Commissioner for Judges of Common Courts".[49]

The release of a landmark resolution by the three chambers of the Supreme Court on the consequences of the ECJ's rulings for the Polish legal system and, in particular, the assessment of the appointment of judges and the legitimacy of the court's staffing in relation to the actions of the NCJ,[50] Radzik concludes, tweeting on the same day, 23 January 2020:

> Today's position of some judges of the three chambers of the Supreme Court is nothing but an illegal attempt to change the system of the Republic of Poland. It has no binding force, and judges who question the legality of the appointment of other judges will be subject to disciplinary action.[51]

It is worth noting the language used by the official and the content of the statement. There is talk of "illegitimate regime change", a reference to the lack of binding force, and a renewed announcement of the prosecution of judges who challenge the appointment of other judges. Despite the limitations of Twitter's character limit, the content is very revealing.

The commissioner also occasionally reviews the actions of other courts hearing disciplinary cases. On 1 June 2020, for example, he wrote:

> The Disciplinary Tribunal in Katowice took as long as 7 months to set the first date for the hearing in the case of Mr. Waldemar Ż.[52] When it finally set the date, the parties turned up – it took 20 minutes to postpone the hearing under any pretext. A retreat does not befit a court.[53]

49 <https://twitter.com/ZRDSSP_Radzik/status/1154748817306279936> accessed 3 May 2024. The position – <http://rzecznik.gov.pl/wp-content/uploads/2019/07/RDSSP_position_24.7.2019_EN.pdf> accessed 3 May 2024.

50 III Chambers Resolution of the Supreme Court of 23 January 2020 – English summary <https://www.iustitia.pl/en/activity/informations/3635-resolution-of-the-civil-criminal-and-labour-social-insurance-chambers-of-the-supreme-court-of-23-january-2020> accessed 3 May 2024, original (Polish) text: <https://www.sn.pl/sites/orzecznictwo/orzeczenia2/bsa%20i-4110-1-20.pdf> accessed 3 May 2024.

51 <https://twitter.com/ZRDSSP_Radzik/status/1220452425582161920> accessed 3 May 2024.

52 "Waldemar Ż." is Judge Waldemar Żurek, from Kraków District Court, a former member of NJC. (It is also an interesting paradox that Waldemar Żurek was a member of the last duly elected NCJ and participated in the adoption of the already quoted paragraph 23 of the rules of professional ethics for judges – supra n. 21).

53 <https://twitter.com/ZRDSSP_Radzik/status/1267473964282109953> accessed 3 May 2024.

Prodigious strategist of the National Judicial Council

Judge Maciej Nawacki is currently serving his second term on the National Judicial Council.[54] He was appointed in 2018 and is known for unconventional behaviour.[55] His Twitter profile (described as private) contains a number of statements on a wide range of issues. On 24 January 2019, Judge Nawacki (an active member of Judges' Association "Iustitia" until his expulsion in 2018[56]) referred to the past practice of judges' promotions and the size of Themis, another judge association, by tweeting:

> Judge Beata Morawiec head of #themis or thereabouts another judges' couch. Member of #KRS from 18 March 2002 to 18 March 2006. On 30 of October 2002, at the age of 38, positively endorsed by a KRS resolution for a vacant position at the District Court in Krakow.[57]

If you browse through Judge Nawacki's profile, among his more than 6,500 tweets (including retweets), you can find a lot of content that links the judge to patriotism, media freedom, and the Catholic Church. There is also an important tweet that was subsequently removed from Nawacki's profile. On 6 February 2022, just over two weeks before the Russian aggression against Ukraine began, the judge posted the following:

> BTW from the point of view of the Kremlin's political interest, a limited attack from Belarus on Volhynia, Rawa Ruska and further towards Lviv would be rational. It cuts Ukraine off from the west, spares the east, and destroys the most anti-Russian regions. Such a partial repeat of the Second World War.[58]

54 So-called "neoKRS" in Polish public debate.

55 For example, there were doubts whether he had reached the required number of 25 signatures, but he did not want to disclose the list of signatures supporting his candidacy. See <https://www.iustitia.pl/79-informacje/3706-nie-ma-krajowej-rady-sadownictwa-poniewaz-maciej-nawacki-nie-zebral-wymaganej-liczby-25-podpisow-sedziow> accessed 3 May 2024. "There is no (lawful) NCJ because Maciej Nawacki didn't collect a proper number of 25 recommendations". Judge Nawacki, as President of the District Court in Olsztyn (appointed by the Minister of Justice and already a member of the NCJ), tore up a draft resolution prepared by the judges during one of the judges' meetings. The photo of Nawacki tearing through a sheet of paper during a meeting (broadcast live on one of the news TV channels) is sometimes used as a meme and has become viral.

56 'Judge Nawacki Expelled from Iustitia', Gazeta Prawna, <https://prawo.gazetaprawna.pl/artykuly/1144603,sedzia-maciej-nawacki-wykluczony-z-ssp-iustitia.html> accessed 3 May 2024.

57 <https://twitter.com/Maciej_Nawacki/status/1088354270926307328> accessed 3 May 2024. Nawacki thus accuses Judge Morawiec of owing her promotion to her position at the NCJ.

58 The deleted post can be found as a screenshot in the author's archive.

On 24 February 2022, Russia launched a violent attack on Ukraine. After a wave of criticism, Judge Nawacki withdrew his post, and since the outbreak of the war, he has also reported on Russian losses and Polish aid to the Ukrainians. He usually contrasts the sacrifice and generosity of the Poles with the behaviour of the Germans after the Second World War and refers to the reparations the Polish government expects from the German government.[59] Nawacki also asks rhetorically whether the European Union intends to support Poland financially in helping the Ukrainians, or whether such aid is reserved for refugees (by implication, migrants from the Global South).

This attitude is combined with a blatant sympathy for the so-called national media, promoting, for example, the TV channel set up by the organisers of the Warsaw Independence March, according to a tweet by Robert Bąkiewicz.[60] He also posted a photo[61] of himself from the march, holding a Polish flag, accompanied by another member of the NCJ, Judge Marek Jaskulski.

On 18 June 2022, the judge went on to retweet a right-wing weekly post, containing the following quote from Archbishop Jędraszewski:[62] "Lech Kaczyński was equal to kings. He was the greatest president of the Third Republic of Poland, a fighter for Polish truth".[63]

Statesman, ministerial secretary, judge, politician?

Judge Łukasz Piebiak adjudicated in the Warsaw Regional Court. From 2010 to 2015, he was also a member of the board of the Iustitia Association. In 2015, he took up the position of Secretary of State in the Ministry of Justice of the United Right government.

59 Tweets about reparations: Robert Bąkiewicz tweet: <https://twitter.com/RBakiewicz/status/1691785618269827511> accessed 3 May 2024 or Polish public TV <https://twitter.com/tvp_info/status/1585931319120482304> accessed 3 May 2024.

60 https://twitter.com/RBakiewicz/status/1635191699084562433> accessed 3 May 2024. Robert Bąkiewicz is the president of the Independence March Association, and he describes his views in this way: Left-wing circles say that this is a war. "Yes, it is a war, and we are joining this war", said President Robert Bąkiewicz, announcing the formation of a new organisation called "National Guard", whose aim will be, among other things, the defence of churches. "We accept that from today, we are at war, and we are putting all our efforts on this front. The time of peace and tolerating barbarians is over", assessed Bąkiewicz at a conference in front of the Holy Cross Basilica in Warsaw. "The 'National Guard' is to be formed by the existing 'Guard of the Independence March'". <https://wiadomosci.onet.pl/kraj/robert-bakiewicz-kim-jest-organizator-marszu-niepodleglosci-i-czlonek-onr/yt6y3ly> accessed 3 May 2024.

61 'Greetings from the Independence March!', <https://twitter.com/Maciej_Nawacki/status/1591088422524887041/photo/1> accessed 3 May 2024.

62 Marek Jędraszewski – https://www.catholic-hierarchy.org/bishop/bjedr.html, example of Jędraszewski's activity <https://www.newwaysministry.org/2019/10/10/polish-archbishop-says-lgbtq-movement-is-great-threat-to-freedom-as-catholics-demand-end-to-violent-rhetoric/> accessed 3 May 2024.

63 <https://twitter.com/wPolityce_pl/status/1538224910132301824> accessed 3 May 2024.

Although he has previously made no secret – including on social media – of his sympathies for a strong state, sovereignty, and patriotism, some of his public statements have been restrained. From time to time since his appointment to a government position, Judge Piebiak has revealed more radical views.

Piebiak has on several occasions expressed his critical attitude towards LGBT+ people,[64] calling them ideologues (just like President Andrzej Duda in the aforementioned election campaign), sinners, or perverts. He commented on an article in the right-wing weekly, entitled "Americans are Fed Up with Social Realism":[65] "Perhaps something they understand, i.e. losses instead of gains, will appeal to the reason of the ideologically inclined? The ultra-left LGBT agenda, among all the other dangers it entails, simply does not pay".

A photograph of a church in France, allegedly converted into a car park, posted by another user of the portal, he commented with the single word "barbaria".[66]

Reposting one of the National Council of Judiciary Twitter messages,[67]on 1 June 2023. Piebiak comments: "It's hard to disagree. If the 'rule of law' expected by the EC consists of following political orders from Brussels, then we will have a hard time agreeing".[68]

Lukasz Piebiak's communication and comments on various events on Twitter were directed to a limited number of issues, and in particular, criticism against European Union activities. In addition, there are also some communist threads as well as tweets from right-wing media.

64 His international political activity is described, i.e. here "The Polish side wanted to draw attention to discrimination against religious groups – Christians and Jews; we cannot allow reality to be distorted in an official EU document", Deputy Justice Minister Łukasz Piebiak told PAP on Thursday.

The Ministry of Justice announced on Thursday that Poland has decided to veto the EU Council conclusions on the application of the EU Charter of Fundamental Rights in 2017. This means that the conclusions will not be adopted. Deputy Minister Łukasz Piebiak, who led the Polish delegation that discussed the text of the conclusions in Brussels, told PAP that the Polish side's aim was to "draw attention in the text of the conclusions to discrimination against religious groups – Christians and Jews – in order to condemn all discriminatory practices with equal force". "Meanwhile, according to what the Austrian Presidency told us, many countries, especially in Western Europe, were not willing to put discriminatory practices against LGBT groups and religious groups on the same level", he added. "From our point of view, this was nonsense, because such discriminatory practices against Christians and Jews exist, especially in Western Europe, and we could not allow this to distort reality in an official EU document", he stressed. – source – <https://www.radiomaryja.pl/bez-kategorii/l-piebiak-nie-moglismy-pozwolic-na-zaklamywanie-rzeczywistosci-w-dokumencie-unijnym/> accessed 3 May 2024. Łukasz Piebiak: "We cannot allow reality to be distorted in an official EU document".

65 <https://twitter.com/LPiebiak/status/1667435511860920321> accessed 3 May 2024.

66 <https://twitter.com/LPiebiak/status/1681255334684553216> accessed 3 May 2024. What is important is that there is no definitive evidence if the picture shows the real church.

67 <https://twitter.com/KRS_RP/status/1664234351754637312> accessed 3 May 2024.

68 https://twitter.com/LPiebiak/status/1664247576785215488

In 2021, for example, Piebiak reached for a note on a centre-right blogging platform and tweeted: "It's worth remembering certain things today. The Advocate-General of the ECJ is the son of a prominent Bulgarian communist[69] and thus encouraged people to read the article".[70]

Judge Piebiak also properly commented on and assessed events in the national legal environment. The Supreme Court has ruled that the hearing of cases in "pandemic" mode, i.e. in a one-man composition and by definition with limited publicity, is a violation of access to a court.

The former deputy minister of justice, on 27 April 2023, commented thus:

> The Supreme Court (or rather four politicians in robes from the Chamber of Labour and Social Security) has taken another big step towards the destruction of the Polish judiciary. As there are so many censored words, I will stop here. I hope that one day they will be called to account.[71]

A spokesman for the Iustitia Association, Judge Bartłomiej Przymusiński, responded to his tweet by writing: "You already remembered how, for the good of Poland (sic!) @ZiobroPL you wanted the Polish government to recognise the position of the plaintiffs against Poland?"[72]

The judge immediately got to Piebiak's reply, who wrote back:

> Are you really that stupid or are you just pretending? What should he do? ZiobroPL a member of the government of @MS_GOV_EN how but to leave the resolution of his own mother's case to the ECtHR? Should he take a procedural position? Would you decide your own mother's case? You probably would, but others have higher standards.[73]

The online exchange did not continue at this level. It is worth noting that Piebiak's second tweet on the matter received almost 6,000 views.

Piebiak announces his participation in the right-wing TV programme:

69 Although the tweet was deleted, there is a screenshot – <https://twitter.com/JarasJarasy/status/1382939011484897281> accessed 3 May 2024. (Evgeni Tanchev – ***author***)

70 <https://www.salon24.pl/u/nick/966285,rzecznik-generalny-tsue-to-syn-prominentnego-komunisty-nagrodzonego-nagroda-lenina> 'The Advocate-General of the ECJ is the Son of a Prominent Bulgarian Communist, Awarded with the Lenin Prize'.

71 <https://twitter.com/LPiebiak/status/1651485109571264512> accessed 3 May 2024.

72 <https://twitter.com/bprzymusinski/status/1651494616527454208> accessed 3 May 2024. Zbigniew Ziobro – Minister of Justice and Prosecutor General – is a deputy prosecutor in the trial of doctors accused of mistreating his deceased father. During the trial, pressure was brought to bear in the Kraków court on both the judge hearing the case, Agnieszka Pilarczyk, and the experts who gave opinions on the case. Zbigniew Ziobro's mother has also taken the case against Poland to the ECHR, as mentioned in the tweet.

73 <https://twitter.com/LPiebiak/status/1651499338600787968> accessed 3 May 2024.

> There's not enough time to talk about all the pathologies of caste, but one thing is certain: they wouldn't exist, and certainly not on this scale, if the system of disciplinary responsibility for judges hadn't been dismantled. Either the political power does something about it, or it will get worse and worse.[74]

The cited statement is more of a political nature (the political power does something about it) than judicial.

The other side's voice

A group of judges also took to Twitter to comment on constitutional issues, reminding the public of European standards, Poland's obligations, and the rule of law. Sometimes they take part in the discussion on the portal – such as judges Dorota Zabłudowska and Bartłomiej Przymusiński, quoted above. It follows from the analysis conducted for the purposes of this chapter, that some judges construct their message in the same way as the average Twitter user – creating their own communiqués, reposting other content, or debating with tweets from politicians or ordinary users. Those judges include Olimpia Barańska-Małuszek, Piotr Gąciarek, and Paweł Strumiński.

The statements of these judges also contain a certain emotional charge – as in the case of Judge Gąciarek, who used Twitter to not only evaluate the Supreme Court's decision on his suspension but also invented his own term for the "new" National Council of Judiciary – the Zbigniew Ziobro Discussion Club – and used it consistently. Another characteristic of Judge Gąciarek's tweets is that he names (and blames) the judges and prosecutors[75] who, in his opinion, are responsible for the suspension of Judge Igor Tuleya, for example, or who owe their promotion to the new NCJ and not necessarily to their merits. The language of Judge Gąciarek's tweets contains strong phrases that he uses consistently, including pseudo-judges, gentlemen of the (disciplinary) chamber, and toga-clad usurpers of the disciplinary chamber.[76]

Judge Paweł Strumiński is equally (or perhaps even more) direct on Twitter. He sometimes comments on the actions of politicians, including those who have nothing to do with the judiciary, or reminds other judges on Twitter of their alleged links to the ruling party. On the activities of Commissioner Radzik, Strumiński commented:

74 <https://twitter.com/LPiebiak/status/1633083520217239552 > accessed 3 May 2024.

75 <https://twitter.com/GaciarekPiotr/status/1678478155647000576> accessed 3 May 2024. – "And once again the names of disgrace: Piotr Niedzielak, Konrad Wytrykowski, Jarosław Sobutka – hese people, the pseudo-judges of the disciplinary chamber, are responsible for the unlawful and groundless suspension of Judge Igor Tuleya".

76 <https://twitter.com/GaciarekPiotr/status/1615578626543570945>, accessed 3 May 2024. <https://twitter.com/GaciarekPiotr/status/1615998949583880192> accessed 3 May 2024.

> #Radzik is such a model of a functionary who carries out orders under the policy of his principal … spitting on judges who oppose the introduction of #Putinisation in the judiciary by party factions … never mind that unjustified, the important thing is that the message about bad judges is to go.[77]

Judge Olimpia Barańska-Małuszek decided to take a different approach to communicating. In particular, she reposts important tweets, even those not directly related to the judiciary but also concerning basic economic knowledge – a kind of civic education on the platform. To a lesser extent, she engages in polemics and focuses on correcting the messages of others. To some extent, her account could serve as a benchmark for judges' activity on Twitter, although at times, it seems to go too far. [78]

The (final) words of a magistrates' schoolteacher

Judge Jakub Iwaniec is also one of the judges active on Twitter. A judge in the criminal division of the Warsaw Court, the deputy disciplinary commissioner also works at the National School of Judges and Prosecutors,[79] and is employed in the teaching department of the Judicial Training Centre. It could be assumed that the standard of expression of a person who is a judge, a disciplinary judge, and a teacher of future judges makes Jakub Iwaniec more responsible for his words than an average judge. But this is not the case.

Judge Iwaniec makes no secret of his beliefs and sympathies and has also overstepped the bounds of freedom of expression towards journalists. Referring to unfavourable material on TVN about the National Council of the Judiciary, he called the station's journalist a "rat".[80]

Elsewhere, the judge explains the current situation in the justice system in these words, using rather familiar rhetoric:

> Facts. There is a group of activists from Iustitia who are loud and somewhat influential, but above all greedy and therefore flexible (useful). Some of them are the nephews and "backpackers" of the families of

77 <https://twitter.com/p_hudini/status/1690710478673084416> accessed 3 May 2024.

78 See, i.e. tweet from 8 July 2023 – "Colleague of the Minister ZiobroPL, who, thanks to his patronage and the political support of the party authorities, has made a career as president of the SAC in Kraków and in the (Law and Justice) neo-KRS, will be locked up for her views.
Is this an announcement of a voluntary surrender to punishment in a future criminal trial?"

79 Judge Jakub Iwaniec has worked in the Education Department of the school.

80 The tweet was deleted, but the screenshot is available here: <https://twitter.com/szarapolka/status/1574337354374041601/photo/1> accesed 3 May 2024. "Pathetic. Journalism has moved past your intelligence and started crying. I was asked nothing by any of your piss, I got nothing. You are a journalistic rat and that's it".

> communist judges, liberated commies or so-called businessmen from property conversions after communist era.[81]

The theme of post-communists, disenfranchisement, estates, and secret agents was also present in Judge Piebiak's tweets or in Judge Nawacki's sympathy for nationalist movements. It is worth remembering that decommunisation of the judiciary is also mentioned in the programme of the United Right.[82]

It is evident how elements of political (right-wing) discourse infiltrate the judges' publicly expressed views. However, these themes are not directly related to the judiciary; they are a reckoning with the legacy of recent history.

There are also themes related to past events; the judges call themselves "pro-state", they reach for the dichotomy of "the third generation of the Home Army[83] against the third generation of the SB"[84] – positioning themselves as continuators of the independence and anti-communist movement. Such positions earn them the applause of the right-wing and public media.[85]

Final remarks – should judges remain silent?

A detailed reading of the judges' tweets from 2018 to 2023 may surprise those who are not used to a certain type of expression and communication. It must be said that, in a significant proportion of cases, these statements are not restrained – on the contrary, they contain quite a lot of opinions, offensive phrases, and sharp polemics.

What are the implications of this new phenomenon for the way we understand judicial communication? There are probably several. First, the time for judges to remain silent at all times (as the "*mouthpiece of the law*") seems to be over. The new phenomenon of vocal judges requires a new paradigm of communication. Leaving the narrative about the courts and the rule of law to individual judges, such as the ones described above, or to others outside of the judiciary (journalists, politicians, and aggrieved parties) will result in an

81 <https://twitter.com/IwaniecKuba/status/1687561068296486912> accessed 3 May 2024.

82 i.e. 'United Right Continues Prime Minister Jan Olszewski's Independence Programme', <https://dzieje.pl/wiadomosci/macierewicz-zjednoczona-prawica-kontynuuje-niepodleglosciowy-program-premiera-jana> accessed 3 May 2024.

83 Armia Krajowa – Home Army – definition <https://ipn.gov.pl/en/brief-history-of-poland/collected-content/9259,COLLECTED-CONTENT-THE-HOME-ARMY.html> accessed 3 May 2024.

84 Służba Bezpieczeństwa – Safety Service, secret police during the Communist Era, more – <https://polishhistory.pl/the-security-services-last-task/> accessed 3 May 2024.

85 "The politicisation of public media in Poland is total. And while most private editorial offices can still exercise their freedom of speech, they then expose themselves to political attacks and financial problems. Journalists are victims of this situation" – more here Karolina Zbytniewska, 7 July 2020 – "How limited is freedom of media in Poland – analysis" <https://www.euractiv.pl/section/demokracja/linksdossier/jak-ograniczana-jest-wolnosc-mediow-w-polsce-analiza-rynku-medialnego/> accessed 3 May 2024.

inability to develop a more moderate judiciary's own narrative, which could win the trust of the society. Perhaps this means giving up a particular tool or platform. In any event, the Twitter/X activity described above calls for a reconsideration of the ways in which judges and the judiciary as a whole should use social media in an effective way, without damaging public confidence in the judiciary.

Second, the often-blunt tweets by judges supporting the ruling party, or posts with content that is not in line with the dignity of the office of a judge[86] not only did not meet with any reaction from the disciplinary ombudsmen, but most of them remain available online. Interestingly, some of these posts have been deleted by their authors. Nevertheless, they show that in a context of politicised judiciary, judges who support the ruling party have unlimited opportunities to express themselves. For example, the authors under scrutiny for this chapter freely attached themselves to (political) ideas or worldviews such as "traditional conservative values" – in particular the promotion of the views of the hierarchy of the Catholic Church, the traditional family model (mother, father, children), or the recognition of homosexuality as a deviation. To the contrary, deviations from a strict standard of neutrality were sanctioned when they came from the opposing side. Such arbitrary use of law shows how the authorities seek to shape the narrative about the judiciary. Norms regulating judicial speech are neutral on their face but are used discriminately to stifle the opinion of those willing to stand in the way of the government's agenda.

Third, the voice of Polish judges has certainly been heard for some time. What remains to be seen is who will hear it, who will listen to it, and whether the listeners will understand it. It will be important to see whether the voice of the judges will lead to an increase in the eroded trust in the judiciary or to a further decline. The current language, the dynamics of the statements and polemics, and the content conveyed do not inspire such confidence. If the judiciary were to have such a "spokesperson" (or, more broadly, a media officer), it would do no good at all in terms of confidence-building.

Fourth, tweeting is a relatively new means of communication and influence, with high dynamics and (in principle) unlimited possibilities for interaction. Certainly, statements with a certain dynamism and energy will attract more interest and generate more lively discussion. It seems that there is no place on Twitter for overly official pronouncements or completely neutral and balanced language. Observing examples of the (hyper)activity of Polish judges on Twitter, serious doubts arise as to the suitability of this platform for judges. A crisis of justice and the rule of law is hardly a justification for the use of a crisis communication tool such as this platform. It would be advisable to leave this digital space to non-governmental organisations (including associations of judges and prosecutors), whose statements could be more controversial and energetic. It can be assumed that the statements of individual judges quoted in

86 See sections II. c., d., and f.

the article would sound different (more appropriate) if they were, for example, the positions of the boards or resolutions of these organisations.[87] In addition, court spokespersons could also use social media as a platform for rapid response and cooperation with the media and citizens,[88] whereas accounts of individual judges may not be appropriate on such platforms. Interestingly, leaders of judicial associations such as Krystian Markiewicz (Iustitia) or Beata Morawiec (Themis) and symbols of judicial resistance such as Igor Tuleya or Paweł Juszczyszyn and Waldemar Żurek do not have accounts on Twitter.

To conclude, not every crisis can be handled and described with crisis communication. It is more valuable for a judge to make a nuanced and well-thought-out statement, not just a dynamic polemic. Simply being on the platform and conforming to its rules should not be the goal of justice, especially in times of breakdown or backsliding when every lapse in communication or hasty word can turn against the judiciary. The efficiency, accuracy, and understanding of the judiciary build trust. Twitter polemics do not.

87 See the position of Iustitia on media freedom in Poland from 28 June 2023 r. – <https://twitter.com/JudgesSsp/status/1674021110587744260> accessed 3 May 2024. It may be questioned whether the issue of threats to the freedom of the (opposition) media should be in the area of interest of a judge, although it may also be questionable whether this falls within the mandate of a judges' association. This statement is rather an expression of solidarity with the journalistic community. "We support journalists and free media ... we are all journalists today". See also position of Themis (The Association of Judges) – appealing to the Minister of Justice. It is hard to imagine (even according to Polish standards) an individual judge doing it: "The Association of Themis Judges appeals to the Minister to take immediate and decisive action to remove from office those persons holding administrative functions and positions in the courts and prosecutor's offices whose attitudes do not guarantee the correct and ethical performance of administrative functions in the said institutions". <http://themis-sedziowie.eu/wp-content/uploads/2023/12/list-otwarty-do-MS-13.12.pdf> accessed 3 May 2024.

88 "When a judge makes such statements not only in his or her personal capacity, but also on behalf of a judicial council, judicial association or other representative body of the judiciary, the protection afforded to that judge will be heightened" – *Żurek vs. Poland*, supra (n. 17).

8 *Working as* a judge or *being* a judge

On the specific features of freedom of expression of the judiciary in Italy

Federica Casarosa

The Italian context

Intense conflicts between the powers of the state have always characterised the Italian socio-political context. It is symbolic that the end of the so-called First Republic in Italy was due to the impact of two different forces: the collapse of Soviet communism and the so-called "Operation Clean Hands" led by the judiciary against widespread political corruption.[1] This tension has not subsided in recent years. Instead, it has been fuelled by several scandals and investigations involving politicians and the judiciary.[2]

In this context, participation by judges in public debate is not perceived as exceptional but instead as a way to gather information from privileged sources that is not only sought after by media outlets but also prioritised and amplified by them to emphasise – and sometimes exacerbate – existing debates, leading in some negative cases to the so-called spectacularisation of justice.[3] There have been several examples of Italian judges expressing their opinions on judicial proceedings presided over by other colleagues, intervening in political debates, and publicly reacting to attacks on their reputation or

1 See the national report dedicated to Italy in AAVV, 'TRIIAL National Reports Belgium, Hungary, Italy, Poland, Portugal, Romania, Slovenia, Spain, The Netherlands', Working Paper, EUI RSC, 2022/52, Centre for Judicial Cooperation, <https://cadmus.eui.eu/handle/1814/74814> accessed 23 January 2023; N. Rossi, 'Il silenzio e la parola dei magistrati. Dall'arte di tacere alla scelta di comunicare', Questione giustizia (2018) 4, < https://www.questionegiustizia.it/rivista/articolo/il-silenzio-e-la-parola-dei-magistrati-dall-arte-di-tacere-alla-scelta-di-comunicare_599.php> accessed 23 January 2023.

2 See, for instance, the "Palamara case" which involved several politicians and magistrates for alleged crimes of corruption and influence peddling, one of them being the former prosecutor and former member of the High Council of the Magistracy, Luca Palamara. See G. Merlo, 'Il caso Palamara e lo scandalo delle nomine al Csm', 23 September 2021 <https://www.internazionale.it/notizie/2021/09/23/palamara-scandalo-csm>, accessed 23 January 2023.

3 Court of Cassation, Joint Chambers, 24 November 2009, 24666; High Court of Magistracy, Disciplinary Chamber, Decision 35/2009; High Court of Magistracy, Disciplinary Chamber, 1/2007.

DOI: 10.4324/9781003470779-10

professionalism.[4] Similarly, the opinions of judges, expressed through their participation in manifestations and debates, were also used by politicians to attack their reputations and, most importantly, their impartiality.[5]

However, such cases should be understood within the framework provided by the constitutional rules and principles that steer judges' institutional (and personal) conduct *vis-à-vis* the media and define the boundaries applicable to exercising freedom of expression by judges in more general terms. If, on the one hand, Article 21 of the Italian Constitution guarantees freedom of expression in general, several other constitutional provisions clarify that the role and institutional activity carried out by judges may require a balancing effort, allowing for some limitations. The balancing exercise is based on the fact that, although judges may exercise their right to freedom of expression as any other individual citizen, their position as civil servants requires that their conduct should never hamper the reputation and paramount features of the judiciary – i.e. independence and impartiality. Consequently, we may affirm that the institutional role of the judge can never be disentangled from his individuality: judges will always *be* judges, even when they do not *work* as judges, i.e. deciding a case.

As clarified in the following analysis, the "appearance" of independence and impartiality is crucial in any legal proceeding involving judges. The concept of "appearance" of impartiality and independence should not be misunderstood as "pretence" or "semblance" where judges only pretend to be impartial and independent while they are not. If that were the case, the judges could be completely partisan towards one of the parties, as long as the citizens are unaware of it. This is not the meaning of "appearance" of impartiality. Judges must "appear" impartial in the process as they should show impartiality in every step of the procedure: they must be able to instil confidence in the parties that, whatever their convictions, opinions, and religious beliefs, they will

4 See P. Dusi, 'Delle esternazioni dei magistrati e di altri problemi connessi', Questione giustizia (1998), 431.

5 See the recent case involving the Ministry of Transport, who posted on his social media profile a video of a public manifestation against the legislation on migration (filmed years earlier by a police officer). The video also included the image of a civil judge participating in such an event. The Ministry connected such participation to the, then, recent decision of the same judge not to validate the detention of three Tunisian migrants, demanding the resignation of the judge from her office. Although the request was discontinued and remained only at the level of political debate, it showed the tight connection between the expression of personal opinions by judges and their perceived impartiality and independence in the eyes of the citizens, as well as their possible exploitation by politicians. See 'Salvini posta un video della giudice Apostolico in corteo. Anm: "Preoccupa lo screening sui giudici"', 5 October 2023, <https://www.rainews.it/articoli/2023/10/salvini-posta-un-video-del-giudice-apostolico-in-corteo-anm-no-a-screening-f8e4359d-ff2f-4d00-8f53-7c15df459458.html> accessed 11 April 2024.

be able to master them. Thus, they will appear to be good arbiters for the dispute at stake.[6]

This approach takes stock of the multilevel system of protection of fundamental rights, including the European Convention on Human Rights and the European Charter of Fundamental Rights, as well as the jurisprudence of the Strasbourg and Luxembourg Courts.[7] It is important to mention that the Court of Justice of the European Union (CJEU) has addressed the social perception of the impartiality and independence of judges, affirming that citizens must not have the impression that the applicable rules and procedures affect the judges' decision-making.[8] In the case law of the CJEU, this standard applies to appointment procedures,[9] disciplinary responsibility,[10] and the possibility of terminating a judicial secondment with a higher court.[11] In these cases, the appearance of independence and impartiality is linked to the need to ensure the separation of powers, ensuring the citizens that there is no external pressure from the executive and the legislative branches over the judiciary. According to the same reasoning, the CJEU affirmed that establishing a judicial body (entrusted with disciplinary powers over judges) could be considered contrary to EU law if the process leading to the creation of such a body gives rise to legitimate doubts regarding its independence.[12]

It must be acknowledged that the above-mentioned case law is never mentioned by the Italian courts (whether civil or disciplinary courts) when addressing cases involving the freedom of expression of judges. On the one hand, this can be justified by the fact that the case law of the CJEU is very recent and refers to specific cases deemed not replicable in the Italian system. On the other hand, the judges deciding these cases prefer to refer to the

6 Giulio Cataldi, 'I giudici, l'imparzialità e la moglie di Cesare, Questione giustizia', 20 October 2023, <https://www.questionegiustizia.it/articolo/i-giudici-l-imparzialita-e-la-moglie-di-cesare> accessed 29 February 2024.

7 See Mohor Fadijga and Sietske Dijkstra in this volume.

8 In the words of the CJEU: "However, the Court has stated that it is still necessary to ensure that the substantive conditions and procedural rules governing the adoption of those appointment decisions are such that they cannot give rise to reasonable doubts in the minds of individuals as to the imperviousness of the judges concerned to external factors and their neutrality with respect to the interests before them, once they have been appointed as judges, and that it is important, inter alia, in that perspective, that those conditions and procedural rules should be such as to preclude not only any direct influence, in the form of instructions, but also types of influence which are more indirect and which are liable to have an effect on the decisions of the judges concerned". See CJEU, 15 July 2021; Case C-791/19, *Commission v Poland* [2021] para 98.

9 See CJEU, 19 November 2018; C-585/18 et al., *A.K. v KRS* [2018].

10 See *Commission v Poland* (n 8) and CJEU, 5 June 2023; Case C-204/21, *Commission v Poland* [2023].

11 CJEU, 16 November 2021; Joined Cases C-748/19 to C-754/19, *Prokuratura Rejonowa w Mińsku Mazowieckim* [2021]. Note that in this case, the CJEU extended its reasoning to include also the self-perceived independence of judges.

12 See *Commission v Poland* (n 8), para 108.

national Constitutional or Supreme Court decisions that directly link freedom of expression with the independence and impartiality of the judiciary as defined by the Italian Constitution. As a matter of fact, since 1981, the Italian Constitutional Court has affirmed that judges' rightful exercise of freedom of expression should be balanced with the need to ensure that judges are – and appear to citizens to be – impartial and independent in their decision-making activity.[13] The jurisprudence of the Disciplinary Chamber of the Italian Court of Cassation follows the guidelines of the Constitutional Court, interpreting the existing legislative provisions and defining the limits applicable to the ethical principles that all legal practitioners should follow.[14]

This well-oiled machine has recently been challenged by two developments that will be the focus of this contribution. The first is an increased use of social media by judges, allowing them to engage in public debates on trivial and sensitive issues. In this case, the role of judges as civil servants impacts not only how they may participate in discussions but also their opportunities to do so. Once again, it is impossible to discontinue a judge's role even online. Second, a recent proposal to create an independent High Court,[15] which could hear cases addressing the conduct of judges, raises some doubts about the ability of this new body to provide an additional pillar supporting the independence of judges and ensuring they can express themselves freely. What happens if the decisions that may qualify the conduct of a judge as being contrary to the national disciplinary provisions are taken by a body that the executive indirectly controls? It is more than probable that the judges will not feel that the decisions evaluating their conduct will be fair, and they will probably refrain from expressing their opinions against the political choices of the executive.[16] Although it is still only a proposal, it shows that there can be hidden threats that may reduce the extent to which judges feel protected from interference by executive power, as the examples emerging in the Polish and Romanian legal systems already show.[17]

This chapter is structured as follows. The next presents the general principles applicable to judges when they exercise their freedom of expression and shows the interpretation of constitutional provisions in the jurisprudence of the Constitutional Court and the Court of Cassation regarding the legislative

13 Constitutional Court, 8 June 1981, 100.

14 Note that the disciplinary sanctions applicable to judges are included in Legislative Decree 109 of 23 February 2006, whereas the ethical code applicable to judges and lawyers dates back to 1994 and was amended in 2010 <https://www.associazionemagistrati.it/codice-etico>, accessed 23 January 2023.

15 Senate Act 2436, 'Amendments to Title IV of Part II of the Constitution Regarding Establishing a High Court', 28 October 2021.

16 *Baka* v *Hungary* App. no. 20261/12 (ECtHR, 27 May 2014).

17 See, in particular the decisions *A.K. and others* (n 9) CJEU, 18 May 2021, Joined cases C-83/19, C-127/19, C-195/19, C-291/19, C-355/19, and C-397/19, *Asociația 'Forumul Judecătorilor din România' and others* [2021].

provisions defining the code of conduct for judges, highlighting the limited interactions occurring with European courts. Specific attention will be devoted to recent jurisprudence addressing the political involvement of judges, which provides for an exception to this behaviour. Then, the chapter addresses the main challenges emerging from judges using social media and shows how, in the absence of specific guidelines by the legislator, the Court of Cassation has also applied general principles to this different communication medium. The proposal for a High Court to handle disciplinary proceedings against judges is discussed next. The proposal will be compared with the standard provided by the CJEU, emphasising how the need to enhance the independence and impartiality of such disciplinary proceedings in the eyes of the public requires serious analysis of the choices adopted on the composition and appointment of the members of this new court. In the absence of such an analysis, the result would instead reduce judges' independence level *vis-à-vis* political power. Concluding remarks follow.

The role of the judiciary according to the Italian Constitution

The Italian Constitution includes several articles that define the role and position of judges in the institutional framework. The most relevant is Article 101, which introduces the section of the Constitution dedicated to the organisation of the judiciary.

Article 101(1) affirms that "Justice is administered in the name of the people". The terminology used in the text is crucial. Unlike other powers, the administration of justice is not exercised by the people but "in the name of the people". Consequently, the jurisdiction of judges is not based on democratic decisions, and it is excluded from the dynamics of majority consensus.[18] Therefore, judges cannot and should not exercise their role and, in practice, adjudicate cases before them, considering the degree of social consensus they are likely to gain. Similarly, any overexposure of judges to media cannot be justified, as judges should not seek any consensus from public opinion. This provision does not exclude interventions aimed at ensuring a certain level of transparency and comprehensibility of their jurisdiction.[19]

The provision affirms that "Judges are subject only to the law". This provision can be read according to a strict interpretation of the principle of

18 M. Luciani, 'L'etica responsabile del magistrato: la prospettiva costituzionalistica', Quaderni della Scuola di Magistratura (2022) 17, <https://www.scuolamagistratura.it/zh/nuovi-quaderni-ssm-frontend>, accessed 23 January 2023.

19 The institutional communication of judicial offices, as well as the relations of the latter with the mass media, is defined by a Resolution of the High Council of the Judiciary, 11 July 2018. These guidelines incorporate the recommendations and opinions of international bodies (e.g. Recommendation 12 of 2010 of the Committee of Ministers of the Council of Europe; the 1 June 2018 report of the European Network of Councils for the Judiciary; and the opinions of the Consultative Council of European Judges of 2005, 2010, and 2011).

tripartition of the powers of the state, which leads to a double set of limits that apply to judges when they express their opinions. First, we can identify an external limit, which represents a safeguard against (undue) interference by other powers of the state. We can then also place an internal limit, which guarantees that judges, when delivering their decisions, should not be subjected to any conditioning by powers outside the scope of their jurisdiction. As a result, judges should not be limited in their discretion when, in exercising their functions, they are called on to interpret the law and make their procedural determinations, provided that these hermeneutical choices are acknowledged in a coherent and comprehensive argument.[20]

Another relevant provision is Article 111, in which the rules on jurisdiction are defined. Paragraphs 1 and 2 affirm that

> Jurisdiction is implemented through due process regulated by law. All court trials are conducted with adversary proceedings, and the parties are entitled to equal conditions before an impartial judge in a third-party position. The law provides for a reasonable duration of trials.

This provision clearly expresses the principle of impartiality of judges, which is indispensable for them to adjudicate in a neutral position. It must be acknowledged that the principles of impartiality and independence, defined in Article 101 of the Constitution, are interconnected, with impartiality qualified as a functional justification for independence.[21]

Within this framework, the equally constitutionally protected right to freedom of expression should be recognised. Article 21(1) of the Constitution affirms that "Anyone has the right to freely express their thoughts in speech, writing or any other form of communication". This provision does not make any distinction based on the role and position of the individual. Therefore, judges, as individual citizens, enjoy this freedom and have the right to express their opinions and thoughts. Interestingly, the constitutional provision does not include any limitation depending on the type of communication, unlike what is provided in Article 10 ECHR, where the limitations of the freedom of expression principle also include "for maintaining the authority and impartiality of the judiciary".[22] Accordingly, restrictions imposed on the freedom of

20 This provision is also connected to Article 111(5), which states as a general rule that "All judicial measures must state the reasons on which they are based". The obligation of motivation is a corollary to the jurisdictional act: as judges cannot exercise political discretion, they are required to justify their decisions. Accordingly, not only does a lack of motivation lead to the nullity of a decision, but it is also a serious violation of the professional duty of the judge.

21 Elena Paciotti, 'Tre interventi per l'autonomia e l'indipendenza della magistratura', Foro It. (1997) V, 138.

22 See *Simić* v *Bosnia and Herzegovina* App. no. 75255/10 (ECtHR, 15 November 2016), para. 33; *Worm* v *Austria*, Reports 1997-V (ECtHR, 29 August 1997), para. 40. Anja Seibert-Fohr, 'Judges' Freedom of Expression and Their Independence: An Ambivalent Relation-

expression should be justified by the existence of a conflicting constitutionally protected right.

The Constitutional Court already addressed the potential conflict between Article 21 and Articles 101 and 111 in 1981 with its Decision 100.[23] The Decision was triggered by a claim of the unconstitutionality of Article 18 of Royal Decree 511/1946, which provided disciplinary sanctions whenever a judge behaved "either in office or out of it, in such a way as to render him undeserving of the trust and consideration which he should enjoy or to compromise the prestige of the judiciary".

At the outset, the Constitutional Court Decision stated that judges enjoy the same rights guaranteed to any other citizen, including the right to express their opinions and thoughts. Still, this fundamental freedom should be subject to limits prescribed by law, provided that they are based on rules and principles established by the Constitution or inferable from it. In fact, according to the Constitution, judges must be impartial and assisted by the guarantee of independence. These values must be protected with specific reference to the concrete exercise of judicial functions and as a deontological rule to be observed in all behaviour. This is because citizens should not doubt the independence and impartiality of judges in performing their institutional role. According to the Court, to reconcile requirements equally guaranteed by the constitutional order, it is necessary to ensure a balance of these interests with the fundamental right to freedom of expression, with the consequence that any form of "abnormal exercise of the right to freedom of expression of one's ideas, i.e. the abuse that comes into existence when the other values mentioned above are infringed"[24] must be considered inadmissible.

The argumentation of the Constitutional Court implies that the duty of impartiality and independence should be interpreted in both a substantial and a formal way: a judge is not only required to *be* impartial and independent but also to *appear* so. Any conduct that hampers perceptions by citizens regarding impartiality and independence should be avoided as it may affect the overall image of the judiciary. Accordingly, the forms and manners in which judges express their opinions and thoughts should take their institutional role into account, as their conduct should not risk undermining the appearance of impartiality and independence.

---

ship', in Maria Elósegui et al. (eds.), *The Rule of Law in Europe* (Springer, 2021) 95. For a more detailed analysis, see Sietske Dijkstra in this volume.

23 See Constitutional Court, 8 June 1981, 100.

24 Ibid.

This approach was confirmed in the jurisprudence[25] of the Disciplinary Chamber of the High Council of the Judiciary,[26] even though the provision regulating disciplinary sanctions applicable to judges was later modified. The provision was initially replaced with the following text: "Judges should not engage in conduct, even if legitimate, that compromises the personal credibility, prestige and decorum of the magistrate or the prestige of the judicial institution", pursuant to Article 1(2) Legislative Decree 109/2006. It was then wholly erased in accordance with Article 1(3)(a) Law 269/2006.

However, Article 3(1)(h) Legislative Decree 109/2006 still includes a provision addressing a specific aspect of freedom of expression, namely political opinion, as it qualifies as a disciplinary offence: "membership or systematic and continual participation in political parties or involvement in the activities of entities operating in the economic or financial sector that may condition the exercise of functions or otherwise compromise the image of the judiciary".[27] In this case, the Court of Cassation provided an interpretation of the provision in light of constitutional principles in a recent decision.[28] Among a set of pleas, the Court dismissed the question of constitutionality raised by the claimant concerning the above-mentioned provision, as it constituted a limit to the right of members of the judiciary to participate in political life at the national level as protected in Article 49 of the Constitution.[29] The Court clarified that due to applying the rule of law, judges cannot participate in political parties.[30] The internal and external features of the independence of judges should be guaranteed, and this cannot occur if they are influenced by the decisions or preferences of the political parties in which they participate. This does not conflict with the constitutional principle that allows all citizens to participate in political debate, as Article 98(3) of the Constitution enables limitations on the right to join political parties for judges and other categories of public officials if

25 See High Council of Magistracy, Disciplinary Chamber, Decision 23/2014; High Council of Magistracy, Disciplinary Chamber, Decision 92/2016; High Council of Magistracy, Disciplinary Chamber, Decision 61/2017; Decision 50/2020.

26 A disciplinary offence is assessed in judicial proceedings before the High Council of the Magistracy following an action brought by the Attorney General at the Court of Cassation or by the Minister of Justice (Article 107 Constitution). An appeal may be lodged against a decision of acquittal or conviction before the Court of Cassation.

27 See European Parliament, 'La libertà di espressione, una prospettiva di diritto comparato – Italia' (2019), <https://www.europarl.europa.eu/thinktank/en/document/EPRS_STU(2019)644172>, accessed 23 January 2023.

28 Court of Cassation, Joint Chambers, 14 May 2020, 8906.

29 Article 49 of the Constitution provides that: "Any citizen has the right to freely establish parties to contribute to determining national policies through democratic processes".

30 For an analysis of the different roles that politics had until the 1970s in Italy and in Europe, see Enrico Scoditti, 'Magistrato e cittadino: l'imparzialità dell'interprete in discussione', Questione giustizia, 22 November 2023, <https://www.questionegiustizia.it/articolo/magistrato-e-cittadino-l-imparzialita-dell-interprete-in-discussione> accessed 29 February 2024.

established by law.[31] The balance between the right of national judges to participate in political life and the protection of their impartiality and independence implies an absolute prohibition on them becoming members of political parties, even if they do not take part in political party activities. To support its arguments, the Court of Cassation also referred to the European Court of Human Rights (ECtHR) jurisprudence and the importance of the "public image of impartiality" that judges should maintain.[32] It is interesting to note that, among the ECtHR cases mentioned by the Court of Cassation, none was directly related to the participation of judges in political parties,[33] but to the general principles related to the evaluation of impartiality according to the subjective and objective test.[34] In particular, they address in detail the absence of personal prejudice or partiality in a judge: although the impartiality of the judge must be presumed until there is proof to the contrary, the party may present proof that shows that the judge, for instance, has displayed hostility or ill will for personal reasons.[35] In this sense, even appearance may play a role and, according to the ECtHR, "[w]hat is at stake is the confidence which the courts in a democratic society must inspire in the public. Thus, any judge in respect of whom there is a legitimate reason to fear a lack of impartiality must withdraw".[36]

The Court of Cassation drew from the standards mentioned above and highlighted that there is a fine line between active participation in political life and the expression of political ideas. Only the latter does not conflict with the duty of impartiality and is, therefore, permitted. The legislative provision prohibits membership or *systematic and continual* participation in political parties. The Court of Cassation acknowledged that the prohibition applies to all judges without exception, including those not currently exercising judicial functions. According to the Court, this extended application is based on the fact that a judge

31 Article 98(3) of the Constitution states that: "The law may set limitations on the right to become members of political parties in the case of magistrates, career military staff in active service, law enforcement officers, and overseas diplomatic and consular representatives".

32 The Court of Cassation mentioned, without discussing them in detail, the following decisions: *Daineliene* v *Lithuania* (ECtHR 16 October 2018); *Kamenos* v *Cyprus* (ECtHR 31 October 2017); *Karelin* v *Russia* (ECtHR 20 September 2016); *Morice* v *France* (ECtHR (Grand Chamber) 23 April 2015); *Dragojevic* v *Croatia* (ECtHR 15 January 2015).

33 See *Otegi Mondragon and Others v Spain* (ECtHR, 6 November 2018) and *M.D.U. v Italy* (ECtHR 28 January 2003).

34 See *Daineliene* v *Lithuania* (n 32) where the subjective and objective tests are described, respectively, as the existence of any personal prejudice or bias by the judge in a given case, and the presence of sufficient guarantees to exclude any legitimate doubt in respect of the impartiality of the tribunal.

35 See *Morice* v *France* (n 32).

36 See *Daineliene* v *Lithuania* (n 32), para 40.

> never stops having his or her institutional role, being called to answer for conduct even outside the exercise of functions (see Legislative Decree No. 109 of 2006, Art. 3, on the subject of so-called extra-functional disciplinary offences); and a political election does not break, not even temporarily, the judge's bond of belonging to the judicial order, because – as the legislation stands – an elected magistrate, once the electoral mandate has ceased, can return to the exercise of jurisdiction.[37]

This confirms what has been affirmed above: the "bond" between the judge and their institutional role cannot be broken, and this appears even in more vital terms when looking at the sensitive case of participation in political life and the expression of political ideas.

Freedom of expression on social media

The sensitive balance between judges' freedom to express opinions and thoughts and the principles of impartiality and independence is even more relevant in the case of judicial communication on social media. In this context, the 'appearance' of impartiality may end up on a slippery slope due to the specific features of social media. Social media are used to communicate, connect, and interact online with other people. Therefore, any personal profile created on a social media platform may directly or indirectly include information about one's unique background, interests, and political views. In this context, it is easy for the private and professional spheres to blend.[38]

Although the rules applicable to the conduct of judges do not distinguish between the media through which the expression is made, but instead the content and the manner of the expression, it is essential to consider that compared to traditional forms of communication, social media present some additional hidden risks that judges need to be aware of. Among the most relevant features that may hamper the appearance of impartiality, the most evident one is the possibility of linking the personal profile of a judge to other people who may be qualified according to the platform as friends or followers.[39] These definitions can be perceived as closer personal relationships than that existing between the judge and the specific persons. Moreover, participation on social media platforms may entail a lower level of control over the privacy of communication. For instance, information posted on social media is easily accessed and disseminated and may not remain private despite strict privacy settings. Additionally, the obligation to avoid actual or perceived bias requires judges

37 See Court of Cassation, 8906/2020 (n 28), point 8.2.

38 Jannika Jahn, 'Social Media Communication by Judges: Assessing Guidelines and New Challenges for Free Speech and Judicial Duties in the Light of the Convention', in Maria Elósegui et al. (eds.), *The Rule of Law in Europe* (Springer, 2021) 145.

39 See *Chaves Fernandes Figueiredo v Switzerland* (ECtHR 28 August 2018).

to not only refrain from making or "liking" inappropriate comments but also to delete such comments made by others from their profiles.[40]

These risks are shared by judges in every legal system, triggering a legislative or soft law intervention in many of them. In Italy, judges' use of social media is not subject to specific regulations, not even in the form of non-binding rules acting as guidelines or recommendations.[41] However, this conduct can be governed by general provisions addressing judicial conduct and ethical rules. This approach has also been confirmed by an intervention by the President of the Republic (also President of the High Council of the Magistracy) on the occasion of the inauguration of training courses at the Superior School of the Magistracy in 2019.[42] In his speech, the President stressed that compliance with the rules of conduct requires strict self-restraint in the use of social networks and mailing lists because these tools, if not managed with attention and discretion, can undermine the confidentiality that must distinguish the actions of magistrates and could tarnish the credibility and prestige of the judicial function.[43]

Although there have been few cases, a couple of recent decisions by the Court of Cassation provide interesting insights into how the general rules of conduct are interpreted and applied in cases regarding social media.

Decision 6965/2017 of the Court of Cassation addressed an intervention by a judge in a blog discussion forum. The judge participated in a heated debate on the efficiency of the public administration. He aggressively defended the public administration at the expense of the reputation of the local bar association.[44] This was condemned by the bar association president and triggered a proceeding before the disciplinary section of the High Council of the Magistracy. This resulted in a disciplinary sanction of the judge for damaging the reputation of the judiciary and incorrect severe conduct in the exercise of judicial functions, pursuant to Article 2(1)(d) and Article 4(1)(d) Legislative

40 Francesco Buffa, 'La libertà di espressione dei magistrati e la Convenzione europea dei diritti dell'uomo', *Questione giustizia* (2022) <https://www.questionegiustizia.it/data/doc/3256/parigibuffa.pdf>, accessed 23 January 2023.

41 It must be acknowledged that at its meeting on 25 March 2021 the Presidential Council of Administrative Justice adopted a resolution on the use of electronic and social media by administrative judges. Although these guidelines do not apply to ordinary magistrates, they are nevertheless important as they recall, first of all, the need for the use of social media to be in such a way as to ensure respect for the rights of citizens and the dignity, integrity, impartiality, and independence of the magistrate and the entire body of administrative judiciary. In addition, with regard to administrative judges, they explain that there is a need to comply with the canon of continual expression, which for ordinary judges can already be deduced from the aforementioned ethical rules that prescribe sobriety and composure of conduct.

42 See the national report dedicated to Italy in AAVV (n 1) 66.

43 See Luca Longhi, 'I magistrati e l'uso dei social. Appunti sulla deontologia professionale di categoria nell'era della comunicazione di massa', Diritto Pubblico Europeo (2019) 1, <http://www.serena.unina.it/index.php/dperonline/article/view/6522>, accessed 23 January 2023.

44 Court of Cassation, Joint Chambers, 17 March 2017, 6965.

Decree 109/2006. The decision was then appealed before the Court of Cassation.

The Court of Cassation overturned the decision of the Disciplinary Chamber. It upheld the appeal that the defamatory statement could not be qualified as a criminal offence in the specific case. The defamation should be addressed to an identified or identifiable victim to be considered a criminal offence. The expression used by the judge did not allow a specific victim to be identified and so could not be sanctioned.

The Court of Cassation then considered whether the judge had lawfully exercised his freedom of expression. In particular, it focused on the possibility of qualifying the judge's expressions as an exercise of his institutional functions, as they were related to the issue of the administration of justice. If this was the case, the conduct could have been sanctioned under Article 2(d) Legislative Decree 109/2006. The interpretation of the Court of Cassation rejected this approach. It affirmed that when the content of the expression concerns opinions on the organisation of a judicial office and its functioning, or on the behaviour of subjects working in that office, the judge is still expressing their personal opinion, which does not qualify as an exercise of their institutional function. This interpretation is extremely relevant as the alternative would have prohibited judges from participating in discussion forums based on the possibility that potential trial parties and defenders may also participate.

Another decision that addressed the use of social media and required interpretation by the Court of Cassation was Decision 18987/2017.[45] In this case, a judge published a comment about the Mayor of Rome on his social network profile. The comment was deemed defamatory, and the judge was subjected to a disciplinary proceeding, dismissing the claim as the offence could not be sanctioned because it was of minor importance, following Article 3*bis* Legislative Decree 109/2006. However, the prosecutor appealed before the Court of Cassation against the decision of the Disciplinary Chamber. The Court of Cassation overturned the decision. In particular, it affirmed that using words and expressions that can be socially interpreted as offensive is crucial in defamation cases. Even though in the case at stake, the addressee of the defamatory statements did not perceive them as offensive, it was still relevant that an individual judge's conduct may taint the judiciary's reputation. As a result, the Court of Cassation affirmed that the seriousness of the offence should not be evaluated according to the victim's attitude.

This case was another example of the intertwining between the role of an individual judge and their membership in the judiciary. Inappropriate use of social networks by a judge cannot go unpunished because published defamatory content damages the institution's reputation. This is in line with the most recent jurisprudence of the ECtHR, which addressed the case of a judge subject to disciplinary sanctions due to the publication of a couple of posts on a

45 Court of Cassation, Joint Chambers, 31 July 2017, 18987.

social network.[46] According to the Strasbourg Court, the criteria to be considered when assessing the attack on the dignity and honour of the judicial profession should be the broader context in which the applicant's statements are made, the fact that the opinions addressed matters of public interest, the qualification as a value judgment, and the potentially chilling effect of the sanction.

Creating a High Court for disciplinary proceedings

As mentioned above, a judge's conduct that may be qualified as a disciplinary offence should be assessed in judicial proceedings before the Disciplinary Chamber of the High Council of the Magistracy. The action can be brought by either the Attorney General in the Court of Cassation or by the Minister of Justice, according to Article 107 of the Constitution. The decision of the Disciplinary Chamber is subject to appeal before the Court of Cassation, which decides in Joint Chambers. This procedure ensures that the conduct is fairly evaluated by fellow judges and is not subject to external pressure or influence.

A proposal to reform this structure has recently been made in Parliament,[47] namely, a constitutional bill submitted to the Senate in October 2021 entitled "Amendments to Title IV of Part II of the Constitution regarding establishing a High Court".[48] The proposed legislation introduces four new articles in the text of the Constitution: Articles 105*bis*, *ter*, *quater*, and *quinquies*. The bill proposes creating a new High Court to hear appeals against disciplinary measures and other measures concerning magistrates adopted by the self-government organs. The High Court would be composed of 15 members: judges chosen from practising and retired judges, including ones retired from the higher courts, ordinary professors of legal subjects, and lawyers with 20 years of experience. The members of the High Court would be appointed in the same way as those of the Constitutional Court: a third appointed by the President

46 See *Danilet v Romania* (ECtHR, 24 February 2024).

47 It should be acknowledged that the proposal to create a High Court is not new. In fact, it has been repeatedly presented in constitutional bills over the last three decades. These are the Senate Act no. 2583 of 1997 (which proposed creating a Court of Justice for the Judiciary composed of nine members elected from their own members by the higher councils of the ordinary and administrative judiciary); the Senate Act 1642 of 2002 (which proposed amending Articles 15, 68, and 105 of the Constitution to create a High Court of Justice in charge not only of disciplinary proceedings but also of authorising proceedings against members of parliament); the House Act 4275 of 2011 (which proposed the creation of a Court for disciplinary proceedings with a section for judges and one for prosecutors, the decisions of which would be appealable in cassation on grounds of legitimacy); and finally the House Act 2709 of 2020 (again proposing a High Court of Justice only in charge of disciplinary proceedings against judges and prosecutors). For a detailed analysis, see Claudio Castelli, 'Il sistema disciplinare dei magistrati: una cosa seria', Costituzionalismo.it (2022), I, 132, <https://www.costituzionalismo.it/wp-content/uploads/1-2022-6.-Castelli.pdf>, accessed 23 January 2023.

48 Senate Act No. 2436, 'Amendments to Title IV of Part II of the Constitution Regarding the Establishment of a High Court', 28 October 2021.

of the Republic, a third by the Parliament, and a third by the supreme ordinary and administrative judiciary. The proceedings before it would be divided into two degrees of jurisdiction: the first degree before a panel of three members and appeals before the plenum.

It should be acknowledged that this bill was triggered by a crisis of credibility that has affected the self-governance body in recent years.[49] The report accompanying the bill stresses that the High Court would provide a solid signal to disentangle the control of acts adopted in the organisational sphere by the High Council of the Judiciary from ones enforcing disciplinary measures.

Although, in theory, this approach may have some positive features, some aspects of the proposed bill raise doubts regarding the independence of judges and their ability to express themselves freely. A first element is that proceedings before the High Court would be wholly disentangled from adjudication before the Court of Cassation and, consequently, from its jurisprudence. In the current structure, an appeal before the Court of Cassation is formally a judgment and falls within the general nomophylactic function of the Court. This means that decisions of the Court of Cassation can reconcile the application of the rules regarding disciplinary sanctions with the more general jurisprudence of the Court.[50] In the proposed structure, instead, decisions by the High Court will not have any link with the jurisprudence of the Court of Cassation, eventually leading to special – or relatively differentiated – treatment for judges.

The second element is that the composition of the High Court would not exclude possible (indirect) interference by the executive in the independence of the judiciary. As mentioned above, among the 15 members of the High Court, only a third would have previous experience in judicial activity. At the same time, the other two-thirds would be composed of lawyers and academics. The aim of the proposal is to introduce an exogenous component in the body in charge of evaluating judges' conduct to enhance the possibility of achieving independence and impartial decisions. However, it is not guaranteed that allocating the appointment of the majority of the members outside the judiciary would ensure a fairer evaluation of conduct. Moreover, the executive would select some members, and the Parliament would appoint a third. How would this appointment procedure ensure that the chosen members do not feel indirect pressure from the government? Or, vice versa, how would this appointment procedure ensure that potential members (judges, lawyers,

49 Ibid.

50 For instance, when a magistrate is charged with the offence covered by Art. 2 (1)(g), Legislative Decree 106/2009, a serious violation of the law brought about by inexcusable ignorance or negligence, the interpretation of the provision by the Disciplinary Chamber of the High Court of Judiciary will be evaluated vis-à-vis the interpretation already defined by the Court of Cassation.

or academics) would not seek the attention of political parties to be elected?[51] It is interesting to mention that these arguments are the same presented by the CJEU in evaluating the impartiality and independence of the Disciplinary Chamber in recent rule of law cases. As mentioned above, the CJEU affirmed that the appointment procedures applicable for the selection of the members of the body responsible for conducting disciplinary investigations and bringing disciplinary proceedings against judges should not "give rise to reasonable doubts that the powers and functions of that body may be used as an instrument to exert pressure on, or political control over, the activity of those judges".[52] If such guarantees are not present, the disciplinary body would be in contrast with Articles 2 and 19 TEU.

Interestingly, some commentators on the proposal have put forward a different composition that would achieve this result: two-thirds of the members selected by the judiciary, chosen from the most senior magistrates, already retired, with participation in the panel adjudicating in the first instance of at least two judges. Only the remaining third of the members would be appointed by the President of the Republic, but from a shortlist of members of the legal profession to be identified with criteria still to be better specified.[53]

Introducing a High Court has been justified by the lack of effectiveness of the current enforcement system in deciding cases of misconduct by judges. Given that judgments on the disciplinary liability of judges are allocated to their self-governing bodies and, on appeal, to the same judicial network to which the judge subject to the proceedings belongs, citizens may perceive that in both trials, the judges evaluating the conduct of their fellows will have difficulty in sanctioning them.[54] This lack of third-party status is a factor that seriously undermines the credibility of the judicial system and public trust. This argument is not without merit, but the proposed bill's choices still do not guarantee, or at least appear to guarantee, the necessary level of independence and impartiality.

51 P. Filippi and Roberto Conti, 'Forum sull'Istituzione dell'Alta Corte. La rivoluzione dell'assetto giurisdizionale in vista dell'istituzione di una giurisdizione speciale per i giudici', interview with V. Zagrebelsky, 23 March 2022, <https://www.giustiziainsieme.it/en/costituzione-e-carta-dei-diritti-fondamentali/2246-forum-sull-istituzione-dell-alta-corte-la-rivoluzione-dell-assetto-giurisdizionale-in-vista-dell-istituzione-di-una-giurisdizione-speciale-per-i-giudici-vladimiro-zagrebelsky>, accessed 23 January 2023.

52 See *Asociația 'Forumul Judecătorilor din România' et al.* (n 17), para 207.

53 Paola Filippi and Roberto Conti, 'Forum sull'Istituzione dell'Alta Corte. La rivoluzione dell'assetto giurisdizionale in vista dell'istituzione di una giurisdizione speciale per i giudici', interview with Maria Alessandra Sandulli, 28 March 2022, <https://www.giustiziainsieme.it/en/costituzione-e-carta-dei-diritti-fondamentali/2252-forum-sull-istituzione-dell-alta-corte-la-rivoluzione-dell-assetto-giurisdizionale-in-vista-dell-istituzione-di-una-giurisdizione-speciale-per-i-giudici-maria-alessandra-sandulli >, accessed 23 January 2023.

54 Contra Castelli, (n 47) 125 ff.

Conclusion

The Italian framework provides an interesting example of a country where participation by judges in public debate has always occurred, showing both the positive and adverse effects that this participation may have. On the one hand, judges can make the justice system accessible to citizens, who have a right to know how justice is administered and how judges, subject only to the law, exercise their judicial power.[55] The form and manner of the expression are crucial when a judge expresses opinions on behalf of the judicial institution and when the opinions are individual. On the other hand, there is a risk of instrumentalising judges' interventions to gain a wider audience with an indirect tarnishing effect on the judiciary's reputation.

In this context, principles enshrined in the Constitution play a crucial role, namely Article 21 on freedom of expression and Article 101 on the role of judges. The Constitutional Court has recognised that judges enjoy the same right to freedom of expression attributed to anyone by Article 21 of the Constitution. Still, at the same time, the Court has acknowledged that the exercise of this right cannot be without limits, specifying that the value of impartiality and that of independence, which Article 101 of the Constitution also protects, "are to be safeguarded not only with specific reference to the concrete exercise of judicial functions but also as a deontological rule to be observed in all behaviour to avoid that [judicial] independence and impartiality may be justifiably doubted".

The precarious balance between freedom of expression and independence and impartiality is even more problematic in the case of social media, where the publication of a "post" (whether it consists of a news item, a comment, or even an image) is, as a rule, followed by a series of reactions, so that through sharing and liking, the users of platforms further disseminate the content. In this regard, the jurisprudence of the Court of Cassation interprets legislative provisions defining the judiciary's code of conduct, meaning that any content

55 See also High Council of the Judiciary, 'Guidelines for the Organisation of Judicial Offices for the Purpose of Effective Public Information and Proper Institutional Communication'. 11 June 2018, which starts with the premise that "the transparency and comprehensibility of judicial proceedings are values that derive from the democratic character of the system and are related to the principles of independence and autonomy of the judiciary and to a modern conception of the responsibility of magistrates" and traces "guidelines inspired by the conviction that transparency and comprehensibility of jurisdiction do not conflict with the confidential, sometimes secret, character of the judicial function" and that "correctly interpreted" they "increase public confidence in justice and the rule of law, strengthen the independence of the judiciary and, more generally, the authority of institutions".

See Luigi Ferrarella, 'Non per dovere, ma per interesse (dei cittadini): i magistrati e la paura di spiegarsi', Questione giustizia (2018), 4, <https://www.questionegiustizia.it/rivista/articolo/non-per-dovere-ma-per-interesse-dei-cittadini-i-magistrati-e-la-paura-di-spiegarsi_610.php> accessed 23 January 2023; Edmondo Bruti Liberati, 'Un punto di arrivo o un punto di partenza?', Questione giustizia (2018), 4, <https://www.questionegiustizia.it/rivista/articolo/un-punto-di-arrivo-o-un-punto-di-partenza-_611.php>, accessed 23 January 2023.

published online by a judge should consider their institutional role. In particular, Decision 18987/2017 of the Court of Cassation shows that even if conduct cannot be sanctioned as a criminal offence, the conduct of an individual judge may still negatively affect the reputation of the judicial institution.

The crisis of legitimacy has affected many Councils of the Magistracy at the European level, not only in the so-called backsliding democracies but also in democratic states such as Spain and Portugal recently.[56] This is primarily due to the fact that self-governance bodies have lost, in the eyes of the public, their reputations as independent bodies for the organisation and enforcement of the judicial system. A similar situation can be found in Italy, where tension between the judiciary and the executive has often triggered the presentation of constitutional reform proposals to move sanctioning powers away from the High Council of the Magistracy in cases of disciplinary proceedings against judges. The proposal presented in October 2021, however, does not consider the implications that the creation of a High Court would entail if its composition and appointment are not carefully evaluated. The risk that emerges is an undue influence of executive power on the decisions of the High Court without any guarantee that participation by members coming from outside the judiciary would be able to comprehend the specific position of judges in the institutional framework.

56 See the national report on Portugal and on Spain, both in AA.VV. (n1), respectively 103 and 173.

Part 3

Epilogue

9 (Personal) reflections on (legal) developments concerning freedom of expression of judges

Boštjan Zalar

Introduction: is freedom of expression of judges an end in itself or a means to protect higher values?

In October 2021, I participated in the "Judges as Citizens: Time to End Self Isolation?" roundtable organised by the Faculty of Law of the University of Ljubljana within the TRIIAL Project. There were two reasons that I accepted invitations to participate in that roundtable and to join the other contributors in this book on the issue of the freedom of expression of judges.

The first reason is the wealth of my personal experience in the area covered by this edited volume. I began to exercise freedom of expression related to my involvement in the judiciary 25 years ago. In 1999, while a researcher and Assistant Professor at the Faculty of Social Sciences of the University of Ljubljana, I started to work as a Senior Expert Associate at the Administrative Court of the Republic of Slovenia. The Open Society Institute selected me to prepare an independent evaluation report on the preparedness of the Slovenian judiciary for accession to the European Union. That project was part of the formal EU accession monitoring programme. At that time, my public interventions at professional events were related to the preparations of Slovenian courts for accession to the European Union.

In 2001, I began to exercise my freedom of expression also in European and international judicial (and legal) communities. This was related to my expertise in human rights law and the effective integration of the case law of the ECtHR into the domestic jurisprudence of the Contracting States. In 2004, I was elected a High Court Judge by the Parliament of the Republic of Slovenia upon the proposal of the Judicial Council. After 2004, I intensified my public interventions in Slovenia and in other (mostly) European countries as a trainer of judges (and lawyers) mostly on the topic of the effective implementation of EU law, especially the Charter of Fundamental Rights of the European Union in conjunction with the case law of the ECtHR in domestic jurisprudence. Around 2006, I gained more formal responsibilities by being selected to be the co-chair of some international judicial networks. These were the Association of European Administrative Judges (AEAJ), where I acted as a co-chair of the Working Group on Asylum and Immigration, and the

DOI: 10.4324/9781003470779-12

International Association of Refugee and Migration Judges (IARMJ), where I had similar functions in various working groups. This was the time when the judgment of the Grand Chamber of the ECtHR in the case *Vilho Eskelinen and Others v Finland* was issued, which opened a path for the eventual protection of various aspects of a judicial career under Article 6 of the Convention for the Protection of Human Rights and Fundamental Freedoms (ECHR).[1] However, in that period, as a judge who had been exercising limited aspects of freedom of expression, I was not attentive to the huge (positive) implications of paragraph 62 of that judgment for the protection of judicial independence.[2] With that paragraph, the ECtHR relativised the concept of the "special bond of trust and loyalty" between a judge as a civil servant and the State as an employer.[3] I realised the importance of the *Vilho Eskelinen* test from paragraph 62 only when I was assigned to be judge rapporteur regarding the first set of cases brought by Slovenian judges to my court against the decisions of the Judicial Council on the dismissal of judges[4] or on the selection of presidents of courts.[5] Thus, in the period from 2013 until 2017, the Administrative Court, based on the case of *Vilho Eskelinen,* started to develop and protect standards under Article 6 of the ECHR in administrative disputes on judicial careers. However, in April 2017, upon the proposal of the Judicial Council, the Parliament adopted a new law, which took away the competence of the Administrative Court to provide judicial control over decisions of the Judicial Council in matters of judicial careers and transferred that competence to the administrative law section of the Supreme Court. The new law introduced a more limited scope of judicial review as it was developed by the Administrative Court in its practice, hence it narrowed effective legal remedies against decisions of the Judicial Council.[6]

1 *Vilho Eskelinen and Others v Finland* App no 63235/00 (ECHR (GC), 19 April 2007).

2 In paragraph 62, the Court stated that in order for the State to be able to rely before the ECtHR on the applicant's status as a civil servant in excluding the protection embodied in Article 6, two conditions must be fulfilled. Firstly, the State in its national law must have expressly excluded access to a court for the post or category of staff in question. Secondly, the exclusion must be justified on objective grounds in the State's interest.

3 Ibid.

4 Among the contested decisions of the Judicial Council, there was also a decision to dismiss a judge because she managed to decide (only) 85% of the expected number of cases per year under the circumstances that no appeal against her judgments was successful before the higher court (judgment of the Administrative Court in the case IV U 213/2014, 5 November 2014). The English summary and analysis of this case are available in the Centre for Judicial Cooperation (the CJC) database: https://cjc.eui.eu/data/data/data?idPermanent=248&triial=1 <accessed 8 May 2024>.

5 Judgment of the Administrative Court in the case I U 1103/2013, 13 May 2013. The English summary and analysis of this case are available in the CJC database: https://cjc.eui.eu/data/data/data?idPermanent=243&triial=1 <accessed 8 May 2024>.

6 Judicial Council Act, Official Journal of the Republic of Slovenia, 23/2017, Articles 36(2) and 36(5). Surprisingly, the Administrative Court remained a competent court to control the legality of decisions concerning the careers of public prosecutors.

From 2011 onwards, I was actively involved in various projects of the European Law Institute (ELI), which is a network of academics, lawyers, judges, and various (inter)national institutions, including around 15 supreme courts. The ELI's projects with my active participation and public interventions ranged from potential reform in EU administrative procedural law, the rule of law in detention cases involving foreigners under EU secondary law on asylum and return, the crisis of judicial independence, common constitutional principles in the European Union and a project on better managing the case-overload at the ECtHR. In 2012, I began to act as a representative of the Slovenian judiciary and of the European Chapter of the IARMJ (IARMJ-Europe) in the Network of Courts and Tribunals of the European Asylum Support Office (EASO, now the European Union Agency for Asylum – EUAA). A lot of effort was needed and is still needed by judges in that network to consolidate the mandate of the EUAA for training of judges and for monitoring courts and tribunals with the principle of judicial independence.

In 2015, I was elected Vice-President of the IARMJ-Europe, which had around 300 members (judges). At that time, I gradually started to include in some of my oral presentations elements for the empowerment of judges in a particular political context and the emerging rule of law crisis in Europe. In June 2016, the Grand Chamber judgment in *Baka v Hungary* was published. In this case, the ECtHR introduced the concept of the "duty" of a judge to promote and protect judicial independence (partly) depending on his or her special position in the judicial system.[7] Two years later, when I began my six-year period of office as President of the IARMJ-Europe, it was a turning point for me because as the President of the IARMJ-Europe, I was particularly attentive to every occasion when I had to react and raise arguments related to judicial independence at international events, regardless of whether the context was partly political or not.

Thus, in the last 25 years, I have participated as a speaker outside Slovenia in around 33 different countries at 142 training events for judges and lawyers organised by (other) public entities, such as the EJTN, ERA, UNHCR, or in other more publicly open forums that were organised by (inter)national (non-governmental) organisations. In addition, I have spoken publicly at around 48 professional events for judges and lawyers in Slovenia. Therefore, this is the first reason for contributing a chapter in this book on my personal reflections on (legal) developments concerning the freedom of expression of judges.

The second reason that I accepted the aforementioned invitations is that, particularly in cases of freedom of expression in public discourse in Slovenia, I have tried to draw and show my colleagues the thin and sensitive borderline between acceptable and unacceptable "freedom" of expression for judges. For example, in 2016, I gave two interviews for weekly editions of supplements to two newspapers in Slovenia, considered by the general public to be two of

7 *Baka v Hungary* App no 20261/12 (ECHR (GC) 23 June 2016), para 168.

the three of the most professional weekly newspapers. These were interviews on the subjects of effective implementation of European human rights law in asylum disputes and in disputes where children are involved. Because of those interviews, two or three superior judicial colleagues initiated a procedure before the Ethics and Integrity Commission in order to verify whether my interviews were in line with the Code of Judicial Ethics. The Ethics and Integrity Commission was at that time a newly established entity attached to the Judicial Council. It was not composed exclusively of judges. The Ethics and Integrity Commission found my interviews to be *prima facie* in line with the Code of Judicial Ethics.[8] However, this is only one example of the "chilling effects" that I have experienced in my judicial career from the relevant judicial actors in Slovenia.[9]

Throughout those 25 years and with the support of the case law of the ECtHR, I learnt to understand more firmly that the right to freedom of expression of a judge is not an end in itself, although it is a fundamental right under Article 10 of the ECHR. Rather, it is a means to preserve higher values – the quality of the justice system, the appearance of, and a general trust in judicial independence, which includes the paramount imperative for the subjective and objective impartiality of judges in each individual case.

In the following five sub-sections, I will put some flesh on the bones of this introductory statement based on my experiences with freedom of expression in the judiciary. I will build on my speech at the roundtable entitled "Judges as Citizens: Time to End Self Isolation?" and will add some thoughts for eventual further reflections on past (legal) developments and future challenges as regards the exercise of freedom of expression of judges. For this, I owe a debt of gratitude to all the other authors in this book since I had a chance to read their draft contributions before finalising mine.

The end of the world as we know it

In 1999, Immanuel Wallerstein wrote a book entitled *The End of the World as We Know It*. The book is divided into two sections: the section on "The World of Capitalism" and the section on "The World of Knowledge". Wallerstein started the book with three premises. His first premise was that progress, unlike what the Enlightenment in all its forms preached, is not at

8 The English summary and analysis of the reasoned opinion of the Ethics and Integrity Commission from 9 November 2016 is available in the CJC database: https://cjc.eui.eu/data/data/data?idPermanent=634&triial=1 <accessed 8 May 2024>.

9 For the concept of "chilling effect" in relation to the exercise and protection of fundamental rights, see: Mohor Fajdiga, 'Chilling Effect: Turning the Poison into an Antidote for Fundamental Rights in Europe', Maastricht Journal of European and Comparative Law, 2024, 31(1), 9–26.

all inevitable.[10] Wallerstein's second premise was that the belief in certainties, a fundamental premise of modernity, is blinding and crippling. His third premise was that in human social systems, the most complex systems in the universe, and therefore the hardest to analyse, the struggle for a good society is a continuing one.[11] Wallerstein also pointed out the problem of the crisis of the legitimacy of political power because of the loss of hope by the popular masses in liberal reformism[12] and he mentioned false assumptions about the inward and outward sovereignty of the state. As regards the latter, he pointed out that the entire corpus of international law represents a series of limitations, while on the other hand, no modern state has ever been truly inwardly sovereign since there has always been internal resistance to its authority, including constitutional laws.[13]

Despite Wallerstein's warnings and several even earlier concerns or predictions of other prominent sociologists,[14] probably very few, if anyone at all, predicted that the centuries-old tradition of the independence of the courts in the United Kingdom would be so easily attacked and harmed after the Brexit ruling in the *Miller* case. When on 4 November 2016 the *Daily Mail* published on the front page a big picture of the three judges of the High Court of England and Wales, including Chief Justice Lord Thomas, with the caption: "Enemies of the People", the Minister for Justice did not want to react properly according to the several-centuries-long legal tradition in that country, where in such circumstances the Minister would protect the independence of the British judiciary. Similarly, no one probably predicted that Catalan politicians and public intellectuals would one day seek asylum in other European countries; or that judges from Eastern Europe would send orders for preliminary rulings to the Court of Justice of the EU (CJEU) under the threat of disciplinary proceedings; or that a judge of the constitutional court

10 No doubt that in this context it is of crucial importance to note the new principle of the rule of law (the so-called non-regression principle) that was introduced by the CJEU in the case of *Repubblika*: "A Member State cannot amend its legislation in such a way as to bring about a reduction in the protection of the value of the rule of law, a value which is given concrete expression by, *inter alia*, Article 19 TEU. The Member States are thus required to ensure that, in the light of that value, any regression of their laws on the organisation of justice is prevented, by refraining from adopting rules which would undermine the independence of the judiciary". (Case C-896/19, *Repubblika*, 20 April 2021, paras 63–64).

11 Immanuel Wallerstein, *The End of the World as We Know It* (University of Minnesota Press 2021), pp. 2–3.

12 Ibid., p. 73.

13 Ibid., p. 60.

14 Niklas Luhmann, for example, already back in 1972, predicted that in the future, the democratic state of law could only be remembered as some unusual, socially unacceptable link in the development of humanity which was dominant only for a short period of time. Twenty-six years later, Jürgen Habermas asked a similar question, whether democracy will survive globalisation at all (Poul Kjaer, *Between Governing and Governance: On the Emergence, Function and Form of Europe's Post-National Constellation* (Hart Publishing 2010), p. 1).

of a Member State of the European Union would ever refer extensively to "media" sources owned and run by the political party in power in support of his separate opinion in a particular case before the constitutional court, while at the same time accusing his colleagues on the bench of politicisation. One cannot exclude from this context the situation when a (successful) candidate for President of the United States in 2016, during his election campaign, said in public: "I could stand in the middle of Fifth Avenue and shoot somebody, and I wouldn't lose any voters, OK?"[15]

These and many other similar circumstances are indeed new, and they have a tremendous impact on the rule of law situation in Europe. We must face them and start changing them for the better immediately and strategically. In my estimation, for example in Slovenia, we would need at least ten years or more to eliminate the new phenomena in the rule of law context – even if we tackled the matter today at the critical points within the judiciary, with competent people and substantial amendments to the Judicial Council Act. Perhaps the turning point was 18 years ago when five judges of the Supreme Court gave strong public support to a political candidate in local elections in the capital city, while the judicial system or the judicial community itself did not process that new phenomenon with sufficient care.[16] Therefore, answers to the question of where those critical points of the rule of law crisis in Europe are embedded substantially differ from country to country, and the answers to the question of to what extent the right to freedom of public expression of judges in a particular country can contribute to solving the problems of the rule of law are also different.

Hence, the main subject behind this book, at least as I see it, is not so much the right to freedom of expression of judges, but rather the crisis of the rule of law and possible means to eliminate certain elements of that crisis. I am referring to the crisis of the rule of law, which is reflected either in cases where the ECtHR found a violation of the right under Article 10 of the ECHR committed by domestic authorities (mostly by judicial councils or similar authorities and domestic courts) or where the ECtHR found a violation of the standards under Article 6 of the ECHR in the context of exercising freedom of expression by judges, or in cases where interferences in judges' freedom of expression by domestic authorities have been in accordance with the ECHR and therefore those judges (applicants) misused their freedoms. The higher the number

15 Colin Dwyer, 'Donald Trump: "I Could … Shoot Somebody, And I wouldn't Lose Any Voters"' (*National Public Radio*, 23 January 2016) <https://www.npr.org/sections/thetwo-way/2016/01/23/464129029/donald-trump-i-could-shoot-somebody-and-i-wouldnt-lose-any-voters> (accessed 8 May 2024).

16 An individual judge questioned this behaviour before the Council of Judicial Ethics of the Slovenian Association of Judges, but eventually, the judge decided to withdraw the request. This led the Council of Judicial Ethics to terminate the procedure (Council of Judicial Ethics of the Slovenian Association of Judges, Order of 9 October 2006 <https://sodnisko-drustvo.si/podpora-sodnika-kandidatu-politicne-stranke/> <accessed 8 May 2024>.

of these three types of cases before the ECtHR, the stronger the signs that in those countries there is a great deal of misunderstanding and weaknesses in the rule of law. Where there are no cases against a particular Contracting State before the ECtHR on freedom of expression of judges, this does not mean that problems of internal or external judicial independence do not exist. In such a case, one needs to analyse decisions and cases on the freedom of expression of judges before domestic authorities, which are responsible particularly for so-called "judicial ethics" issues and for disciplinary sanctions against judges.

I doubt very much that judges really need the right to freedom of expression as much as this is perhaps visible in expanded academic literature and in the case law of the ECtHR in the last ten years. What judges really need are good and necessary conditions so that they can professionally, independently, and impartially adjudicate cases in a working environment of collegiality. In such ("normal") circumstances, the freedom of expression of judges would not be an issue at all in the case-flow of the ECtHR. Rather, from time to time, judges would ask for guidelines or would refer questions to specially designed collegiate bodies for judicial ethics, composed exclusively of judges, on how to act or what would be ethically unproblematic behaviour or conduct in a particular situation. Such collegiate bodies would then develop good practices, standards and recommendations as guiding principles for the behaviour of judges in their private and professional life. That would be a "normal" situation, which unfortunately no longer exists in many countries. In Slovenia, for example, we had this idea and some (but not sufficient) practice in place until 2017 within the structure of the Slovenian Association of Judges (SAJ, founded in 1971). In 2001, the SAJ adopted the Code of Judicial Ethics and its commentary. However, in Slovenia, judges did not manage to preserve and further develop that idea of autonomously managing ethical questions in the judiciary, which is an essential aspect of quality and knowledge management in the judiciary. Instead, with the new Judicial Council Act in 2017, we entered a period where we have legal disputes initiated by judges against judges under the rules of the Ethics and Integrity Commission, while the Council of Judicial Ethics at the Slovenian Association of Judges completely lost its function and is today a dormant entity.

Therefore, what light has been shed thus far by the ECtHR on legal disputes concerning judges' freedom of expression, which could partly assist us in finding the way forward for a more meaningful realisation of judges' right to freedom of expression without having frequent legal disputes among judges themselves on these matters?

Judges: loyal to whom or loyal to what?

At the very start of the development of the case law on freedom of expression for judges related to the ECHR, in *Hans-Christian Leiningen-Weserburg v Austria*, the Commission of Human Rights stated that the "authority of the judiciary" and the "protection of the reputation of other colleagues" (judges) is a legitimate aim for which an interference with the right of a judge under Article 10 of the ECHR may be compatible with the ECHR. For an interference to be necessary in response to a pressing social need, the national authorities must provide "relevant and sufficient" reasons. In this context, a margin of appreciation was mentioned. In that Austrian case, a judge sanctioned in disciplinary proceedings had said: "The judiciary is a whore". He made a disparaging remark about a colleague in a conversation with a journalist. His statement accused the judiciary of lacking impartiality and insinuated that the courts were open to bribery. The Commission of Human Rights concluded that such criticism of a judge went far beyond normal criticism and that it could undermine the credibility of the judiciary. The domestic courts considered all the circumstances of the case, which included the argument of excessive criticism that lacked a factual basis, and the fact that the applicant ought to have been aware of the risk that those statements would be published.[17]

At first glance, it seems that – apart from the aforementioned *Vilho Eskelinen* test from 2007 – since the case of *Hans-Christian Leiningen-Weserburg*, the ECtHR has not significantly changed the methodology for dealing with the right to freedom of expression of judges, although cases on the expression of judges which have come before the ECtHR since 1997 have been quite different, and some of them have brought significant (solely) positive implications for the freedom of expression of judges. However, almost 20 years later, in the landmark judgment in the case *Baka v Hungary*, the Grand Chamber added or reiterated several important (new) legal dimensions concerning the freedom of expression of judges.

In *Baka v Hungary*, the ECtHR used the argument that "given the prominent place among State organs that the judiciary occupies in a democratic society", judiciary is not part of the ordinary civil service.[18] This is a very important starting point, although this argument is put somewhere in the middle of the ECtHR's argumentation. Certainly, the reiterated or the added value added of this judgment is also a methodological approach by which the ECtHR confirmed a possible link between the freedom of expression of judges, the right to access to court, and the protection of the independence of judges;[19] but at the same time, the ECtHR importantly differentiates in the context of Article 10 of the ECHR between the situation where the measure complained of is essentially related to the freedom of expression of a judge and the situation where the measure complained of is related to the applicant's eligibility for judicial service or his or her professional ability to exercise judicial functions (appraisal of his or her professional qualifications).[20] Under the former

17 *Hans-Christian Leiningen-Weserburg v Austria* App no 26601/95 (ECHR, 20 January 1997) (admissibility decision).

18 *Baka* (n 7), para 163.

19 Ibid., paras 108–109, 121, 156, 165, 172. In this respect, see also the much earlier case *Wille v Liechtenstein* App no 28396/95 (ECHR, 28 October 1999), paras 8, 37, 61(ii), 68–69.

20 *Baka* (n 7), paras 141–142, 149, 156.

situation, it is not the "right", but a "duty" of the president of the court to express his or her opinion on legislative reforms, which were likely to have an impact on the judiciary and its independence.[21] Another value added by the judgment in the case of *Baka* relates to the part where the ECtHR states that there is little scope for restrictions on political speech or debate on matters of public interest, and as a consequence, a higher level of protection of freedom of speech in matters of public interest brings in a narrow margin of appreciation in respect of the principle of proportionality;[22] in such circumstances, the "close scrutiny" test is conducted by the ECtHR.[23] A very important aspect is the methodological aspect of the Baka case as regards the standard of proof, burden of proof, and evidentiary assessment.[24]

However, a part of this judgment that I would particularly like to point out for the purposes of this contribution is the paragraph where the ECtHR states that judicial authorities, insofar as the exercise of their adjudicatory function is concerned, "are required to exercise maximum discretion with regard to the cases with which they deal in order to preserve their image as impartial judges".[25] This is reiterated in more recent judgments,[26] and in the case where the ECtHR has stated that it "is the higher demands of justice and the elevated nature of judicial office which impose that duty. Judges must show restraint when they express criticisms about their fellow civil servants, in particular other judges".[27]

In my experience, this is the essence that needs to be protected, and the eventual right(s) of a judge who expressed his or her opinion in public must be assessed through this perspective. However, the ECtHR often uses in its argumentation the protected value of the "impartiality" of the judiciary together with the protected value of the "authority" of the judiciary.[28] In my view, these are not two equally protected values, since the Grand Chamber of the

21 Ibid., para 168.
22 Ibid., paras 159, 161, 171.
23 Ibid. para 165. More recent cases, like *Danileț*, which relate to critical expressions by a judge via Facebook concerning political influences in the justice system, show that the so-called "close scrutiny" test among other things, means that the exercise of balancing competing interests must also take into account the circumstances in which declarations have been made, the broader context and, of course, the content and factual basis of those declarations (*Danileț v Romania* App no 16915/21 (ECHR, 20 February 2024), paras 58, 66, 70, 82). In the case of *Żurek*, the ECtHR adds that the sequence of relevant events in their entirety must be taken into account rather than as separate and distinct incidents (*Żurek v Poland* App no 39650/18 (ECHR, 16 June 2022), paras 203, 211).
24 *Baka* (n 7), paras 143–149.
25 Ibid., para 164. See also *Buscemi v Italy* App no 29569/95 (ECHR, 16 September 1999), para 67.
26 See, for example, *Danileț* (n 23), paras 55, 65; *Sarisu Pehlivan v Turkey* App no 63029/19 (ECHR, 6 June 2023), para 36.
27 *Eminağaoğlu v Turkey* App no 76521/12 (ECHR, 9 March 2021), para 136.
28 *Sarisu Pehlivan* (n 26), paras 36 38; *Baka* (n 7), para 164.

ECtHR in the case *Grzęda v Poland* reiterated the position that was taken in the earlier case of *Bilgen v Turkey*[29] that:

> [E]mployment relationship of judges with the State must be understood in the light of the specific guarantees essential for judicial independence. Thus, when referring to the special trust and loyalty that they must observe, it is loyalty to the rule of law and democracy and not to holders of State power.[30]

Hence, the standards under Article 6 of the ECHR on subjective and particularly objective tests of impartiality are in my view inseparable from the context of examining the (un)acceptable exercise of the freedom of expression of judges. According to these tests, if there is sufficient evidence that a judge has displayed personal bias, the domestic courts or judicial councils should examine the case under the objective impartiality test, which provides for a further guarantee.[31] As to the objective test, it must be determined whether, quite apart from the judge's conduct, there are ascertainable facts which may raise doubts as to his or her impartiality. This implies that, in deciding whether in a particular case there is a legitimate reason to fear that a particular judge or a body sitting as a bench lacks impartiality, the standpoint of the person concerned is important but not decisive. What is decisive is whether this fear can be held to be objectively justified. In this connection, even appearances may be of a certain importance or, in other words, "justice must not only be done, it must also be seen to be done".[32] This is essential and it is the highest protected value also in the context of freedom of expression of judges.

For example, core members of IARMJ-Europe had a vivid discussion about whether IARMJ-Europe should join other international associations of judges in a public statement in support of judges under sanctions in Turkey after the attempted *coup d'état*. The argument that prevailed was to not intervene with such a statement, because our members could be assigned to cases that might be brought by applicants for international protection who are judges from Turkey. The argument of the protected values of objective and subjective impartiality prevailed (over freedom of expression and solidarity with judges in Türkiye) and IARMJ-Europe remained silent.

29 *Bilgen v Turkey* App no 1571/07 (ECHR, 9 March 2021), para 79.

30 *Grzęda v Poland* App no 43572/18 (ECHR (GC), 15 March 2022), para 264. See also: *Juszczyszyn v Poland* App no 35599/20 (ECHR, 6 October 2022), para 136.

31 *Micallef v Malta* App no 17056/06 (ECHR (GC), 15 October 2009) paras 100–101.

32 *Ramos Nunes de Carvalho E Sá v Portugal* App no 55391/13, 57728/13, 74041/13 (ECHR (GC), 6 November 2018), paras 148–149.

Legal challenges ahead

The interventions of judges in public space can take different forms. Most typically, these are written or oral critiques of proposals for legislative reforms, which are prepared by the executive branch of government or by civic society entities. Such reforms may (negatively) affect constitutional principles, such as the rule of law (including access to justice), the separation of powers, judicial independence, the adequacy of the transposition of EU law and the case law of the ECtHR into domestic legislation, and they may elevate the risks of the ineffective protection of human rights in the respective field of law. In public, judges also sometimes provide detailed explanations of complex legal issues to make them understandable for the professional and general public, mostly during interviews or in written publications. The public intervention of a judge can also take the form of active participation in the drafting process in a particular contested legislative area, which can subsequently, after its adoption, become part of a dispute before the same court where that judge exercises his or her judicial function. There are also situations involving the oral or written interventions of judges in public that are not strictly limited or subordinated to matters related to the rule of law (mentioned previously) but can be considered predominantly political or in some other way questionable from the perspective of the integrity of someone who performs judicial service. There are, unfortunately, also incidents of public comments made by a judge on a particular legal or factual situation, which is already exposed in public and which may be expected to reach a court. Similar incidents could occur in the case of critical comments directed towards another public officer or colleague in the judiciary, either in relation to that person's practice of the administration of justice/office, adjudication, or other professional or private conduct. Unacceptable comments given orally or in written form in relation to pending cases in public happen in practice more rarely.

Since the ECtHR and the CJEU have already done what is in their respective competence to protect judicial independence in circumstances of harmful successive judicial reforms aimed at weakening judicial independence in particular countries, and since the ECtHR has also set standards in cases of more or less isolated incidents of the misuse of the freedom of expression by judges, I see further challenges for domestic courts and for the ECtHR in cases of much more subtle interferences in the "freedom of expression" of judges in their exercise of independent and impartial adjudication through various forms of "chilling effects". The modalities of "chilling effect" on the freedom of expression of judges and their independent and impartial adjudication are present and remain in practice in relation to different aspects of the so-called internal judicial independence, such as the selection, promotion, and performance evaluation of judges and the assessment of ethical behaviour of judges even in countries that did not experience brutal reforms attacking judicial independence and where there are no visible systemic deficiencies in the respective justice system.

A very specific dimension of the case of *Baka v Hungary* includes "attempts" of judges in their concurring opinions to defend the need to recognise a subjective right of a judge under the ECHR to his or her independence to be guaranteed and respected by the State.[33] Judge Sicilianos emphasised particularly that judges, in their individual capacity, must be free from internal influence within the judiciary.[34] Judges must be free not just from "fear and favour" from the outside,[35] but also from "fear and favour" from the inside. The internal aspect has been recognised as equally important as external independence in many cases before the ECtHR.[36]

In the words of Advocate General Emiliou, so far, before the CJEU, the emphasis was rarely placed on the internal aspect because cases concerning the independence of the judiciary from other branches of government reach the CJEU's docket more often. They strike at the heart of the doctrine of separation of powers, which makes them both easier to spot and to flag as potentially problematic. Cases regarding the influence exercised by certain members of the judiciary over their peers are more subtle.[37] In his opinion in the case of AFRJ, Advocate General Emiliou says:

> it is certainly possible, and not at all difficult to imagine, that certain forms of judicial self-governance may generate a system of dependent judges within an independent judiciary, with undue influence being exercised by judicial officials, such as presidents of courts or officials of judicial self-administration bodies, within the judiciary.[38]

It is precisely in these aspects of internal judicial independence (not only in the countries of Central and Eastern Europe) that I see the actual legal challenges for effective protection of judicial independence and impartiality, also in the context of the freedom of expression of judges. Whether the case law of the ECtHR will go in the direction of the subjective right of a judge to their independence remains to be seen. The Grand Chamber of the ECtHR in the case *Grzęda v Poland* followed the aforementioned argument of concurring opinions in the case of *Baka* by saying that

33 *Baka* (n 7), Joint Concurring Opinion of Judges Pinto de Albuquerque and Dedov, paras 19–20, 25; Concurring Opinion of Judge Sicilianos, paras 5, 7, 12, 13–15.

34 Ibid., para 4.

35 *Grzęda* (n 30), para 264.

36 See, for example: *Guðmundur Andri Ástráðsson v Iceland* App no 26374/18 (ECHR (GC), 1 December 2020), para 226; *Reczkowicz v Poland*, App no 43447/19 (ECHR, 22 July 2021), para 218.

37 Opinion of Advocate General Emiliou delivered on 16 February 2023, Case C-216/21, *Asociația 'Forumul Judecătorilor din România'*, paras 61–62.

38 Ibid. paras 61–62. See also the judgment in this case from 7 July 2023, paras 65–66, 71, 75, 78–82.

> it would be a fallacy to assume that judges can uphold the rule of law and give effect to the Convention if domestic law deprives them [of] guarantees of the Articles of the Convention on matters directly touching upon their individual independence and impartiality.[39]

However, in my firm view, the legal developments regarding the eventual subjective right of a judge to their independence and impartiality will certainly not resolve a persistent rule of law crisis or trends of more subtle elements of deprofessionalisation of judicial services in Europe that I briefly address in the final two subsections.

An unexamined life is not worth living: the pursuit of better knowledge management in the judiciary

The famous quote in the context of the pursuit of wisdom that the "unexamined life is not worth living", which was recorded in Plato's *Apology*, is a dictum uttered by Socrates. Socrates advocated knowledge over opinions, and he willingly accepted a death penalty based on the court decision in Athens in May 399 BC for exercising his freedom of speech.[40] Taking into account the three premises of Immanuel Wallerstein mentioned earlier, I do not see a reason why the same approach should not apply to each court in its pursuit of justice through continuous questioning, self-criticism, examining relevant data, analysing relevant case law, particularly of the ECtHR and CJEU, and the deliberation of logical conclusions and arguments based on all these about what needs to be improved based on the inclusive and meaningful participation of the members of courts who know the most in particular fields of case law concerning the "life" (challenges, deficiencies, and systemic errors) of a particular court and the judiciary as a whole. However, what hinders the development of such a strategic approach towards the pursuit of justice is the global trend of bureaucratization of judicial systems, accompanied by rituals, which cover up the real challenges in the judiciary.[41] Namely, far too often the aforementioned enormous efforts of court management and judicial councils happen without the collection and analysis of the strategic and key facts and data that could contribute to the constant self-examination, change, and raising of the genuine quality of the judiciary. However, excessive and resource-intensive, but often useless, bureaucratization does not come inevitably and by itself. It is a by-product of something else, which is a typical phenomenon of all highly professionalised services that are based on knowledge

39 *Grzęda* (n 30), para 264.

40 There were 360 votes for his death penalty and 141 for his acquittal. Only 31 less votes for his death penalty would have brought his acquittal. However, he irritated the narcissism of the "judges" by his defence, saying that he should have been rewarded for his conduct, not punished (Platon, *Sokratov zagovor* (Družba sv. Mohorja 1923), p. 48).

41 This is, of course, a global problem, not restricted to the field of the judiciary.

and professional experience. That something else is a gradual abandonment of meritocracy within the judiciary (and within other professionalised subsystems in a society).

Towards a conclusion: meritocracy in the judiciary as a "myth" or as a precondition for the meaningful exercise of the freedom of expression of judges?

The *conditio sine qua non* for going in the direction of a "self-examined life" of courts and the judiciary as a whole is the establishment and continuing nourishment of the meritocratic system concerning the appointment, selection, performance evaluation, and promotion of judges and experts in all positions within the judiciary, including, of course, within judicial councils.

My assessment is that the great majority of the cases before the ECtHR concerning the freedom of speech of judges, where a violation or non-violation of the rights under the ECHR has been established, relate to those countries where there exists no or merely a rhetoric of meritocracy and where there are a lot of unexplored opportunities for the genuine implementation of meritocratic principles in judiciaries. I would even say that the mere rhetoric on meritocracy in those countries substantially increases the chances of dysfunctions and the misuse of freedom of speech by judges, which are today visible in the extensive case law of the ECHR, particularly against the countries of Central and Eastern Europe. As Michael Sandel has affirmed in his book *Tyranny of the Merits*, populism, extreme polarisation, deep distrust of governments, and the political project of liberalism are expressions of brewing anger and frustration; it is a revolt against the tyranny of meritocracy as this has been experienced by those who feel humiliated by a mere declaratory approach to meritocracy.[42]

However, at least as regards judicial systems in Europe, all necessary (minimum) legal conditions for the introduction and development of meritocracy in judiciaries are already set by the ECtHR and CJEU in their case law, developed particularly since February 2018.[43] The requirement of a court or a tribunal to be "established by law", this being a stand-alone right[44] under Article 6 of the ECHR or Article 47 of the Charter of Fundamental Rights of the European Union (in conjunction with the second sub-paragraph of Article 19(1) of the TEU), encompasses the process of the initial appointment of a judge to office, meaning that judges must be selected on the basis of merit and

42 Michael Sandel, *The Tyranny of Merit: What's Become of the Common Good?* (Farrar, Straus and Giroux 2020). See also other works on meritocracy as a myth: Stephen J. McNamee, *The Meritocracy Myth* (4th edn, Rowman & Littlefield Publishers 2018); Jo Littler, *Against Meritocracy: Culture, Power and Myths of Mobility* (Routledge 2017).

43 The turning points were cases: Case C-64/16, *ASJP*, 28 February 2018, para 34; Case T-639/16 P, *FV v Council*, 23 January 2018; Joined cases C-542/18 RX-II and C-543/18 RX-II, *Simpson v Council*, 26 March 2020; *Guðmundur Andri Ástráðsson* (n 36).

44 *Besnik Cani v Albania* App no 37474/20 (ECHR, 4 October 2022), para 107.

objective criteria, not only to ensure public confidence in the judiciary but also to supplement the guarantee of the personal independence of judges.[45] This is equally relevant for the promotion of judges.[46] Thus, appointment and promotion procedures should introduce, publish and give effect to objective criteria, with the aim of ensuring that the selection and career of judges are based on merit, having regard to "qualifications, integrity, ability and efficiency"; there should be a rigorous process for the appointment and promotion of ordinary judges to ensure that the "most qualified candidates" – both in terms of technical competence and moral integrity – are appointed to judicial posts;[47] in this respect, the criterion of "independent state of mind" is mentioned, too.[48] The relevant domestic law on judicial appointments and promotions should be couched in unequivocal terms, to the extent possible, so as not to allow arbitrary interferences in such processes.[49] Under the standards of the case law of the CJEU, information taken into consideration for the purposes of those assessments must be sufficiently varied and verifiable, which limits the risk of the procedure for effective promotion being discretionary.[50] The ECtHR adds that "it goes without saying that the higher a tribunal is placed in the judicial hierarchy, the more demanding the applicable selection criteria should be".[51] Procedural fairness under Article 6 of the ECHR or Article 47 of the Charter in cases involving the selection, appointment, and career of judges among other fairness standards,[52] such as the right to a defence as a general principle of law,[53] demands that "adequate" or "solid" reasons have to be given throughout such processes.[54] Without requiring a detailed answer to every argument advanced by the complainant, this obligation presupposes

45 *Guðmundur Andri Ástráðsson* (n 36), para 228; *Gloveli v Georgia* App no 18952/18 (ECHR, 7 April 2022), para 50.

46 *Tsanova-Gecheva v Bulgaria* App no 43800/12 (ECHR, 15 September 2015), para 63.

47 *Guðmundur Andri Ástráðsson* (n 36), paras 221–222, 230, 234; *Gloveli* (n 45), para 50; *Xero Flor w Polsce sp. z.o.o. v Poland* App no 4907/18, (ECHR, 7 May 2021), para 244; *Xhoxhaj v Albania* App no 15227/19 (ECHR, 9 February 2021), para 291; *Reczkowicz* (n 36), para 261. See also: Case C-216/21, *Asociația 'Forumul Judecătorilor din România'*, 7 July 2023, para 86.

48 *Guðmundur Andri Ástráðsson* (n 36), para 230.

49 See: ibid. paras 229–230, 231–233; *Besnik Cani* (n 44), paras 86–87.

50 Case C-216/21, *Asociația 'Forumul Judecătorilor din România'* (n 47). Pay attention to the difference between the English version of the judgment (which uses the term "discriminatory") and Slovene, Croatian, Italian, and French versions which all use the term "discretionary", similarly to Advocate General Emiliou who uses the term "undue discretion" (see para 70 of his opinion from 16 February 2023).

51 *Guðmundur Andri Ástráðsson* (n 36), para 222; *Besnik Cani* (n 44), para 84.

52 See, for example: *Baka* (n 7), paras 143–149.

53 For this right, see *mutatis mutandis*: Case C-249/13, *Boudjlida*, 11 December 2014, paras 30–59.

54 *Gloveli* (n 45), paras 58–59; *Guðmundur Andri Ástráðsson* (n 36), paras 263–265, 268–272; Case C-619/18, *Commission v Poland* 24 June 2019, paras 114–117; Joined cases C-748/19 to C-754/19, *WB and others*, 16 November 2021, paras 78–79.

that a judge can expect to receive a specific and explicit reply to the arguments which are decisive for the outcome of those proceedings.[55] There must be a sufficient judicial review of a decision on various aspects of judicial careers and competition,[56] which may also lead to the invalidation of unlawful decisions.[57] These requirements for meritocracy *mutatis mutandis* should be applicable to all other relevant selections and appointments in the judiciary, such as heads of departments, and the members of the judicial councils and judicial bodies that are responsible for the evaluation of the performance of judges. Those with the greatest responsibilities in the judiciary should be advocates of knowledge – that is, advocates of the concept of knowledge, which does not separate European law so vigorously from national law, since these are two inseparable bodies of knowledge.

Therefore, there should be no doubt whatsoever: meritocracy (at least) in the judiciary should not be just a "myth" and should not (continue to) become fake news in postmodern societies. It is the legal, professional, and ethical responsibility of judicial councils, courts which control the legality of decisions on the careers of judges, the presidents of courts and other relevant (quasi) judicial entities involved in decisions affecting professional aspects of the careers of judges, to implement those European minimum legal standards on meritocracy into daily practice and decision-making processes. Then, the fundamental right of an acting judge to express his or her opinion in public, including in his or her judgments, decisions, and orders, would no longer be a contentious issue, and the practice of disputes initiated by judges against judges will end. Thus, the concept of human rights protection in the field of the freedom of speech could return to its original and normal purpose, which is primarily to protect private parties from the State.[58] It appears that after judges, independent public intellectuals and scientists might be the next target group in relation to Article 10 of the ECHR.

55 *Alonso Saura v Spain* App no 18326/19 (ECHR, 8 June 2023), para 34.

56 For details on the scope and intensity of judicial control of those decisions, see: C-619/18, *Commission v Poland* (n 54), paras 114–117; Joined cases C-748/19 to C-754/19, *WB and others* (n 54); Joined cases C-585/18, C-624/18, C-625/18, *A.K. and others*, 19 November 2019, para 145; Case C-824/18, 2 March 2021, *A.B. and others*, paras 128, 167; *Guðmundur Andri Ástráðsson* (n 36), paras 222, 226, 243–252, 281–283; *Xero Flor w Polsce sp. z.o.o. v Poland* App no 4907/18, (ECHR, 7 May 2021), para 245; *Reczkowicz* (n 36), para 218; *Dolinska-Ficek and Ozimek v Poland*, App nos 49868/19 and 57511/19 (ECHR, 8 November 2021), para 274; *Gloveli* (n 45), paras 51, 56, 57; *Alonso Saura v Spain* (n 55), para 38.

57 *Guðmundur Andri Ástráðsson* (n 36), para 283.

58 According to Article 34 of the Convention, the Court may receive applications from "any person, non-governmental organisation or group of individuals" claiming to be the victim of a violation by one of the High Contracting Parties of the rights set forth in the Convention or the Protocols.

Index

FSC
www.fsc.org
MIX
Papier | Fördert
gute Waldnutzung
FSC® C083411

Kolibri 360 GmbH
Ferdinand-Jühlke-Straße 7
99095 Erfurt, Deutschland
produktsicherheit@kolibri360.de